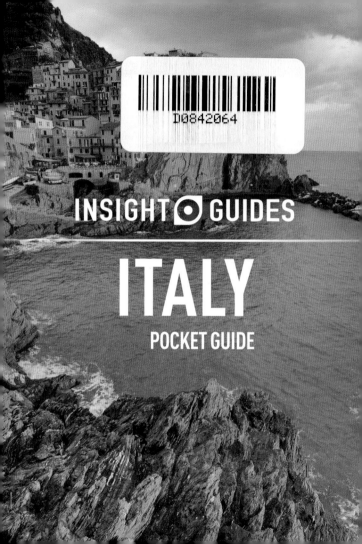

ID0842064

INSIGHT ⊙ GUIDES

ITALY

POCKET GUIDE

◎ Walking Eye App

YOUR FREE EBOOK AVAILABLE THROUGH THE WALKING EYE APP

Your guide now includes a free eBook to your chosen destination,
for the same great price as before. Simply download the Walking Eye
App from the App Store or Google Play to access your free eBook.

HOW THE WALKING EYE APP WORKS

Through the Walking Eye App, you can purchase a range of eBooks and destination
content. However, when you buy this book, you can download the corresponding
eBook for free. Just see below in the grey panel where to find your free content and
then scan the QR code at the bottom of this page.

Destinations: Download essential destination
content featuring recommended sights and
attractions, restaurants, hotels and an A–Z of
practical information, all available for purchase.

Ships: Interested in ship reviews? Find independent reviews of river and ocean ships in this
section, all available for purchase.

eBooks: You can download your free accompanying digital version of this guide here. You
will also find a whole range of other eBooks,
all available for purchase.

Free access to travel-related blog articles
about different destinations, updated on a
daily basis.

HOW THE EBOOKS WORK

The eBooks are provided in EPUB file format. Please note that you will need an eBook reader installed on your device to open the file. Many devices come with this as standard, but you may still need to install one manually from Google Play.

The eBook content is identical to the content in the printed guide.

HOW TO DOWNLOAD THE WALKING EYE APP

1. Download the Walking Eye App from the App Store or Google Play.
2. Open the app and select the scanning function from the main menu.
3. Scan the QR code on this page – you will then be asked a security question to verify ownership of the book.
4. Once this has been verified, you will see your eBook in the purchased ebook section, where you will be able to download it.

Other destination apps and eBooks are available for purchase separately or are free with the purchase of the Insight Guide book.

TOP 10 ATTRACTIONS

SIENA
Piazza del Campo is the gorgeous main square of this perfect town. See page 100.

THE LAKE DISTRICT
The ravishing lake and mountain scenery is irresistible. See page 156.

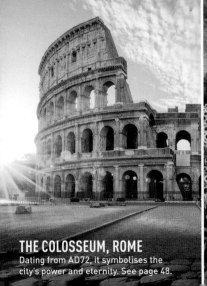

THE COLOSSEUM, ROME
Dating from AD72, it symbolises the city's power and eternity. See page 48.

TUSCANY
Cypresses, sunflowers, hill towns and much more. See page 70.

Tuttle

Concise
Japanese
Dictionary

Japanese-English
English-Japanese

Samuel E. Martin

Revised and Updated by Sayaka Khan and Fred Perry

TUTTLE Publishing
Tokyo | Rutland, Vermont | Singapore

The Tuttle Story: "Books to Span the East and West"

Most people are surprised to learn that the world's largest publisher of books on Asia had its humble beginnings in the tiny American state of Vermont. The company's founder, Charles E. Tuttle, belonged to a New England family steeped in publishing. And his first love was naturally books—especially old and rare editions.

Immediately after WW II, serving in Tokyo under General Douglas MacArthur, Tuttle was tasked with reviving the Japanese publishing industry. He later founded the Charles E. Tuttle Publishing Company, which thrives today as one of the world's leading independent publishers.

Though a westerner, Tuttle was hugely instrumental in bringing a knowledge of Japan and Asia to a world hungry for information about the East. By the time of his death in 1993, Tuttle had published over 6,000 books on Asian culture, history and art—a legacy honored by the Japanese emperor with the "Order of the Sacred Treasure," the highest tribute Japan can bestow upon a non-Japanese.

With a backlist of 1,500 titles, Tuttle Publishing is more active today than at any time in its past—inspired by Charles Tuttle's core mission to publish fine books to span the East and West and provide a greater understanding of each.

Published by Periplus Editions (HK) Ltd.

www.tuttlepublishing.com

© 2008 by Samuel Martin
This revised edition © 2012 by Periplus
Editions (HK) Ltd

ISBN 978-4-8053-1139-4

15 14 13 12   7 6 5 4 3 2 1   1207EP

Printed in Hong Kong

TUTTLE PUBLISHING® is a registered trademark of Tuttle Publishing, a division of Periplus Editions (HK) Ltd.

Distributed by:

Japan
Tuttle Publishing
Yaekari Bldg., 3rd Floor, 5-4-12 Osaki,
Shinagawa-ku, Tokyo 141-0032
Tel: (81) 3 5437-0171
Fax: (81) 3 5437-0755
sales@ tuttle.co.jp
www.tuttle.co.jp

North America, Latin America, and Europe
Tuttle Publishing
364 Innovation Drive, North Clarendon,
VT 05759-9436 USA.
Tel: 1 (802) 773-8930
Fax: 1 (802) 773-6993
info@tuttlepublishing.com
www.tuttlepublishing.com

Asia Pacific
Berkeley Books Pte. Ltd.
61 Tai Seng Avenue
#02-12 Singapore 534167
Tel: (65) 6280-1330
Fax: (65) 6280-6290
inquiries@periplus.com.sg
www.periplus.com

POMPEII
Walk the streets of this beautifully preserved Roman town. See page 178.

PORTOFINO
The jewel of the Italian Riviera. See page 166.

THE SISTINE CHAPEL, ROME
Michelangelo's masterful ceiling frescoes in the Vatican are a visual and spiritual feast. See page 67.

THE GRAND CANAL, VENICE
This magical highway winds past waterside palaces to Piazza San Marco. See page 114.

THE DUOMO, FLORENCE
A perfect symbol of the premier city of arts. See page 72.

GREEK TEMPLES, PAESTUM
Magnificent legacy of Italy's Greek colonies. See page 186.

A PERFECT DAY

9.00am

Breakfast
Start your day in Trastevere at Caffè delle Arance (Piazza Santa Maria 2) where, along with espresso and cornettos, the house speciality is freshly squeezed orange juice (served with ice cubes on the side) and great people-watching right on the piazza.

12.30pm

Across the Tiber
Cross pedestrian Ponte Sisto and go straight up Via Pettinari. Turn left on Via dei Giubbonari for great shopping and stop for lunch or snacks right on Campo de Fiori, where the city's most picturesque market is still held.

11.30am

Galleries
Head down through Trastevere's winding streets towards Piazza Trilussa and the Tiber, checking out the boutiques and galleries.

1.30pm

Piazza Navona
Cross busy traffic-filled Corso Vittorio Emanuele and take Corso Rinascimento. To the left is the sprawling Piazza Navona. Check out Bernini's fountain in the centre and grab a classy, if pricey espresso, or better still, the dark chocolate ice cream *tartufo* at bar Tre Scalini (www.trescalini.it).

10.00am

Views from the Janiculum Hill
Take Via Garibaldi to Piazzale Garibaldi at the top of Janiculum Hill for splendid views of the city and the dome of St Peter's. On your way up, veer off towards San Pietro in Montorio church for a peek at Bramante's Tempietto.

N ROME

3.00pm

Spanish Steps and beyond
Walk east along the narrow Via dei Pastini and follow the shopping streets Via del Corso and Via Condotti to Piazza di Spagna. Give your credit cards a break at the Keats-Shelley House at the base of the Spanish Steps, then head down Via del Babuino to the sculptor Canova's old studio at no.150, which has been transformed into a caffè (www.canovatadolini.com) with marble masterpieces at every corner.

10.30pm

Trendy bar
Walk up the street for fancy drinks at Doney (www.restaurantdoney. com), which is as posh and popular with today's cool set as it was at the time of *la dolce vita*.

2.15pm

Pantheon
To the right of Corso Rinascimento on the parallel Via Di S. Giovanna D'Arco, you will find the San Luigi dei Francesi church at no. 5. Inside are three of Caravaggio's most famous paintings, including *The Calling of St Matthew*. Take Via del Seminario and you will reach the Pantheon.

7.30pm

Dinner
Catch bus 61 and get off at the last stop inside the park. Cross under the arch and into Via Veneto. Dine at the excellent restaurant inside the Hotel Majestic for unforgettable traditional Italian cuisine; be sure to book a table on the patio in good weather.

5.30pm

Art in the park
Walk through Villa Borghese Park and check out the Carlo Bilotti Modern Art Collection (http://en. museocarlobilotti.it).

CONTENTS

INTRODUCTION

From the Alps down to the southern tip of Sicily, Italy provides the most tangible proof that the world is indeed a wondrous stage. Architects and sculptors treat the myriad parks and gardens as set designs, and nature turns the landscapes – replete with statuesque cypresses, tortuous olive and fig trees, and rows of vineyards – into so many artful backdrops for the daily brio and histrionics of *La Vita Italiana*.

In the cities, the cathedrals, palazzi, monumental public buildings and open-air piazzas, are planned as if harmonious elements in unrivalled stage sets. Venice's dazzling basilica, the Doge's Palace and the 500-year-old Clock Tower, all within the sprawling Piazza San Marco and adjacent Piazzetta, are the focus of the city's life. The same is true of Rome's grand squares – Navona, del Popolo and di Spagna, Siena's unique Campo, and Florence's elegant Piazza della Signoria. Conceived as a theatre and emphasising the decorative space as much as the buildings surrounding it, the piazza satisfies the Mediterranean desire to conduct life in the open air.

A NATION OF ACTORS

We must not overlook the players. In each town, at that magic moment of the *passeggiata* at the end of each afternoon, they stroll across the piazza, find themselves a well-placed seat at their favourite caffè, or stand in groups to argue business, politics or football. Their celebrated gift for gesticulation aids the inherent air of drama that reassures Italians of the appreciation of their audience – no people more joyfully live

People vs State

The Italian people have long held a deep mistrust for the State. A popular saying, *fatta la legge, trovato l'inganno* (a law is passed, a way past is found), has now become a national motto.

up to their legendary image than the Italians. As Orson Welles put it, all 60-odd million of them are actors, with only a few bad ones, and those, he added most unfairly, are found on the stage and in films.

Watch them at the wheel of a car: long ago, driving became a major opportunity for the Italians to display their dramatic talents. An Italian designer observed that a nation's cars are like

One of Gucci's Rome stores

its people: Scandinavian and German models are solid, strong and reliable, built to resist an accident; Italian cars tend to be more fragile, but slick and spirited, built to avoid an accident. They are designed, above all, to indulge the national sense of style. The imaginative flair of a Neapolitan taxi driver zig-zagging out of a traffic jam forces the admiration of any nerve-shattered back-seat passenger.

The world also reveres Italian cuisine. In the simplest trattoria or most elegant of restaurants, the experience often begins before you sit down. Not with the menu, but with the artistically presented display across a long table as you enter: seafood antipasti, stuffed aubergines and courgettes, grilled peppers in red, yellow and green, and whatever bounty that morning's market yielded.

THE LAY OF THE LAND

If you take a train the length of the peninsula, Italy offers a constantly changing mosaic of landscapes. In the north, the snow-capped Alps and jagged pink pinnacles of the Dolomites; the gleaming Alpine-backed lakes of Como, Garda and Maggiore; the

Il mare or la montagna – the Italians' choice for summer

fertile and industrial plain of the Po, stretching from Turin and Milan across to ancient Verona; the Palladian villa-studded hills of Vicenza, and the romantic canals of Venice.

On the northwest coast, the Italian Riviera curves from Ventimiglia on the French border to La Spezia, with venerable Genoa in the centre. Behind the alternating rocky and sandy coastline, from the marble quarries of Carrara, the mountain chain of the Apennines reaches south into Tuscany. Here you will find the ageless beauties of Florence, Lucca, Pisa and Siena, not to mention the smaller, and perhaps more magical, hillside towns of Montepulciano, San Gimignano and Volterra.

Landlocked Umbria's rich green countryside surrounds a golden triangle of historic cities: the Assisi of St Francis, the noble university hillside town of Perugia and the medieval mountain post of Gubbio. To the east, the grand Byzantine citadel of Ravenna dominates the seaside resorts lining the Adriatic.

The Eternal City, Rome, lies halfway down the west coast. For more than 26 centuries it has witnessed countless declines, falls and rebirths, and today continues to resist the assaults of brutal modernity in its time-locked, colour-rich historical centre.

The exhilarating chaos of Naples commands its magnificent bay, the visible isles of Ischia and Capri, and the ruins of Pompeii in the shadow of Vesuvius, its still active volcano. To the south, the former fishing villages of Sorrento and Positano spill down the craggy cliffs of the serpentine Amalfi coast, justifiably famed as one of the world's most beautiful drives. On the other side of the peninsula, off the tourist track in the peninsula's 'heel', are the curiously romantic landscapes of Puglia, featuring its centuries-old *trulli* constructions (see page 189) and medieval fortresses of the German emperors.

Italy's western approaches are guarded by two of the Mediterranean's largest islands, Sardinia and Sicily; both rugged, mysterious and steeped in history. Smaller islands with fabled names such as Elba, Lípari and Stromboli, fill in the necklace of floating gems, many reached only by boat, where the lifestyle is often that of the Mediterranean one hundred years ago.

A DIVERSE PEOPLE

The Italian people – with Latins and Etruscans mixing over the millennia with Greeks, Lombards, Normans, French and Spaniards – are as fascinatingly diverse as the panoply of landscapes. The country was historically divided into the city-states, duchies, kingdoms and republics of Florence, Naples, Venice, Lombardy, Piedmont and Sicily. Today, each region still sustains a solid and pugnacious local pride. Nurtured within the geographical separations of the Alps, the Po valley and the coasts on either side of the Apennines, it was this very diversity that created the richness of Italian art and its competing regional schools of painting and architecture. Significantly, the move towards national unity in the 19th century coincided with a dramatic artistic decline, from which the country is only now recovering.

Given its comparatively short history as a unified nation, much of Italy's patriotic sense seems to be most visible in the national football team. After the devastating experience of Mussolini's Fascism, national government is rarely regarded as an obvious solution to the population's daily problems. If some form of government proves necessary, Italians prefer the local town hall to the parliament in Rome.

Most Italians are naturally cheerful and friendly towards foreign visitors, reserving their scorn for each other – Venetians and Romans

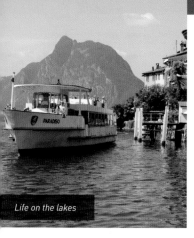

Life on the lakes

or Milanese and Neapolitans have a strong regional identity and rivalry. They bemoan the EU-imposed automobile licence plates that no longer designate the origin of the driver.

Beyond the country's regional identifications, Italy remains strongly divided culturally, economically and psychologically between the prosperous, industrial North and the less developed South, or *Mezzogiorno* (Midday). This division was perpetuated by centuries of feudal rule in 'The Two Kingdoms' of Naples and Sicily, while the North, closer to the rest of Europe, developed more progressive forms of economy and government. The division has come almost to the point of regarding the South as Italy's own Third World, and has only worsened with the recent recession.

However, the warm-hearted, high-spirited Neapolitans in no way feel themselves inferior to the cool, pragmatic 'managerial' types of the prosperous northern cities. Italy's two halves come face to face in Turin, where Fiat's car factories have for generations attracted thousands of workers from the *Mezzogiorno*. Sociologists have noted that the transplanted southerners tend to support the populist Juventus football team, owned by Fiat's Agnelli family, while the other, more bourgeois local team, Torino, is favoured by the longer-established Turin citizenry.

Foreign visitors are not obliged to take sides. We are free to fall in love with the entire country and invariably do: it is a glorious lifelong love affair.

⊘ FACTS AND FIGURES

Geography: The Italian landmass covers 301,245 sq km (116,228 sq miles). The familiar boot-like silhouette stretches 1,200km (850 miles) from the northwest Alpine frontier with France to the south-east 'heel' of Puglia. Below the three great lakes, Maggiore, Como and Garda, the fertile plain of the River Po separates the Alps from the rugged chain of the Apennines, running like a wall down the middle of the peninsula to the arid south. Italy's other major rivers include the Tiber in Rome, the Arno in Tuscany, and the Adige in the Tyrolean Dolomites.

Off the Tyrrhenian coast are the islands of Sardinia (and the south of France's Corsica) and Sicily (off the boot's 'toe'), largest of the Mediterranean islands. Three major volcanoes in the south, Naples' Vesuvius, and Sicily's Stromboli and Etna, are still active. The highest point in the country (and in western Europe) is Mont Blanc (Monte Bianco), at 4,807m (15,772ft), on the Swiss and French borders.

Population: 60.8 million. The birth rate, at 1.3, is one of the lowest in Europe.

Capital: Rome (pop. 2.8 million).

Other major cities: Milan (1.3 million), Naples (989,000), Turin (892,000), Palermo (674,000), Genoa (854,000), Bologna (386,000), Florence (382,000), Bari (326,000), Venice (including mainland, 264,000, historic city 59,000).

Government: Italy became a republic in 1946, and is divided into 15 regions and five autonomous regions. Parliament consists of two houses: the 630-strong Chamber of Deputies and the Senate with 315 members. The two Houses have equal powers. A parliamentary mandate is five years. The elected president has honorary rather than political powers, while the prime minister is the head of the government. Since World War II, Italy has had 64 governments and only one has lasted the full five-year term.

A BRIEF HISTORY

Italy has only existed as a nation since 1871. Before then, despite the peninsula's obvious geographical unity bounded by the Alps and the Mediterranean, its story is a fragmented tale of independent-minded cities, regions and islands – and the outside powers who coveted them.

We have abundant evidence of the ancient Etruscan, Greek and Roman communities in Italy, but know very little of the country's earlier, prehistoric settlers. Vestiges of dwellings survive – cabins on stilts in the frequently flooded Po Valley, larger clay houses on the western marshlands of Tuscany, and Sardinia's still visible domed dry-stone *nuraghi* (see page 197). But the inhabitants? Perhaps North Africans and eastern Europeans peopled the Ligurian coast, while people from the Balkans and Asia Minor may have settled the Adriatic and south.

ETRUSCANS AND GREEKS

Nobody knows much about the early Etruscans. Some historians believe that they were the first native Italians; others believe they arrived from Asia Minor. During the millennium before the Christian era, their civilisation reached north beyond Tuscany to the Po Valley and south towards Naples. At a time when early Roman and other Latin tribes were still primitive, Etruscan society – itself savage in many respects – was also aristocratic and highly sophisticated. Solid gold workmanship and other metal ornaments and tools show a Greek influence, but the Etruscans' vaulted architecture, town planning, and irrigation systems were indigenous.

Arriving in the 8th century BC, the Greeks set up city-states in Sicily, dominated by Syracuse, as well as other settlements on the Italian mainland, such as Naples, Paestum and Taranto. Together they formed Magna Graecia, whose zenith was reached during the 6th and 5th centuries BC. The Etruscan Empire faded in the 4th century BC, after defeats by Greeks in the south, Latins in the centre, and Gallic invaders in the north. As Greek colonial power grew weak from Athens–Sparta rivalry back home and pressure from Phoenicians in Sicily, the vacuum was filled by a confederation of Latin and Sabine tribes living on seven hills known collectively as Rome.

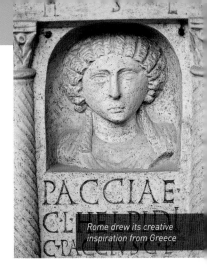

PACCIAE
CL TELPIDI
G PACCIN SCE

Rome drew its creative inspiration from Greece

THE ROMANS

Legend says Rome was founded by Romulus, sired with his twin brother Remus by Mars of a Vestal Virgin and abandoned on the Palatine Hill to be suckled by a she-wolf. Historians agree that the myth's site and traditional founding date of 753 BC are just about right.

Under Etruscan domination, Rome had been a monarchy until a revolt in 510 BC established a patrician republic, which lasted some five centuries. In contrast to other Italian cities, which were weakened by internal rivalries and unstable government, Rome drew strength from a solid aristocracy of consuls and senate ruling over plebeians proud of their citizenship and only rarely rebellious.

Recovering quickly from a Gallic invasion in 390 BC, the Romans took effective control of the peninsula by a military conquest reinforced by a network of roads with names that exist to this day: Via Appia, Flaminia, Aurelia. All roads did indeed lead to – and from – Rome. By 250 BC, the city's population had grown to an impressive 100,000. Roman power extended throughout the Mediterranean with a victory in the Punic Wars against Carthage (now Tunisia) and conquests in Macedonia, Asia Minor, Spain and southern France.

Mosaic of Emperor Justinian in Ravenna's San Vitale Basilica

Under Julius Caesar, elected in 59 BC, provincial towns won the privileges of Roman citizenship. His reformist dictatorship, bypassing the senate to combat unemployment and ease the tax burden, made dangerous enemies. After being appointed dictator for life, he was assassinated by Brutus, among others, on 15 March (the Ides of March) 44 BC. This led to civil war and the despotic rule of Octavius, nephew and heir of Julius Caesar, whose title of Augustus Caesar signified the collapse of the Republic and the beginning of the Roman Empire in 27 BC.

Conquest of the Greeks accelerated rather than halted the influence of their culture in Italy. Romans infused Greek refinement with their own energy to create a unique mixture of elegance and realism, delicacy and strength, which have remained the essence of Italian life and art.

CHRISTIAN BEGINNINGS

Christianity spread throughout the Empire, despite the dramatic persecution under Nero in the 1st century AD in which the Apostles Peter and Paul were martyred in Rome. Constantine the Great declared

Christianity the official state religion in AD 313, later transferring the capital to Byzantium, renaming it Constantinople (modern-day Istanbul) in 324. At the end of the 4th century, Emperor Theodosius the Great organised the Church into dioceses, making Ravenna the new capital of the Western Empire, with Constantinople as capital of the Eastern Empire. Rome would never be the same again. The position of the Bishop of Rome as primate of the Western Church ('pope' derived from *papa*, the Latin for father), first claimed in the 2nd century, was later asserted by Pope Leo I (440–61), who traced the succession back to St Peter.

The Western Empire came to an end in 476 following the invasion of Attila's Huns and the Goths and Vandals who came to sack Rome, and the subsequent abdication of Emperor Romulus Augustus.

AFTER THE EMPIRE

Italian unity was prevented by ongoing wars between the Goths and Byzantines, followed by yet more invasions. The dual influence of Greek and Latin culture persisted. Emperor Justinian (527–65) and his wife Theodora re-annexed Italy to the Byzantine Empire and codified Roman law as the state's legal system. Under Emperor Heraclius (610–41), Greek was extended to Italy to become its official language.

⊙ ARCHITECTURAL INNOVATION

In architecture, the Romans made a quantum leap forward from the Greek structures of columns and beams, by developing the arch, vault and dome, well suited to the needs of the empire. They built basilicas for public administration, pioneered the engineering of aqueducts and bridges and erected triumphal arches for victorious armies. They adopted the Greeks' gods, giving them Roman names (Zeus became Jupiter, Aphrodite Venus) and placing the emperor – serving the interests of the Roman state – at the apex of the gods.

Byzantine ritual coloured Roman liturgy and architecture. The Roman basilica's colonnaded nave leading to an apse gave way to the Greek cross with a central space surrounded by arches and topped by a dome. Sculptural reliefs flattened out, painting and mosaics became more formal, and spiritual preoccupations turned to mystic contemplation of the ineffable hereafter.

Things were much too ineffable, it seems, for Italian tastes. The monastic movement, founded by St Benedict of Umbria in the 6th century, reasserted involvement in the realities of social life. The Benedictine order emphasised moderation. Flagellation and similar rigours introduced into other Italian monasteries by the Irish monk Columbanus were modified.

By the 8th century, the Byzantines held the balance of power with the Germanic Lombards who had invaded Italy in 568 and set up their capital at Pavia four years later. The Lombards controlled the interior in a loose confederation of independent duchies. Lombard territory split Byzantine Italy into segments ruled from the coasts. The divisions resulted in Veneto (Venice and its hinterland), Emilia (between Ravenna and Modena) and Pentapolo (between Rimini and Perugia), plus Rome and Naples (with Sicily and Calabria).

THE HOLY ROMAN EMPIRE

In Rome, the popes played the Lombard duchies against those of the Byzantine Empire. They cited a forged document, the 'Donation of Constantine', supposedly bequeathing them political authority over all of Italy. Seeking the support of the Franks, Pope Leo III crowned their king, Charlemagne, Emperor of the West on Christmas Day in 800. But in turn, the pope had to kneel in allegiance. This exchange of spiritual blessing for military protection laid the seeds of conflict between the papacy and secular rulers, compounded in 962 when Otto I was crowned emperor of the new Holy Roman Empire.

Venice, founded on its islets and lagoons in the 6th century by mainland refugees fleeing Lombard raiders, prospered from a privileged relationship with Byzantium and from a readiness to trade with Muslims and others further east. The merchants of Venice who formed the backbone of the Most Serene Republic were only too happy to disseminate their Oriental cargoes of exotic goods to the Lombards in the Po Valley and the courts of northern Europe.

Naples held on to its autonomy by combining links with Rome and Constantinople. When Arabs conquered Sicily in the 9th century and turned to the mainland, Naples sought an alliance. But as the invaders advanced on Rome, Naples linked up with the maritime republic of neighbouring Amalfi. The Arabs remained on the Italian scene for two centuries, leaving a lasting influence on sciences and food.

THE MIDDLE AGES

In the 11th century, the adventurous Normans put an end to Arab control of Sicily and southern Italy. Exploiting a natural genius for assimilating the useful elements of the local culture rather than

Venetian wealth depicted in the Pala d'Oro, St Mark's Basilica

indiscriminately imposing their own, they adopted Arab-style tax collectors and customs officials, and Byzantine admirals commanded their navy. In Palermo, churches and mosques stood side-by-side, feudal castles next to Oriental palaces and gardens.

The Crusades against Islam brought great prosperity to Italy's port cities. Pisa sided with the Normans in Sicily and profits from its new commercial empire in the western Mediterranean paid for its magnificent cathedral, baptistery, and campanile (the Leaning Tower). Genoa's equally powerful merchant empire spread from Algeria to Syria.

Supreme master of the art of playing all sides, Venice stayed out of the First Crusade to expand its trade with the faraway East while ferrying pilgrims to Palestine. In 1204, when Byzantium threatened its eastern trading privileges, Venice persuaded the armies of the Fourth Crusade to attack Constantinople; the conquest of Byzantium strengthened its position even further.

The Po Valley's economic expansion through land clearance and irrigation works brought a rapid decline of feudalism. Dukes, administrators and clergy lived in towns rather than isolated castles, absorbing the hinterland into communes, forerunners of the city-states.

THE GUELFS AND THE GHIBELLINES

The communes were strong enough to confine German Emperor Frederick Barbarossa's Italian ambitions to the south, where he secured Sicily for his Hohenstaufen heirs by marrying his son into the Norman royal family. Ruling from Palermo, Barbarossa's highly cultured but brutal grandson Frederick II (1194–1250) was a prototype for the future Renaissance prince.

His power struggle with the papacy divided the country into two – Guelfs supporting the pope and Ghibellines supporting the emperor. The backbone of the Guelfs was in communes such as Florence and Genoa. In 1266, they financed the mercenary army of Charles d'Anjou to defeat the imperial forces – and take the Sicilian throne. But Palermo rose up against the French in the Sicilian Vespers of 1282, when local people massacred everyone who spoke Italian with a French accent, and forced Charles to move his capital to Naples. The Sicilians offered their crown to the Spanish house of Aragon.

The Guelf–Ghibelline conflict became a pretext for settling family feuds (such as the one between the Montagues and Capulets in Shakespeare's *Romeo and Juliet*) or communal rivalries, from which Genoa and Florence emerged stronger than ever. In Rome, the dissolute popes repeatedly switched factions for temporary advantage and lost all political and moral authority.

FRANCIS OF ASSISI

The Church needed spiritual renewal, finding the perfect ally in Francis of Assisi (1182–1226), pious without being troublesomely militant. His sermons had great popular appeal. He chose not to attack Church corruption but instead to preach the values of a Christ-like life. The Franciscan order provided a much needed revival. The architecture of

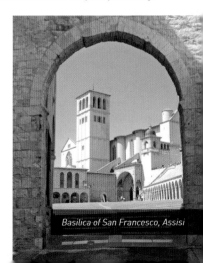

Basilica of San Francesco, Assisi

the church constructed in his name at Assisi contradicted Francis's humble testament denouncing 'temples of great dimension and rich ornament.' But Assisi's frescoes of the saint's life, painted by Cimabue and disciples of Giotto, were an effective act of propaganda against the prevalent libertinism and heresy.

THE CITY-STATES

By the late 13th century, with the independently minded communes growing into city-states, Italy was not to be subjugated to the will of one ruler. The Middle Ages saw the founding of Europe's first university in Bologna in the 11th century, followed by institutions of learning in Padua, Naples, Modena, Siena, Salerno and Palermo. In the absence of political unification, it was the universities that awakened the national consciousness. Travelling scholars needed a common tongue beyond the elitist Latin to break through the barriers of regional dialects. German Emperor Frederick II launched the movement for a national language at his court in Palermo, but Florentine-born Dante Alighieri (1265–1321) provided the ardour, moral leadership and literary example to bring it to fruition.

The maritime republic of Genoa rose to challenge Venice's supremacy. It dislodged Pisa in the western Mediterranean, whittled down Venice's hold on eastern ports, and set up colonies on the Black Sea for trade with Russia and faraway Cathay (China). But Genoa's participation in the Chioggia War of 1381 on the Venetian lagoon exhausted its resources.

Venice and its Repubblica Serena (Serene Republic) rebounded and turned to the mainland, extending its Veneto territory from Padua across the Po Valley as far as Bergamo, creating a new land-owning aristocracy in the process.

In the fertile Po Valley, Milan prospered from trade with Germany, principally in textiles and armour. Escaping unscathed from the Black Death of 1348 and subsequent plagues, it built up a sound economic base and maintained a strong army.

Florence was the first Italian town to mint its own gold coin (*fiorino* or florin), a prestigious instrument for trade in European markets, and it organised textile manufacture on a grand scale. Despite uprisings such as that of the *Ciompi* (wool-workers), the resilient Florentines were well-fed and highly literate compared to the residents of the rest of the country. The wealthy, ambitious Medici

Dante Alighieri, Italian author

emerged as the dominant merchant family. Cosimo the Elder (1389–1464) became the city's ruler and founder of the Medici dynasty in 1434.

Divided in the 14th century between the Spanish in Sicily and the French in Naples, southern Italy remained solidly feudal. Its agricultural economy suffered more than the north from plague and drought, which brought the inevitable famine. As Palermo was in decline, Naples flourished as a brilliant cosmopolitan capital. It was reunited with Sicily and known as the Kingdom of the Two Sicilies under the Spanish king Alfonso V of Aragon in 1442.

With the papacy in exile in Avignon since 1309, the brutal rule of the Orsini and Colonna families reduced Rome to a backwater village. Self-educated visionary Cola di Rienzo governed briefly in 1347 until the nobles drove him out. After 30 years, the papacy returned.

THE HIGH RENAISSANCE

A new national fraternity of scholars with expertise in the arts, sciences and law emerged as itinerant consultants to visionary rulers eager to make their city-states centres of cultural prestige and political propaganda. Men such as Leon Battista Alberti, the brilliant architect-mathematician-poet, brought about a new spirit of inquiry and scepticism. From their detailed study and translation of the Greek philosophers, they developed principles of objective scientific research, independent of the political, religious and emotional bias of earlier times.

Leonardo da Vinci eagerly applied the new method to architecture, civil and military engineering, urban planning, geography and map-making. This cultural explosion was dubbed a *rinascita*, or rebirth, of the glories of Italy's Greco-Roman past. But even more, it proved, with the humanism of both Leonardo and Michelangelo and the political realism of Machiavelli, to be the birth of our modern age.

Unfortunately, the creative ferment by no means precluded new horrors of war, assassination, persecution, plunder and rape. It was the heyday of the brilliant but lethal Spanish-Italian Borgias: lecherous Rodrigo, who became Pope Alexander VI, and treacherous son Cesare, who stopped at nothing to control and expand papal lands. His sister Lucrezia, forever smeared by anti-Spanish propaganda of the day as mistress of both her father and brother, was in fact, as duchess of Ferrara, a generous patron of the arts and benefactor of the poor.

In Florence, where his family had to fight to hold on to their supremacy, Lorenzo 'il Magnifico' de' Medici (1449–92) found time to encourage the art of Perugino, Ghirlandaio, Botticelli, young Leonardo and tempestuous Michelangelo.

On the international scene, the Turkish conquest of Constantinople in 1453 closed Genoa's Black Sea markets, but competitor Venice worked out a new deal in Cyprus and even a *modus vivendi* in Constantinople. But the Venetians' empire declined as they lost their taste for commerce in favour of the safety of their landholdings. From 1494 to 1530, the Spanish Habsburgs and the French

The spectacular ceiling of the Medici Chapel, Florence

turned Italy into a battleground for the Kingdom of Naples and the Duchy of Milan. Genoa sided with the Spanish to give Emperor Charles V access, via Milan, to his German territories, and later became a lucrative clearinghouse for Spain's newly discovered American silver. Rome was plundered by imperial armies in 1527; the Medici were driven out of Florence and returned to power under tutelage of the Spanish, who won effective control of the whole country.

When the dust of war settled, it was the dazzling cultural achievements that left their mark on the age. The father of Rome's High Renaissance, Pope Julius II (1503–13) began the new St Peter's cathedral, and commissioned Michelangelo to paint the ceiling of the Vatican's Sistine Chapel, and Raphael to decorate the Stanze. The architect Donato Bramante was nick-named *maestro ruinante* because of all the ancient monuments he dismantled to make way for the pope's building plans. With the treasures uncovered in the process, Julius founded the Vatican's magnificent collection of ancient sculpture.

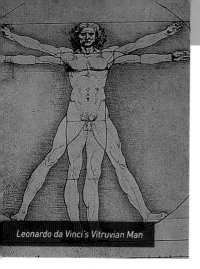
Leonardo da Vinci's Vitruvian Man

COUNTER-REFORMATION

Badly shaken by the Protestant Reformation in northern Europe, the Catholic Church convoked the Council of Trent (north of Lake Garda) in 1545. Non-Italian bishops urged the Church to carry out its own reform, hoping to democratise relations with the pope. But the threat of Lutherans, Calvinists and other heretics shifted the emphasis to repression, culminating in the Counter-Reformation formally proclaimed in 1563. The Church reinforced the Holy Office's Inquisition and the Index to censor the arts. The Jesuits, founded in 1534, became an army of theologians to combat heresy. Italian Protestants fled and Jews in Rome were restricted to a ghetto (50 years later than the Venice ghetto, Europe's first) and expelled from Genoa and Lucca.

Cardinal Carlo Borromeo, nephew of Pope Pius IV and Archbishop of Milan (1565–84), was the exemplary spiritual leader of Italy's Counter-Reformation. In alliance with the Jesuits, he weeded out corrupt clerics. As a symbol of his crusading spirit, he consecrated Milan's new cathedral, which took centuries to complete and remains one of the world's largest and most famous Gothic structures.

In the south, the 16th century saw Naples become the largest town in Europe, but it was oppressed and impoverished. In Sicily and Naples the army crushed revolts against taxes and conscription for Spain's wars in northern Europe.

TOWARDS NATIONHOOD

Lacking the solidarity to unite and too weak to resist by themselves, Italian kingdoms and duchies were reduced to handy pawns in Europe's 18th-century dynastic power plays. At the end of the Wars of Spanish, Austrian and Polish Succession, the Austrians had taken over northern Italy from the Spanish. The Age of Enlightenment engendered a new cultural ferment. In Milan, the theatre of La Scala opened, while La Fenice opened in Venice. Stimulated by the ideas of Voltaire, Rousseau and Diderot, the country's intellectuals were more keenly aware of being not only Europeans, but also *Italians*.

The hopes of progressives were raised by Austrian reforms in Lombardy and Tuscany (where the Medici dynasty had fizzled out by 1737). The results included fairer taxes, less Church influence in schools, more public education and removal of the Inquisition, Jesuits, the death penalty and instruments of torture. Outside the Austrian sphere of influence, Italy remained solidly conservative.

⊘ CULTURAL PROPAGANDA

Art proved a major instrument of Counter-Reformation propaganda, but it had to undergo some important changes. The vigour and intellectual integrity of the High Renaissance had softened into the stylised sophistication of Mannerism, the transition from the Renaissance to the Baroque. Condemning the preoccupation with pagan gods and decadence, the Church urged artists to deliver a strong, clear message to bring the troubled flock back to the fold. The Madonna and saints of Annibale Carracci further paved the way for the Baroque, attracting the faithful with a sensuous image of ideal beauty, while Caravaggio made a more brutal, but no less effective, appeal with a proletarian Mary and barefoot Apostles.

Venice stagnated under the rule of its elite, drawing nostalgic comfort from the city's beauty as painted in the *vedute* of Guardi and Canaletto. The papacy in Rome had lost prestige with the dissolution of the Jesuits and the loss of revenue from the Habsburg Church reforms. The South's aristocracy resisted all significant social reforms proposed by the Spanish. Don Carlos, a descendant of Louis XIV, saw himself as a southern Sun King, with Caserta Palace as his Versailles.

On the northwestern Alpine frontier, a new state had appeared on the scene, destined to lead the movement to a united Italy. With Savoy split in the 16th century between France and Switzerland, Piedmont, its foothill region southeast of the Alps, had come into the Italian orbit. Sidestepping the stagnant economic burden of Spanish domination, the sparsely populated duchy expanded quickly. Turin was little more than a fortified village of 40,000 inhabitants in 1600, but it rose to 93,000 a century later. The pragmatic dukes of Piedmont favoured French-style absolutist monarchy tempered with a parliament to bypass local fiefdoms. They copied Louis XIV's centralised administration and tax-collection and, by the 18th century, Turin was a sparkling royal capital.

NAPOLEON'S 'LIBERATION'

Napoleon Bonaparte, with his ideas of Italian 'independence', was welcomed after driving out the Austrians and Spanish in 1797. But the Italian treasuries were soon used to support the French war effort and the Bonaparte family. If Napoleon did not 'liberate' Italy, he did shake up the old conservatism from Lombardy to Naples by creating new universities and high schools, streamlining the bureaucracy, creating a new legal system with his Napoleonic Code, and awakening the forces of Italian nationalism.

Caution was the watchword among Italian rulers restored to their lands after Napoleon's defeat. Austria seized the chance to add the Veneto to its territories. The 1823 conclave elected

Royal Palace at Caserta, in Campania

arch-conservative Leo XII to help the papacy recover from its Napoleonic shock. On the lookout for any progressive movement, the Austrians helped Bourbon king Ferdinand of Naples crush an 1821 revolt for constitutional monarchy and foiled an uprising in Piedmont. In 1831 insurrection spread through Bologna, Modena and Parma to the Papal States of central Italy, but the Austrians defeated a rebel government of 'united Italian provinces', weakened by regional rivalries and conflicting personal ambitions.

THE RISORGIMENTO

The Risorgimento, the 'resurrection' of national identity, took two paths. Genoese-born Giuseppe Mazzini's *Giovane Italia* (Young Italy) movement sought national unity by popular-based insurrection. He opposed Piedmontese patricians and intellectuals of the Moderates party, seeking reform through a privilege-conscious confederation of Italian princes blessed by the papacy – with Piedmont providing the military muscle. The Moderates feared a proletarian militancy among factory workers. Landowners bringing in cheap migrant labour faced peasant resentment. Food riots broke out in Lombardy, revolts in Tuscany, and southern peasants demanded a share of common land.

Outright rebellion erupted in Milan on 18 March 1848, the year of revolution across Europe. Milan was freed from its 14,000-strong Austrian garrison. The Venetians restored their republic, a Piedmontese army joined with troops from Tuscany, the Papal States and Naples, and a new democratic Roman Republic was proclaimed. However, the hesitant Carlo Alberto of Piedmont gave the Austrians time to re-establish their authority and Italian gains toppled.

Conceding the need for more reform, the new king of Piedmont, Vittorio Emanuele II, became a constitutional monarch with a parliament dominated by Moderates. His prime minister, Count Cavour, was a hard-nosed political realist who won over left-wing support for a programme of free-trade capitalism and large-scale public works. Among the political exiles flocking to Piedmont was a veteran of the earlier revolts, Giuseppe Garibaldi.

With their French allies, Piedmont defeated Austria at Magenta and Solferino to secure Lombardy in 1859. A year later, Cavour negotiated the handover of Emilia and Tuscany. But it was the adventure of Garibaldi's Red Shirts that imposed the unification of the peninsula in 1860. They seized Bourbon Sicily and

Garibaldini statue in Varese

crossed to the mainland. At
Teano, outside Naples, they
met Vittorio Emanuele, who
was proclaimed the first King
of Italy. National unity was
completed with the annexation of the Veneto in 1866
and Rome was made the new
capital in 1871.

Verdi

The composer Giuseppe
Verdi was the towering
artist of the Risorgimento.
The romantic humanism of
his operas inspired fellow
patriots, who saw in the
Nabucco Freedom Chorus a
positive call to action.

THE MODERN ERA

Italy took its place among modern nations as an unexceptional centralised state. It was careful to protect the interests of its industrial
and financial establishment and granted reforms to the working
classes only under the pressure of their united action.

Both the political left and right wanted Italy to join the European
race for colonies – their eyes fixed on Ethiopia and Libya. Conservatives supported expansion for reasons of national prestige.
Socialists talked of Italy's 'civilising mission' in the Mediterranean,
seeking to divert the flow of emigrants (heading increasingly to
the Americas) to experimental collective land management in new
African colonies in Tripoli and Cyrenaica.

At home, in addition to traditional textiles, industry was expand-
ing fast in metallurgy, chemicals and machinery. The national love
affair with cars had begun – from seven produced in 1900 and 70 in
1907, there were 9,200 rolling out of the factories by 1914, most of
them from Fiat, which was founded in 1899.

With Prime Minister Giovanni Giolitti manoeuvring the capital and labour forces, Italy began the 20th century in a blithe
state of calm and prosperity known as *Italietta*, and remained
neutral when war broke out in 1914. The following year, acting
with what Prime Minister Antonio Salandra acknowledged to be
'*sacro egoismo*', Italy signed a secret treaty to enter the war on

the side of Britain, France and Russia in exchange for the post-war annexation of Austrian-held Trento, South Tyrol (now Alto Adige) and Trieste.

The people were at first cool to the war, despite the jingoism of Fascist sympathiser, aristocrat and author Gabriele D'Annunzio and his friend, Benito Mussolini. The Italian army was the least well prepared of the combatants, lacking artillery, guns, trucks and trained officers, but the infantry showed great courage in the trenches. After the disaster at Caporetto, the planned Austro-German 1917 advance across the Veneto plain was held until the Italian counter-attack of October–November 1918 permitted a triumphant entry into Trento and Trieste. For most ordinary Italians, war in uniform was their first real experience of Italian nationality. War-supporters such as D'Annunzio, who captured the popular imagination by flying over Vienna to drop propaganda leaflets, were acclaimed as patriots, while democrats and pacifist republicans were dismissed as defeatists. Parliament, which was denied knowledge of the secret war treaty until the Peace Conference of 1919, was exposed as impotent.

THE RISE OF FASCISM

The political left was in disarray. The Socialists won the elections but split over support for the Russian Revolution, leading to the formation in 1921 of the Italian Communist Party. In an atmosphere of economic crisis – stagnant productivity, bank closures and rising unemployment – conservatives wanted somebody tougher and more dynamic than the eternally compromising old-style politicians. As the black-shirted *Fasci Italiani di Combattimento* (Italian combat groups) beat up Slavs in Trieste and trades union workers in Bologna, Mussolini filled the role. Threatened by the Fascists' March on Rome in 1922, King Vittorio Emanuele III caved in and invited Mussolini, *Il Duce*, to form a government.

The now all-too-familiar process of totalitarianism set in: opposition leaders were assassinated; their parties, free unions and the free press were abolished. Yet Italian Fascism remained more of a style than a coherent ideology, characterised by bombastic architecture and the arrogant harangues of Mussolini from the Palazzo Venezia's 'heroic balcony' in Rome.

Most Italians survived with lip-service and good humour, while Communists re-allied with Socialists in the anti-Fascist underground, whose partisans linked up with the Allies during World War II. In 1936, Mussolini invaded Ethiopia to divert attention from the worsening economic climate at home. Italian war planes joined Hitler's Luftwaffe on General Franco's side in the Spanish Civil War (5,000 Italian Communists and Socialists fought on the Republican side).

Following the Germans' lead in 1938, racist legislation was introduced against the country's 57,000 Jews. The next year, Italy invaded Albania and, after the collapse of France in June 1940, plunged with Germany into World War II. Its poorly equipped armies were defeated by the British in the African desert and by the mountain snows in the Balkans. The Allies landed in Sicily in June 1943 and liberated Rome one year later. Mussolini, toppled soon after the Allied landings and re-instated briefly as a German puppet in the north, was caught fleeing in German uniform to the Swiss border. He was executed in April 1945.

National Fascist Party poster, 1925

Post-war hardships – unemployment, the black market and prostitution – have been made familiar by the films of Rossellini, de Sica and Fellini.

POST-WAR RECOVERY AND THE 21ST CENTURY

By popular mandate, Italy became a republic in 1945 and the monarchy was exiled. Italians did not take easily to national government. They had existed through most of their history without it and Mussolini had spoiled their appetite. Fatigued by 'Il Duce's' excesses, they rejected the militant left for a little *dolce vita* with the less adventurous but less disturbing Christian Democrats. Fuelled by financial aid from the US, Italy achieved her economic miracle in the 1950s and early 1960s, becoming a leading industrial nation. However, the country fell into economic and political turmoil in the late 1960s, and terrorist activities became commonplace, continuing through the next decade. In the 1980s, a pragmatic Socialist coalition government with the Christian Democrats brought a few years of unusual stability. Corruption and tax-evasion continued, but the police clamped down on the political terrorism of the Red Brigades and neo-Fascists, as well as the age-old criminality of the Mafia.

THE RISE AND FALL OF SILVIO BERLUSCONI

In the early 1990s a series of bribery and corruption scandals (known as *Tangentopoli* or 'Bribesville') revealed the dirty and deep-rooted hold of politicians and business tycoons. Politics has been dominated by Italy's most powerful media magnate, Silvio Berlusconi, who was head of Italy's longest-lasting post-war government. Depicting himself as the new face of Italy he headed a right-wing, short-lived coalition in 1994, then in 2001, was swept to power on a tide of populism and nationalism. Voted out in the 2006 election, he was back in power again in 2008. In 2013, after a two month political stalemate, Berlusconi emerged as a winner again when a coalition, headed by Enrico Letta, brought the media

tycoon's party back to power. Berlusconi was facing three criminal trials at the time.

Berlusconi's final fall from grace came in August 2013 when Italy's Supreme Court upheld his four-year jail sentence for conviction for tax fraud. He had faced 17 major criminal indictments in the past but had always managed to escape prosecution by forcing through legislation or letting charges expire under Italy's statute of limitations. A 2006 amnesty law reduced Berlusconi's four-year jail sentence to one, and given his age at the time of 76, his custodial sentence was upheld in favour of community service. Consequently, he was expelled from the Senate and barred from serving in any legislative capacity for six years, which finally put an end to his long political career. With the fall of Berlusconi, the reins of the country were taken over briefly by Enrico Letta, who was quickly replaced by Matteo Renzi, who embarked on an ambitious programme of political and economic reforms. Renzi was forced to resign in December 2016 after losing a key referendum on constitutional law. He was replaced by Paolo Gentiloni.

HISTORICAL LANDMARKS

9th century BC First signs of pre-Roman Etruscans.

8th century BC Greeks colonise Sicily and other southern regions.

753 BC Rome founded.

510 BC Establishment of Roman Republic.

44 BC Julius Caesar assassinated on 15 March.

27 BC Octavius (Augustus Caesar), the nephew and heir of Julius Caesar, founds the Roman Empire.

AD 79 Vesuvius volcano buries Pompeii.

306–37 Emperor Constantine makes Constantinople the capital and Christianity the state religion.

410 Visigoths sack Rome.

476 The fall of the Roman Empire; the Dark Ages begin.

800 Pope crowns Charlemagne Holy Roman Emperor.

827–1060 Arabs invade and settle in Sicily.

1000–1100 Normans conquer the south; First Crusade.

1309–77 Papacy exiled from Rome to Avignon, France.

1442 Alfonso V of Aragon crowned king of 'Two Sicilies' (Naples and Sicily).

1503–13 Rome is the centre of the Renaissance.

1545–63 Council of Trent starts the Counter-Reformation.

1700–13 War of the Spanish Succession ends and Austria becomes the major foreign power.

1796–1814 Napoleon invades the north then much of Italy.

1815–32 Austrians crush insurrection; the *Risorgimento*, a national political movement, begins.

1831 Mazzini founds *la Giovane Italia* to combat Austria.

1859 Franco-Piedmontese alliance takes Lombardy.

1860 Garibaldi's 'Thousand' conquer Naples and Sicily.

1861 Kingdom of Italy proclaimed with Turin as capital and Vittorio Emanuele II as king.

1871 Rome named capital of unified Italy.

1915 Italy joins the British, French and Russians in World War I.

1922 Mussolini begins Fascist regime with march on Rome, declaring himself prime minister, then Duce.

1929 Lateran Treaty establishes separate Vatican state.

1936 Mussolini annexes Abyssinia (Ethiopia).

1940 Italy joins Germany in World War II.

1943–4 Allies liberate Sicily, then Rome; Mussolini arrested. Rescued by the Germans, he founds a puppet state in the north.

1945 Execution of Mussolini and his mistress.

1946 Abdication of Vittorio Emanuele III; proclamation of the Republic.

1957 Treaty of Rome institutes the EEC, forerunner of the European Union (EU), of which Italy is one of the six founder members.

1970s–80s Shadowy far-left group, the Red Brigade, causes instability in a campaign of kidnapping and murder.

Early 1990s Widespread economic and political corruption scandals. Two anti-Mafia judges assassinated in Sicily.

2001 Media magnate Silvio Berlusconi is elected prime minister.

2002 The euro replaces the lira. An earthquake in Puglia kills 26 children.

2005 Pope John Paul II dies. Cardinal Joseph Ratzinger elected to replace him.

2006 Turin hosts Winter Olympics.

2008 Prodi resigns and Berlusconi returns to power.

2009 Earthquake strikes Abruzzo, killing 308 people.

2011 Berlusconi is forced to resign. Technocrat Mario Monti is chosen to sort out Italy's economic crisis.

2013 The Five Star Movement (M5S), co-founded by comedian Beppe Grillo, stuns mainstream political parties by taking a quarter of the votes in the general election. Pope Benedict XVI resigns. Cardinal Jorge Bergoglio of Argentina is elected the 26th Pope and takes the name of Pope Francis I.

2014 Matteo Renzi is elected prime minster, forms a left-right coalition government and embarks on major political and economic reforms.

2015 Sergio Mattarella is elected Italy's first president from Sicily. The refugee crisis intensifies as more than 1,500 people drown trying to reach Italy by boat.

2016 A 6.2-magnitude earthquake devastates the town of Amatrice, killing nearly 300 people. Parliament adopts a law legalising same-sex unions. Renzi announces a referendum on major constitutional reform. Another powerful earthquake hits central Italy, destroying the Basilica of Saint Benedict in Norcia. Renzi is defeated in the referendum and resigns as PM and is replaced by Paolo Gentiloni.

Sunset over Rome

 # WHERE TO GO

Planning a trip to Italy entails a series of difficult decisions. 'Doing' Italy is a lifetime's job and many devotees are so in love with the place that they won't even think of an alternative destination. After a predictable first romance with Rome, Venice or Florence, they spend the rest of their lives systematically working their way through the small but wildly varied country, region by region, visit after visit. If this is your first trip, you would do well to establish an overall impression. If the seduction works – and it usually does – you will want to come back time and again.

GETTING AROUND

This section is divided into six areas and includes all the most important towns and regions. Five of the six areas have a principal city as a focus or starting point: **Rome** for central Italy; **Florence** for Tuscany, with Umbria and the Adriatic seaside resorts to the east; **Venice** for Veneto, the Dolomites and Emilia-Romagna's historic towns from Parma to Ravenna; **Milan** for Lombardy, Piedmont and the Italian Riviera to the west; and **Naples** for the south. The sixth area focuses on Italy's two largest islands, **Sicily** and **Sardinia**.

Those with a passion for the big city can combine Rome with the artistic delights of Florence and Tuscany, or Milan with the magical romance of Venice. For those who like to be active, mountains, lakes and wind lend themselves to myriad year-round sporting activities. Italy has 7,600km (4,722 miles) of coastline and when the summer heat gets too much, you can cool off at one of the many seaside resorts or any of the gem-like islands.

Nowhere is it easier or more delightful to overdose on museums and monuments than in Italy. While it would be a crime to ignore the churches, palazzi and museums chronicling the glories of

Bike-sharing scheme in Rome

Italy's history, the best way to enjoy them is to also spend plenty of time soaking up the atmosphere from a front-row seat in a caffè, joining the early evening street *passeggiata* (promenade) or watching seaside life unfold from under a beach umbrella. The siesta is one of the greatest of all Mediterranean institutions and the most important Italian expression you may ever learn is *dolce far niente* (the sweetness of doing nothing).

ROME AND LAZIO

Crowning seven hills along the winding banks of the River Tiber, **Rome ❶** has numerous personalities: ancient Rome of imperial ruins; Catholic Rome of Vatican City and countless churches; the Renaissance city of Michelangelo and Raphael; and the Baroque of Bernini and Borromini. It is also a modern metropolis of interminable traffic jams, fashionable boutiques and caffès, as well as factories and characterless post-war suburbs. The secret of the Eternal City's magic is that it lives and relishes all its ages: churches are built on the ruins of Roman baths or pagan temples, while the trendy caffè crowd on Piazza Navona draw inspiration from Bernini's grandiose 17th-century fountain.

To attempt to know its every nook and cranny is daunting, but by starting with the ancient city around the Colosseum or the Vatican, you will come to know one age at a time.

CLASSICAL ROME

The nucleus of Classical Rome is around the Forum, with the Colosseum to the east, and the Palatine Hill and Baths of Caracalla to the south. Take them in your stride, avoid the midday sun in the shade-less Forum and enjoy a picnic and siesta on the Palatine. Even if you're not interested in archaeology, it's worth at least an hour or two to stand among the debris of an empire and wonder whether Fifth Avenue, Piccadilly or the Champs-Elysées will look any better 2,000 years from now.

⊙ MUSEUM TIPS

Museum-going in Italy is not always simple. Even the local tourist office cannot always keep up with the changes in opening hours. Some museums are closed temporarily – for days, months or even years – for *restauro* (restoration). This is a blanket term covering budgetary problems for museum staff and modern security systems, or genuine, long overdue programmes to renovate the buildings and restore the paintings. Many ancient Roman monuments may also go into prolonged hiding under protective scaffolding.

When you visit one of the huge museums such as the Uffizi or the Vatican, treat it like Italy itself. Unless you're a museum-fiend, don't try to see it all. Before you begin, study the museum plan at the entrance, then head for the things that capture your interest. Or, if you prefer serendipity – stumbling across beautiful surprises – just wander around, but not for much more than a few hours. Otherwise, you may struggle to recall the next day, let alone years later, just what masterpieces you saw. Many cities offer cost-effective tourist passes that include entry to museums. For major sights, pre-booking tickets is recommended.

The Roman Forum

With a leap of the imagination, you can stand among the columns, arches and porticoes of the **Roman Forum Ⓐ** (daily Nov–mid-Feb 8.30am–4.30pm, mid-Feb–Mar until 5pm, Apr–Sept until 7pm, Oct until 6.30pm; last entry one hour before closing) and picture the civic, commercial and religious hub of the city, the first in Europe to house a million inhabitants. Earthquake, fire, flood and the plunder of barbarians and Renaissance architects reduced the area to a cow pasture until the 19th-century excavations. A detailed map and audio guide, rented at the entrance (on Via dei Fori Imperiali), will help you trace the layout of the ancient buildings.

Part of the **Curia**, home of the Roman Senate, still stands. Steps nearby lead underground to the **Lapis Niger**, a black marble pavement laid by Julius Caesar over the presumed grave of Romulus, the city's founder. To the south of it are remains of the Basilica Julia law court and the **Rostra** orators' platform from which Mark Antony informed the people of Caesar's assassination. Countless Renaissance and Baroque sculptors have drawn inspiration from the friezes on the **Arch of Septimius Severus** (a 3rd-century emperor).

The **Temple of Saturn** doubled as state treasury and site of the debauchery known as the Saturnalia, pagan precursor of Christmas. In the circular **Temple of Vesta**, the sacred flame of Rome was tended by six Vestal Virgins who would be buried alive if they broke their 30-year vow of chastity. At the end of Via Sacra, the **Arch of Titus** commemorates the sacking of Jerusalem in AD70.

Of the Imperial Forums, built as an adjunct to the Roman Forum in honour of Julius Caesar, Augustus, Trajan, Vespasian and Domitian, the most sumptuous was Trajan's. The beautifully designed **Museum of the Imperial Forums** (Museo dei Fiori Imperiali; www.mercati ditraiano.it; daily 9.30am–6.30pm) gives access to Trajan's Markets, a tiered semi-circular structure of shops that sold everything from silks and spices to fish and flowers. The soaring **Trajan's Column** (AD113) celebrates the emperor's campaigns against the Dacians

The Forum, hub of ancient Rome

in what is now Romania, the detailed friezes spiralling around the column constitute a textbook of Roman warfare. St Peter's statue on top replaced that of the emperor in 1587.

The Palatine Hill

South of the Forum, a slope leads to the **Palatine Hill** (Colle Palatino; daily, same hours as the Roman Forum), legendary birthplace of Rome, the history of which is charted in the **Palatine Museum**. Today the hill is a romantic garden, dotted with toppled columns among the wild flowers and acanthus shrubs. Only rows of cypress trees and pavilions remain from the 16th-century botanical gardens. Nearby lie the ruins of the huge **Domus Augustana** Ⓑ (House of Augustus; www.coopculture.it; Mon–Fri 9am–1pm, 2–5pm, Sat 9am–2pm; guided tours only, two-day ticket also valid for the Forum and Colosseum; free on the first Sunday of the month; to book tel: 06-3996 7700). After years of restoration, exquisite, vividly coloured frescoes in four of the rooms are accessible. Expect long queues – only five visitors are allowed in at a time. Enjoy

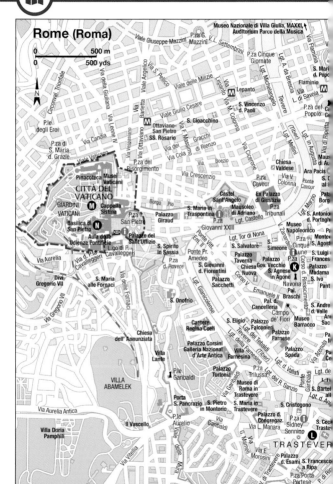

Rome (Roma)

0 _____ 500 m
0 _____ 500 yds

N

Museo Nazionale di Villa Giulia, MAXXI,
Auditorium Parco della Musica

Viale Giuseppe Mazzini
P.za G. Mazzini
V.le L. Settembrini
Via Flaminia

Viale Angelico
Via S. Pellico
Via della Giuliana
Circonval. Trionfale
P.le degli Eroi
Via Candia
Via Leone IV
Via Vespasiano
Via Ottaviano
Viale Vaticano

Via delle Milizie
Viale Giulio Cesare
Via Barletta
Lepanto M
Via F. Massimo
Gracchi
Via Cola di Rienzo
P.za del Risorgimento
Via Crescenzio
Borgo Pio

Via M. Colonna
Via Marianna Dionigi
Via Lepanto
Lgt. A. da Brescia
Via Michelangelo
Tevere
P.za Cinque Giornate
S. Mari d. Popo
Flaminio
Via di Savoia
P.za del P Popolo G

Lgt. in Augusta
(Tiber)
Lgt. di Ripetta
Maus di Au
Ara Pacis
S. C. al

Ottaviano-San Pietro M
S. Gioacchino
SS. Rosario
Via dei Gracchi
Via Cicerone
Via Boezio
Chiesa Valdese

P.za Cavour
Via V. Colonna
Ponte Cavour
Lgt. Marzio
Via Tomacelli
S. Antonio d. Portoghe
Pa Borg
Pe

Pinacoteca Musei Vaticani
CITTÀ DEL VATICANO
GIARDINI VATICANI M
Cappella Sistina N
Basilica di San Pietro
Aula delle Udienze Pontificie
Lgo. di P. Cavalleggeri
Via di P. Cavalleggeri

Palazzo Giraud
P.za San Pietro
Palazzo del Sant'Uffizio

Castel Sant'Angelo
S. Maria in Traspontina
Mausoleo di Adriano
P.za Pia
Lgt. Castello
Ponte Vitt. Em. II
S. Spirito in Sassia
Giovanni XXIII
Lgt. Tor di Nona

Ex Palazzo di Giustizia
P.za Tribunali
Museo Napoleonico
S. Salvatore
S. Simeone
P.za Cinque Lune
S. Agostino
S. Luigi dei Francesi
Palazzo Madama
S. Ivo
Pant

Via Aurelia
Divi Gregorio VII
Via di Gregorio VII

S. Maria alle Fornaci
Via delle Fornaci
S. Onofrio

P.za d. Rovere
Ponte Pr. Amedeo
S. Giovanni d. Fiorentini
Palazzo Sacchetti
Palazzo Taverna
Chiesa Nuova
Gov. Vecchio
S. Agnese in Agone
Corso V. Emanuele II
Pal. Braschi
Pal. d. Cancelleria
Corso del Rinascimento
P.za Navona K
Palazzo Madama
S. Andre d. Valle
Are Sac

Carcere Regina Coeli
Chiesa dell'Annunziata
Villa Lante

S. Eligio
Palazzo Falconieri
Lgt. dei Tebaldi
Lgt. Farnesina (Tiber)
Campo de' Fiori
Palazzo Farnese
Museo Barracco
Palazzo Spada
Pa
Via Arenula
Ce

VILLA ABAMELEK

Palazzo Corsini Galleria Nazional d'Arte Antica
Villa Farnesina
Palazzo Tortonia
P.za Trilussa
P.le Garibaldi
Museo di Roma in Trastevere
Lgt. della Farnesina
Lgt. R. Sanzio
P.za di S. Vallati
Via Garibaldi
Lgt. de
S. Bartol all
Lgt. d. An

Via Aurelia Antica
Villa Doria Pamphili
Porta S. Pancrazio
Il Vascello
P.le Aurelio
S. Pietro in Montorio
Via Garibaldi
S. Maria in Trastevere
Palazzo d. Congregaz.
Via L. Manara
S. Cristogono
P.za i
Sidney Sonnino L
S. Ce Traste

Via Vitellia
Via di Porta S. Pancrazio
Via E Morosini
Palazzo d. Esami
S. Francesco a Ripa
P.za Porta Portese
TRASTEVER
P. di Ri

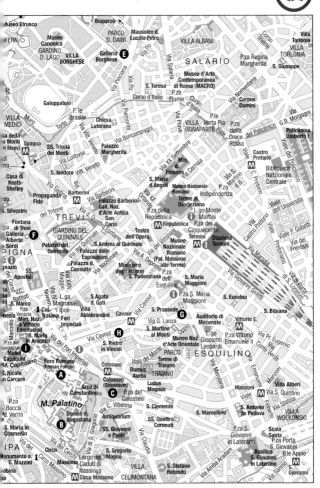

Museo Etrusco
Bioparco
FERN.
Museo Canonica
GIARDINO D. LAGO
VILLA BORGHESE
PARCO D. DAINI
Mausoleo d. Lucillo Petro
VILLA ALBANI
Galleria Borghese **E**
SALARIO
Villa Torlonia
VILLA TORLONIA
S. Giuseppe

Pza Regina Margherita

Galoppatoio
P.le Brasile
Chiesa Luterana
S. Teresa
Corso d'Italia
Museo d'Arte Contemporanea di Roma (MACRO)
Via Nomentana
Corpus Domini

VILLA MEDICI
Muro Torto
a della i Monti Steps)
Spagna **M**
P.le Brasile
Via Veneto
Pza Fiume
Via XX Settembre
Pza della Croce Rossa
G.B. Morgagni
Policlinico Umberto I.

SS. Trinita dei Monti
Chiesa Luterana
VILLA BONAPARTE
P.le Porta Pia
Via del Policlinico

Casa di Keats-Shelley
zo
S. Silvestro
S. Isodoro
Vitt. Veneto
Palazzo Margherita
Castro Pretorio
Biblioteca Nazionale Centrale

Propaganda Fide
Via Sistina
S. Maria d.Angeli
Min. d. Finanza
Museo Nazionale Romano Terme di Diocleziano
Via S. Marino d.B.
Via C. Pretorio

Barberini **M**
Palazzo Barberini-Gall. Naz. d'Arte Antica San Carlo
Pza della Repubblica
Indipendenza
Via dell'Università

Fontana di Trevi Galleria Alberto Sordi **F**
TREVI
GIARDINO DEL QUIRINALE
Teatro dell'Opera
Repubblica **M**
Lgo Monte Martini
Pza dei Cinquecento
Via P. Gobetti

PIGNA
SS. Apostoli
Palazzo del Quirinale
S.Andrea al Quirinale
Palazzo delle Esposizioni
Museo Nazionale Romano (Pal. Massimo alle Terme)
Stazione Termini
Termini **M**
Via dei Frentani

Ignazio
del Corso
Battisti
S. Marco
Mon. Naz. a Vittorio Emanuele II
Palazzo d. Consulta
Ministero degli Interni
S. Pudenziana
Pza dell' Esquilino
S. Maria Maggiore
Via Giovanni Giolitti
S. Bibiana

Venezia
Col. Traiana
L.ga Magnana poli
Villa Aldobrandini
Fori Imperiali
Cavour **M**
P.za S. Maria Maggiore
S. Eusebio
Vittorio E. **M**
Via Pr. Eugenio Conte Verde

Pza del
Musei Capitolini
M. Capitolino
S. Nicola n Carcere
S. Maria in Aracoeli **I**
Via Cavour
S. Prassede **G**
Via G. Lanza
Auditorio di Mecenate
Pza Vittorio Emanuele II
Manzoni **M**

Foro Romano (Roman Forum) **A**
S. Pietro in Vincoli **H**
S. Martino ai Monti
Museo Naz. d'Arte Orientale
Lgo Giacomo Leopardi
ESQUILINO
Villa Altieri
Via S. Quintino

S. Maria in Cosmedin
Colosseo
Colosseo (Colosseum) **C**
Domus Aurea
PARCO DI TRAIANO
S. Antonio de Padova
VILLA WOLKONSKI

M. Palatino
Domus d. Augustana **B**
Arco di Constantino
Pza del Colosseo
Ludus Magnus
S. Clemente
S. Marcellino
Pza S. Giovanni in Laterano
Scala Santa

Pza Bocca d. Verita
Antiquarium
Via C. Vibenna
SS. Giovanni e Paolo
SS. Quattro Coronati
Pza Porta S. Giovanni

IPA
Monumento a. G. Mazzini
Circo Massimo
S. Gregorio Magno
VILLA
S. Stefano Rotondo
Basilica S. Giovanni in Laterano
P.le Appio
S. Giovanni **M**

Circo
Largo del Circo Massimo Caduti di Nassiriya
Circo Massimo **M**
CELIMONTANA
Via Amba Aradam
Via San. Gio.

the fine view southwards over the **Circus Maximus**, where chariot races were held for crowds of up to 200,000.

The Colosseum

Of Rome's countless inspirational churches, palazzi and monuments, it is the Roman Empire's largest amphitheatre, the **Colosseum** Ⓒ (daily Nov–mid-Feb 8.30am–4.30pm, mid-Feb–Mar until 5pm, Apr–Sept until 7pm, Oct until 6.30pm; last entry one hour before closing) that is the symbol of the city's eternity. The building that Lord Byron called 'the gladiator's bloody circus' was begun by Emperor Vespasian in AD72; the four-tiered elliptical amphitheatre seated more than 50,000 spectators. Flowing in and out of 80 arched passageways known as *vomitoria*, aristocrats and plebians came to see blood: bears, lions, tigers, leopards and other wild beasts were starved into fighting each other and against criminals, war captives and (according to some historians) Christians. Gladiators, once criminals and slaves but later professional warriors, fought to the crowds' cries of *Jugula!* ('Slit his throat!')

For their churches and private palaces, popes and princes have stripped the Colosseum of its precious marble, travertine and metal. In the arena's basin, they have left a ruined maze of cells and corridors that funnelled men and beasts to the slaughter. The horror has disappeared and what remains is the thrill of the monument's endurance. In his *Childe Harold's Pilgrimage* (1812–18), Byron wrote: 'While stands the Colosseum, Rome shall stand; when falls the

Palatine ticket

A ticket for the Palatine Hill and Museum includes entry to the Colosseum. Buying your ticket here allows you to bypass the lengthy queues at the city's most iconic Roman building (see page 48). Or you can buy a ticket online at www.coopculture.it.

The Colosseum

Colosseum, Rome shall fall; and when Rome falls, with it shall fall the world.' There is reason to believe it shall stand forever. Restoration is an ongoing process and Tod's, the luxury shoemaker, is contributing €25 million to shore up the monument. The first stage of the restoration was completed in 2016, with the reopening of the underground and the third ring (9am–5pm, shorter hours in winter; guided tours only).

The nearby **Arch of Constantine** celebrates the 4th-century emperor's battlefield conversion to Christianity. A frugal Senate took a number of fragments from monuments of earlier rulers Trajan, Hadrian and Marcus Aurelius in order to decorate the arch.

Northeast of the Colosseum is the **Domus Aurea**, a fabulous villa built by Emperor Nero, who spent just a few years in his 'Golden House' (the facade was clad in solid gold) before killing himself in AD68. On a site once 25 times the size of the Colosseum, the palace had 250 rooms (www.coopculture.it; Sat–Sun, guided tours only, tours in English at 9.45, 11.30, noon, 3pm).

South Towards the Via Appia

Just 1km (0.66 miles) south of the Colosseum, the 3rd-century **Baths of Caracalla** (Terme di Caracalla; http://archeoroma.beni culturali.it or www.coopculture.it; from 9am to Apr–Aug 7.15pm, Sep 7pm, Oct 6.30pm, Nov–mid Feb 4.30pm, mid Feb–mid Mar 5pm, mid Mar–end Mar 5.30pm; free the first Sun of the month) were built for 1,600 people to bathe in luxury. The baths and gymnasia were of alabaster and granite, decorated with statues and frescoes. Public bathing was a prolonged social event, as merchants and senators passed from the *calidarium* (hot room) to cool down in the *tepidarium* and *frigidarium*. In 2012 a new museum opened in the basement, showcasing 45 archaeological findings in a beautifully arranged exhibition space.

South of the baths begins the **Old Appian Way** (Via Appia Antica), built in 312BC for the Roman legions who marched to coastal Brindisi to set sail for the Levant and North Africa. On either side lie the ruins of sepulchres of 20 generations of patrician families. The 17th-century chapel of Domine Quo Vadis marks the site where St Peter, fleeing persecution in Rome, is said to have encountered Christ. Further along the Via Appia are three of Rome's most celebrated catacombs, including those of **St Callisto** (daily 9am–noon, 2–5pm), the largest of some 50 underground Christian cemeteries.

STREETS AND SQUARES

Beyond the ancient ruins, the streets of the Eternal City display its hugely varied heritage, from early Christian basilicas and graceful Renaissance palaces to the theatrical piazzas and flamboyant fountains of the Baroque. Take time to pause and soak up the atmosphere in a piazza, admiring the play of sunlight on russet and ochre facades, as you listen to the fountains and enjoy a refreshing drink.

Piazza di Spagna

Named after a palace used as the Spanish Embassy, the **Spanish Steps** (Scalinata della Trinità dei Monti) and the **Piazza di Spagna** are the heart of the city's most exclusive shopping enclave. The piazza's 17th-century fountain, Fontana della Barcaccia, is by Bernini's father. Babington's Tea Rooms nearby are a relic of the days when Romans called the piazza the 'English ghetto'. More essentially Roman, on nearby Via Condotti, is the city's oldest

The Spanish Steps

coffee house, the 18th-century Caffè Greco – popular, as you will
see from pictures, busts and autographs, with Liszt, Baudelaire,
Byron, Keats, Goethe, Casanova and Fellini.

The steps themselves are a hang-out for Rome's youths, lovers, trinket peddlers and tourists. The pleasant daze induced on
the three-tiered, flower-festooned staircase was celebrated by
John Keats, who died here in 1821, as a 'blissful cloud of summer indolence'. His house at the foot of the steps has been preserved as the **Keats-Shelley House** (www.keats-shelley-house.
org; Mon–Sat 10am–1pm and 2–6pm). At the top of the steps, its
twin belfries looming over the piazza, is the 16th-century French
church, **Trinità dei Monti**.

To the west of the Piazza di Spagna, close to the Tiber's banks,
the **Ara Pacis** (Altar of Peace; daily 9.30am–7.30pm; www.ara
pacis.it), built in 13BC by Emperor Augustus, is a superb example
of Classical Roman art. In 2006 a controversial glass and travertine complex, designed by US architect Richard Meier, was built to
showcase the monument.

Piazza del Popolo

North of here you will find the **Piazza del Popolo**. The gracefully curving piazza is an open-air urban theatre designed in 1816 by Napoleon's architect Giuseppe Valadier.

On the north side of the square, the church of **Santa Maria del Popolo** (www.santamariadelpopolo.it; Mon–Thu 7.15am–12.30pm, Fri–Sat 7.15am–7pm, Sun 7.30am–1.30pm, 4.30–7.30pm) is important for Raphael's handsome Chigi Chapel, exquisite frescoes by Pinturicchio and two profoundly disturbing early 17th-century paintings executed by Caravaggio, the *Conversion of St Paul* and *Crucifixion of St Peter*.

Next to the church, a 16th-century gateway marks what was the entrance to ancient and medieval Rome along the Via Flaminia, leading from Rimini on the Adriatic coast. The **obelisk** in the piazza's centre, dating from the Egypt of Ramesses II (13th century BC), was brought here from the Circus Maximus and re-erected by Pope Sixtus V in 1589.

Rounding off the south side are the twin Baroque churches, **Santa Maria dei Miracoli** (daily 7am–12.30pm, 4–7.30pm) and **Santa Maria in Montesanto** (Mon–Fri 5–8pm, Sun 10.30am–1.30pm), completed by masters Gianlorenzo Bernini and Carlo Fontana.

Pincio Gardens and Villa Borghese

Above Piazza del Popolo to the east, the **Pincio Gardens** (close at sunset) offer a magical view of the city. The ascending Pincio promenade lined with umbrella pines takes you past **Villa Medici**, back towards the Spanish steps.

Stretching north from Pincio Gardens is the large and leafy **Villa Borghese** park, once the estate of Cardinal Scipione Borghese, the nephew of Pope Paul V. Italy's most important Etruscan museum, the **Museo Nazionale Etrusco**, can be found in the 16th-century **Villa Giulia** (www.villagiulia.beniculturali.it; Tue–Sun 8.30am–7.30pm, last entry 6.30pm) in the northwest area of the park. The collection includes finds from major excavations in Lazio and Tuscany, countless Etruscan artefacts and a reconstructed Etruscan temple.

The **Galleria Borghese** E (tel: 06-32810, www.galleriaborghese.it; Tue–Sun 8.30am–7.30pm, last admission 6.30pm; booking essential) is housed in the Baroque Villa Borghese in the east of the park. The villa was inspired by Hadrian's Villa at Tivoli (see page 68), but with Italian formal gardens transformed into an English-style landscaped park. One of Italy's loveliest and most important small museums, its highlights include sculptures by Bernini and Canova, and paintings by Botticelli, Caravaggio, Correggio, Cranach, Dürer, Raphael, Rubens and Titian.

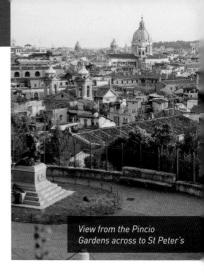
View from the Pincio Gardens across to St Peter's

Around the Trevi Fountain

This is the general area of the **Trevi Fountain** F (Fontana di Trevi), which benefited from Fellini's keen sense of Baroque aesthetics when he dipped the dazzling Anita Ekberg in its legendarily purifying waters for his 1960 film *La Dolce Vita*. Nicola Salvi's 18th-century fountain is, in fact, a triumphal arch and palace facade (to the old Palazzo Poli) framing mythical creatures, with Neptune as the centrepiece, in a riot of rocks and pools, with a rearing horse symbolising the ocean's turmoil and a calmer steed a symbol of its tranquillity. Tucked away behind alleys, this extravaganza is out of all proportion to its tiny piazza, and no amount of signposts leading to it can prepare you for the shock of discovery.

The Trevi Fountain

On one of the seven hills of ancient Rome, the fortress-like **Palazzo del Quirinale** (guided visits by prior reservation only; www.quirinale. it), once summer residence to popes fleeing the malarial swamps of the Vatican down by the Tiber, housed the new king of Italy after 1870 and, since 1947 has been the presidential palace. The only embellishment on its formidable facade is Bernini's graceful porch, but its piazza is worth the climb for the view over the city and the Vatican.

On the Via delle Quattro Fontane is the **Palazzo Barberini**, also known as the **National Gallery of Antique Art** (Galleria Nazionale d'Arte Antica; http://galleriabarberini.beniculturali.it; Tue–Sun 8.30am–7pm). This is another architectural battleground for rivals Borromini and Bernini, worth a visit as much for its Baroque decor as for its 13th- to 17th-century paintings.

That other symbol of *la dolce vita*, the **Via Veneto**, has been deserted by its starlets and *paparazzi* (derived from Paparazzo, a news photographer in Fellini's *La Dolce Vita*) and only the expensive caffès, stylish shops and five-star hotels remain.

Three Churches

Built in the 4th century on the Esquiline Hill site of a Roman temple to the goddess Juno is the largest and most splendid of the churches dedicated to the Virgin, **Santa Maria Maggiore** (daily 7am–7pm). Christmas is especially popular here, when pilgrims come to admire relics of the holy crib. The most spectacular art treasures are its Byzantine mosaics, shimmering Old Testament scenes high on the walls and a Mary and Jesus enthroned in the apse over the high altar. The coffered Renaissance ceiling glitters with the gold of the first shipments from the New World.

In a nearby side street, **Santa Prassede G** (daily 7.30am–noon, 4–6.30pm) is unprepossessing from the outside but the intimate interior is enchanting. The richly coloured 9th-century Byzantine mosaics of Jesus and four angels make the Chapel of St Zeno the city's most important Byzantine monument. To the right of the chapel is a fragment of rare jasper said to come from the column to which Jesus was tied for his flagellation.

San Pietro in Vincoli H (St Peter in Chains; daily 8am–12.30pm, 3–7pm, Oct–Mar until 6pm) might not attract a second look if it didn't contain one of Michelangelo's greatest sculptures, his formidable Moses (1515). On each side, the figures of Jacob's wives were Michelangelo's last completed sculptures. In the Reliquary are St Peter's two *vincoli* (chains), which, it is said, shackled him while he was held in the Mamertine Prison.

Piazza Venezia

You couldn't miss **Piazza Venezia** if you tried – and many do try, because of its endless traffic jams and the overpowering, ungainly white marble **Il Vittoriano** (Vittorio Emanuele Monument). The monument, known familiarly as the 'Wedding Cake', celebrates the first king of unified Italy, as well as the Tomb of the Unknown Soldier, with inimitable 19th-century pomposity.

Northwest of the monument, the 15th-century **Palazzo**

Return to Rome

You must throw two coins into the Trevi Fountain, with your right hand over your left shoulder, the first for a wish, the second to ensure a return to Rome. Donations are made to the Red Cross from the collected coins.

Venezia (Tue–Sun 8.30am–7.30pm) is a fine example of severe but elegant early Renaissance architecture, now home to a museum of medieval and Renaissance arms, furniture and sculpture. Mussolini had his office here and spoke to his followers from the balcony.

Off the piazza, the **Palazzo Doria Pamphilj** (www.doriapamphilj.it; daily 9am–7pm) houses over 400 paintings, representing one of the city's most important private late Renaissance collections. The family's apartments are exquisitely furnished, and the gallery includes masterpieces such as Titian's *Salome with the head of St John* and Caravaggio's *St John the Baptist*. There is also a fine collection of Dutch and Flemish works.

The church of **Il Gesù**, (www.chiesadelgesu.org; daily 7am–12.30pm, 4–7.45pm), severe and relatively discreet on its own square west of the Piazza Venezia, was a major element in the Jesuits' Counter-Reformation campaign. Begun as their Roman

◎ THE WEDDING CAKE

Few edifices have known such universal hostility as Il Vittoriano (the Vittorio Emanuele Monument). Popularly known as the 'Wedding Cake' or 'Rome's False Teeth', the bombastic colonnade with its equestrian bronzes and almost unscalable steps is a true monument of urban catastrophe. Begun in 1885, the 40-year construction entailed the demolition of a piece of the ancient Capitoline Hill. Parts of the Palazzo Venezia were dismantled for a clearer view. The gigantic proportions completely dwarf the surrounding splendours of ancient Rome and the dazzling white Brescia marble clashes with the city's preference for gentle amber, ochre or pink travertine. In 1944, art historians were said to have pleaded with the Allies to suspend Rome's status as an open city – protecting it against bombardment – just long enough to destroy the Vittoriano.

The giant marble monument to Vittorio Emanuele

'headquarters' and the city's first Jesuit church in 1568, its open ground plan was the model for the Congregational churches that were to regain popular support from the Protestant faith. While its facade is more sober than the Baroque churches constructed later, the interior glorifies the new militancy in gleaming bronze, gold, marble and precious stones. The most elaborate ornament is the **altar of St Ignatius Loyola** (Sant'Ignazio), covering the tomb of the Jesuits' Spanish founder in the left transept.

In gentle contrast, the nearby church of **Sant'Ignazio** (http://sant ignazio.gesuiti.it; Mon–Sat 7.30am–7pm, Sun from 9am) stands in an enchanting rococo stage-set of 17th-century houses. Inside, Andrea Pozzo (a Jesuit priest and designer of the saint's tomb at Gesù church) painted a superb trompe l'oeil ceiling fresco (1685) depicting St Ignatius' entry into paradise.

The Capitoline Hill

Beside the Piazza Venezia, a steep staircase leads up to the austere 13th-century **Santa Maria in Aracoeli,** while another, more graceful and gradual, takes you up between the statues of Castor and Pollux to Michelangelo's beautifully proportioned square of the **Campidoglio ❶** (Capitoline Hill). This traffic-free haven, where sacrifices were once made to Jupiter and Juno, forges a superb link between the Renaissance and ancient Rome's most sacred site. Michelangelo also remodelled the **Palazzo Senatorio**, Rome's former town hall, and planned the two palaces that flank it, the **Palazzo dei Conservatori** and the **Palazzo Nuovo**. The bronze equestrian **statue of Marcus Aurelius** at the piazza's centre is a copy; the original is in the courtyard of the Palazzo Nuovo.

Forming the **Capitoline Museums** (Musei Capitolini; www.musei capitolini.org; daily 9.30am–6.30pm), the two palaces' extensive Greek and Roman collections provide an excellent introduction to the ancient Roman Forum that spreads below.

Among the rich collection of ancient sculpture in the **Palazzo dei Conservatori** are fragments of the bronze colossus of Constantine and the celebrated Etruscan bronze **Capitoline SheWolf** (*Lupa Capitolina*), symbol of the city. The wolf dates from around the 5th century BC, but the Romulus and Remus are Renaissance additions by Pollaiuolo. The top-floor gallery has works by Bellini, Titian, Tintoretto, Veronese, Rubens and Caravaggio. A tunnel links Palazzo dei Conservatori to Palazzo Nuovo across the piazza. The palace is packed with ancient sculpture including busts of Emperors and philosophers, the *Capitoline Venus* and the *Dying Gaul*.

Pantheon and Piazza Navona

The circular **Pantheon ❷** (Piazza della Rotonda; Mon–Sat 9am–7.30pm, Sun 9am–6pm) is the best-preserved monument of ancient Rome and rivals the Colosseum in its combination of quiet elegance and massive power. Built by Emperor Hadrian around AD120 on the site of an earlier building destroyed by fire, it achieved a marvel of engineering with its magnificent coffered dome: more than 43m (141ft) in interior diameter (larger than the cupola of St Peter's

Basilica), exactly equal to its height. Bronze that once embellished the entrance was carted away and recycled as Bernini's canopy for the high altar in St Peter's. On fine days a shaft of sunlight illuminates the windowless vault through the circular hole *(oculus)* in the dome (it also lets in the rain). This 'Temple of all the Gods' today contains the tombs of Renaissance masters such as Raphael, as well as the

The Pantheon interior

first king of Italy, Vittorio Emanuele II, and his son Umberto I.

Some of Caravaggio's greatest masterpieces are in the neighbourhood: the *St Matthew* trilogy (1597–1602) in the fine Baroque church of **San Luigi dei Francesi** and the moving *Madonna of the Pilgrims* (1609) in the Renaissance church of **Sant'Agostino**.

Pause a moment at a caffè in that most serene of city squares: nowhere in Rome is the spectacle of Italian street life more pleasantly indulged than in the **Piazza Navona Ⓚ**. The elongated oval piazza was laid out around AD79 by Emperor Domitian as an athletics stadium for the *Circus Agonalis* – a sporting tradition that was continued in the Middle Ages with jousting tournaments and with other events in the centuries that followed. The 17th century contributed its sublime Baroque decor and today it is protected as Rome's most beloved square. In the centre, Bernini's **Fountain of the Four Rivers** *(Fontana dei Quattro Fiumi)* celebrates the great rivers of the four continents: the Americas (Río de la Plata), Europe (Danube), Asia (Ganges) and Africa (Nile). Romans who delight in Bernini's scorn for his rivals suggest that the Nile god covers his head rather than look at Borromini's church of **Sant'Agnese in Agone** (closed Mon), and the river god of the Americas is poised to catch it in case it collapses. In fact, the fountain was completed several years *before* Borromini's structurally impeccable facade and dome.

Just north of Piazza Navona is a superb collection of Classical sculpture housed in one of Rome's finest Renaissance buildings. The **Palazzo Altemps** (Piazza Sant'Apollinare, 46; Tue–Sun 9am–7.45pm) is part of the Museo Nazionale Romano, set around a delightful courtyard.

Campo de'Fiori and the Jewish Ghetto

A large and boisterous fruit, vegetable and flower market takes place in the mornings (Mon–Sat 7am–2pm), in the **Campo de' Fiori**, and for the rest of the day and evening it is a popular spot for bar-life. The square is overseen by the statue of philosopher Giordano Bruno who was burnt at the stake here by the Counter-Reformation in 1600 for his preposterous idea that the universe was infinite, with many more galaxies than ours. An even more famous death occurred at the nearby Piazza del Biscione, more precisely the res-taurant Da Pancrazio (www.dapancrazio.it; tel: 06-686 1246) at No. 92, whose cellar shelters ruins of Pompey's Theatre where Julius Caesar was assassinated.

Although generally closed to the public, the glorious **Palazzo Farnese**, built by Antonio da Sangallo the Younger, Michelangelo and Giacomo della Porta from 1514, now houses the French Embassy. Only the inner courtyard of Rome's finest Renaissance palace is accessible to the public, but its grand portico and the handsome stuccoed vestibule leading to it make it well worth a visit. Narrow streets southeast of the Campo dei Fiori take you to the **Jewish Ghetto** near the ruins of the ancient Roman Theatre of Marcellus (*Teatro di Marcello*), architectural model for the Colosseum. Jews have been a permanent feature of Roman life for over 2,500 years but were forced into a ghetto in the 16th century. A small Jewish

The market at Campo de' Fiori

community is still based around the Via del Portico d'Ottavia. The hefty neo-Babylonian **synagogue**, inaugurated in 1904, with the **Museo Ebraico** (Jewish Museum; www.museoebraico.roma.it; Sun–Thu 10am–7pm, until 5pm in winter, Fri 10am–4pm, until 2pm in winter) next door, is by the riverbank.

Trastevere

The neighbourhood west of the Tiber, **Trastevere** , literally 'across the Tiber', has long been renowned as the most popular quarter of Rome. It is good to wander among the narrow streets and markets to sample the authentic life of the city, highlighted by the *Noantri* ('We Others') street festival of music, food and fireworks, in the last two weeks of July. Another sort of festival atmosphere prevails every Sunday, when the Porta Portese section of Trastevere hosts Rome's liveliest and largest flea market.

Inevitably, 'authentic' became chic and incomers able to afford the higher rents have changed the ambience somewhat. But the true Trasteverini hang on, mainly in the area around **Santa Maria in**

Trastevere (daily 7.30am–9pm), reputedly the oldest church in the city. Its foundation may date from the 3rd century, but the present structure is the work of Pope Innocent II, himself a Trasteverino, c.1140. It is known for a wonderful Byzantine-influenced facade and interior pavements and **mosaic** apse ceiling of Mary enthroned with Jesus.

THE VATICAN

The power of Rome endures both in the spirituality evoked by every stone of St Peter's Basilica and in the almost physical awe inspired by the splendours of the **Vatican City** Ⓜ. At their best, the popes and cardinals replaced military conquest with moral leadership and per-suasion; at their worst, they could show the same hunger for politi-cal power and wealth as any Caesar or grand duke. A visit to the

⊙ MEETING THE POPE

It may be possible to see the Pope when he is not abroad on official visits. He holds a public audience most Wednesdays at 10.30am in the Vatican's Papal Audience Hall or in St Peter's Square. You can usually get tickets (free) one, two or three days in advance from the Pontifical Prefect's Office (Mon–Sat, tel: 06-6988 5863) through the bronze gates in St Peter's Square. A visitor's bishop at home can arrange a private audience. Alter-natively, write to the Prefecture of the Papal Household (check http://w2.vatican.va, 'Info' section) at least 10 days in advance. On Sunday at noon (except July and August, when he is at Castel Gandolfo), the Pope appears at the window of his apartments in the Apostolic Palace, delivers a brief homily, says the Angelus and blesses the crowd. On a few major holy days, he celebrates high Mass in St Peter's. Note the strict dress code (no shorts, bare shoulders or midriffs).

Vatican (http://w2.vatican.va) is an object lesson for faithful and sceptic alike.

Named after the hill on which it stands, the Vatican has been a papal residence for over 600 years, but a sovereign state independent of Italy only since the Lateran Treaty signed by Mussolini in 1929. It is preferable to visit St Peter's Basilica and the Vatican Museums on separate days to avoid fatigue and visual overload. Check with the tourist office for opening times.

Swiss Guard in traditional uniform

To appreciate the panorama of St Peter's Basilica and its 1 sq km (0.66 sq mile) piazza, approach it on foot as countless pilgrims have done before you. Cross at the beautiful **Sant'Angelo Bridge**, one of 20 crossing the Tiber River. Adorned with 10 angel sculptures by Bernini and his studio, it arrives at the **Castel Sant'Angelo** (www.castelsantangelo.com; daily 9am–7.30pm; free on the first Sun of the month), originally built as Hadrian's mausoleum in AD139. Its name derives from Pope Gregory's vision of the Archangel Michael heralding the end of a plague in 590. Sixth-century barbarians commandeered the round, brick pile as a fortress, using ancient statues as missiles to hurl onto their enemies below. Linked to the Vatican by a thick-walled passage, it served as a hide-out for popes, notably for Pope Clement VII, holed up here for a month during the sack of Rome by Habsburg troops in 1527 (see page 27). The Papal Apartments are a contrast to the dungeons, both open to the public, where the philosopher and monk Giordano Bruno and the sculptor-goldsmith Benvenuto Cellini were imprisoned.

St Peter's

In **St Peter's Square** (Piazza San Pietro), Bernini has performed one of the world's most exciting pieces of architectural orchestration. The sweeping curves of the colonnades reach out to the stream of pilgrims from Rome and the whole world, *urbi et orbi*, to take them into the bosom of the church beyond. Bernini completed the 284 travertine columns, 88 pilasters and 140 statues of the saints in just 11 years (1656–67). Stand on either of the circular paving stones set between the square's twin 17th-century fountains and the red granite Egyptian obelisk to appreciate the harmony of the quadruple rows of Doric columns, so perfectly aligned that they seem like a single row.

St Peter's Basilica (daily Apr–Sept 7am–7pm, Oct–Mar 7am–6.30pm) is the largest of all Roman Catholic churches and by any standards a grandiose achievement, but it suffered from the competing visions of all the architects called in to collaborate –Bramante, Giuliano da Sangallo, Raphael, Baldassare Peruzzi, Michelangelo, Giacomo Della Porta, Domenico Fontana and Carlo Maderno. From 1506 to 1626, it changed from the simple ground plan of a Greek cross, with four arms of equal length, as favoured by Bramante and Michelangelo, to the final form of Maderno's Latin cross extended by a long nave, as demanded by the Counter-Reformation popes. One result is that Maderno's porticoed facade and nave obstruct a clear view of Michelangelo's dome from the square.

The church's dimensions are impressive: 212m (695ft) exterior length, 187m (613ft) inside length; 132m (435ft) to the tip of the dome (diameter 42.45m/139ft). As you go in, note St Peter's keys inlaid in the doorway paving. Set in the floor by the central door is the large round slab of red porphyry where Charlemagne knelt for his coronation as the first Holy Roman Emperor in AD800.

You will find the basilica's most treasured work of art, Michelangelo's *Pietà* – Mary with the dead Jesus on her lap – in its own chapel to the right of the entrance. The Florentine artist was 25 and proud enough of his work to append his signature (the only surviving example), visible on the Madonna's sash. Since a religious fanatic attacked it with a hammer in 1972, the statue has been protected by bullet-proof glass. Reverence can also cause damage: on the 13th-century bronze **statue of St Peter** near the main altar, attributed to Arnolfo di Cambio, the lips and fingers of countless pilgrims have worn away the toes of its right foot.

Michelangelo's dome

Beneath the dome, Bernini's great **baldacchino** (canopy), cast out of bronze beams taken from the Pantheon's porch (see page 58), soars above the high altar. It was built right over St Peter's tomb and reserved exclusively for the pope's Mass. In the apse beyond, the Baroque master gives full vent to his exuberance with his bronze and marble **Cathedra of St Peter**, the throne of the Apostle's successors.

Vatican Treasures

The greatest patron that painters, sculptors and architects have ever known, the Catholic Church, houses in its headquarters one of the world's richest collections of art. The 7km (4 miles) of rooms and galleries of the **Vatican Museums** (Musei Vaticani; www.musei vaticani.va; Mon–Sat 9am–6pm, last Sun of the month 9am–2pm, last entry two hours before closing, free Sun; to avoid queues book online at https://biglietteriamusei.vatican.va) are made up of eight museums, five galleries, the Apostolic Library, the Borgia Apartments, the Raphael Stanze (Rooms) and the incomparable Sistine Chapel.

Shuttle buses run regularly from St Peter's Square to the museum entrance and back, which otherwise would be a 20-minute walk.

To avoid the inevitable queues, consider taking a guided tour or go there first thing in the morning (don't forget your binoculars for details on the ceiling).

With the booty from the ruthless dismantling of ancient monuments to make way for the Renaissance city in the 16th century, the **Pio Clementino Museum** has assembled a wonderful collection of Roman and Greek art. Most celebrated is the tortured *Laocoön* group from Rhodes.

Pope Julius II took a risk in 1508 when he called in a relatively untried 26-year-old to do the interior decoration of his new apartments. The result was the four **Raphael Rooms** (Stanze di Raffaello). In the central Stanza della Segnatura are the two masterly frescoes, *Dispute over the Holy Sacrament* and the famous *School of Athens*, confronting theological with philosophical wisdom.

In stark contrast to Raphael's grand manner, seek out the gentle beauty of Fra Angelico's frescoes in the **Chapel of Nicholas V** (Cappella del Beato Angelico). The lives of Sts Lawrence and Stephen are depicted in subdued pinks and blues.

The lavishly decorated **Borgia Apartments** contain Pinturicchio's frescoes with portraits of the Spanish Borgia Pope Alexander VI and his notorious son Cesare and daughter Lucrezia, and lead into the collection of modern religious artwork opened in 1973 by Pope Paul VI. The latter includes Rodin bronzes, Picasso ceramics, Matisse's Madonna sketches and designs for ecclesiastical robes and, rather unexpectedly, a grotesque Francis Bacon pope.

'I am no painter'

The Sistine Chapel was sculptor Michelangelo's first fresco painting. After Pope Julius II threatened to throw him off the scaffolding if he didn't hurry up, he wrote to a friend: 'I am not in a good place, and I am no painter.'

Michelangelo's famous Sistine Chapel ceiling

The Sistine Chapel

Nothing can prepare you for the visual feast of the **Sistine Chapel** (Cappella Sistina; same hours as Vatican Museums, see page 65), built for Sixtus IV in the 15th century. Returned to its original colours after a 20-year restoration, the fresco is overwhelming. Despite the distraction of the constant crowds (quiet is requested), visitors seem to yield to the power of Michelangelo's ceiling and his *Last Judgement*. The other wonderful wall frescoes by Botticelli, Pinturicchio, Ghirlandaio and Signorelli are barely given attention. In this private papal chapel, where cardinals hold their conclave to elect a new pope, the glory of the Catholic Church achieves its finest artistic expression.

The chapel portrays the story of man, in three parts: from Adam to Noah; the giving of the Law to Moses; and from the birth of Jesus to the Last Judgement. Towards the centre of Michelangelo's **ceiling**, you will make out the celebrated outstretched finger of man's creation, filled out by the drunkenness of Noah, the turmoil of the Flood. But most overwhelming of all is the impression of the whole –best appreciated from the bench by the chapel's exit.

Hadrian's Villa

On the chapel's altar wall is Michelangelo's tempestuous **Last Judgement**, begun 23 years after the ceiling's completion in 1512, when he was 60, and imbued with religious soul-searching. It is said that the artist's agonising self-portrait can be made out in the flayed skin of St Bartholomew, to the right below Jesus.

Amid all the Vatican's treasures, the 15 rooms of the **Picture Gallery** (Pinacoteca Vaticana), located in a separate wing of the palace, get short shrift. This collection of nine centuries of paintings includes works by Giotto, Fra Angelico, Perugino, Raphael's *Transfiguration* (his last great work), Leonardo da Vinci's unfinished St Jerome, Bellini's *Pietà* and Caravaggio's *Descent from the Cross*.

EXCURSION TO TIVOLI

Follow the old Roman chariot road of Via Tiburtina 30km (19 miles) east of the capital to the ruins of **Hadrian's Villa** (Villa Adriana; www.villaadriana.beniculturali.it; daily 9am–5pm, until 6-7.30pm in spring and summer; free first Sun of the month), situated near the town of **Tivoli ❷**, at the foot of the Sabine Hills. Sprawling across 70 hectares (173 acres), this retirement hideaway of the great emperor was designed to recapture some of the architectural marvels of his empire. Barbarians and museum curators have removed most of the villa's treasures, but a stroll through the remaining pillars, arches and mosaic fragments in gardens running wild among the olive trees, cypresses and pines can be marvellously evocative.

Located in the centre is the delightful **Villa dell' Isola**. This pavilion, surrounded by a little reflecting pool and circular portico, epitomises the magic of the place.

Set in Tivoli itself, overlooking the Roman plain, the **Villa d'Este** (Tue–Sun 8.30am–6.45pm, until 4pm in winter; www.villadestetivoli.info), is a 16th-century counterpart that celebrates all the extravagance of the late Renaissance period. From the former home of Cardinal Ippolito d'Este, visitors can survey the terraced gardens that are the real reason for Tivoli's fame: alleys of cypresses and soaring fountains (some 500, including Bernini's *Bicchierone*), grottoes, waterfalls and pools. The hydraulic **Organ Fountain** operates at 10.30am, 12.30pm, 2.30pm, 4.30pm and 6.30pm, while the **Fountain della Civetta** is currently out of action.

ALBAN HILLS AND CASTEL GANDOLFO

The region southeast of Rome is known locally as the Castelli Romani (Roman Castles) for the fortified hilltop refuges built during the medieval civil wars. Today it is the summer heat that drives the Romans out on day trips to the vineyards of the Alban hills and lakes. The country villages of **Frascati, Grottaferrata, Marino** and **Rocca di Papa** make delightful stops, not least for a cool glass of white wine, especially during the autumn grape-harvest festivals. The pope's summer palace is at **Castel Gandolfo**, on the shores of Lake Albano – note that his Wednesday and Sunday blessings here in summer are not guaranteed. Pope Francis also opened the beautiful **Barberini Gardens** to the public, which overlook the lake. The Gallery of the Pontiffs (guided tours only, www.museivaticani.va, booking essential, see https://biglietteriamusei.vatican.va) is also well worth a visit.

NORTHERN LAZIO

The A12 *autostrada* and the old Via Aurelia (which ends up in Arles in French Provence) take you to **Tarquinia**. Most important of the original 12 towns of the Etruscan confederation, it dominated Rome in

its 6th- to 7th-century BC heyday. Today, the paintings and sculptures found in its **Necropolis** (www.tarquinia-cerveteri.it; Tue–Sun 8.30am–dusk) of more than 5,700 tombs provide evidence of the brilliant Etruscan civilisation. Visits to the tombs outside town are organised from the **National Museum** (Tue–Sun 8.30am–7.30pm) in the fine 15th-century Gothic-Renaissance Palazzo Vitelleschi as you enter Tarquinia. The museum exhibits sarcophagi, Etruscan and imported Greek vases, and wall paintings – all in reconstructed tombs.

Tuscania is a quiet little fortified town, shaken in 1971 by an earthquake that fortunately did not harm its two fine Romanesque churches, which are situated on the eastern outskirts (check with the tourist office on Piazza Basile for the churches' erratic opening hours).

In the restful charm of its medieval quarters, **Viterbo** makes a good overnight stop. The oldest neighbourhood, with narrow streets and little market squares, is around the Via San Pellegrino. On the equally attractive Piazza San Lorenzo, the Palazzo Papale has an impressive 13th-century Gothic loggia, opposite the Romanesque Cathedral with a Renaissance facade.

TUSCANY AND UMBRIA

Light is the secret of Tuscany's magic. In that apparently miraculous collision of imagination and intellect that sparked the Renaissance in 15th-century Florence, its painters and architects had the constant inspiration of the dramatic changes in Tuscan light from dawn to dusk. And more than anywhere else in the country, Tuscany and neighbouring land-locked Umbria present the ideal green Italian landscape, dotted with stalwart hilltop towns, where cypress-tree sentinels watch over twisted olive groves and vineyards blanket the gentle rolling hills.

Florence lies at the heart of the northern Apennines, in a basin of the Arno River that runs out to Pisa and the sea. Siena, its proud historic rival, dominates the Tuscan hill towns to the south, while

Quintessential Tuscany: cypress trees and sunflowers

the university towns of Perugia and Assisi are the keys to Umbria's luminous beauty. With some careful timing, today's visitors can capture a glimpse of that miracle of light. Arrive early in the morning for your first look across the hills from the grey-stone towers of San Gimignano (sometimes called a 'medieval Manhattan'), or visit Siena's Piazza del Campo at sunset. The dazzling white marble of Pisa's Duomo and leaning campanile is breathtaking in the noonday sun, but late afternoon is the blessed moment for the brilliant mosaic facade of Orvieto's cathedral.

FLORENCE (FIRENZE)

Florence ❸ is one of the world's great tourist magnets and has architecture, history and artwork in quantities found nowhere else in the world. Our itineraries divide the city's heart into four quarters: from the Duomo north to Piazza San Marco; from Piazza della Signoria, Palazzo Vecchio and the Uffizi Galleries east to Piazza Santa Croce; from the Mercato Nuovo west to Piazza Santa Maria Novella; and the southern 'Left Bank' of the Arno River around the

Pitti Palace and Piazzale Michelangelo. The city is easily covered on foot, particularly since the city centre was pedestrianised in 2009.

From the Duomo to Piazza San Marco

The **Duomo** (Cathedral; www.operaduomo.firenze.it; Mon–Wed, Fri 10am–5pm, Thu 10am–4.45pm, Sat 10am–4.45pm, Sun 1.30–4.45pm, closed first Tue of each month; free), officially called Santa Maria del Fiore, proclaims the inordinate but justified civic pride of the Florentines. The very heart of the city's *centro storico* (historical centre), the building was begun in 1296 under Arnolfo di Cambio, although the imposing green, white and rose marble neo-Gothic facade was completed six centuries later. The first of its glories is the free-standing **campanile** (daily 8.15am–6.50pm), designed by Giotto. The 85m (267ft) bell-tower (it's a 414-stair climb to the top) is decorated on its lower sections by hexagonal bas-reliefs sculpted by Andrea Pisano and Luca della Robbia, based on Giotto's drawings. Characteristic of the city's civic consciousness, they portray the Life of Man from Adam's creation to the rise of civilisation through the arts and sciences – music, architecture, metallurgy – pursued so earnestly by the Florentine guilds that commissioned the work.

Brunelleschi's masterpiece, the terracotta **cupola** (Mon–Fri 8.30am–6.20pm, Sat until 5pm, Sun 1–4pm), with eight white stone ribs curving to the marble lantern at the top, is the city's symbol, visible from the Tuscan hills far beyond. Completed in 1436, it measures 45.5m (149ft) in diameter. The 463 steps to its top climb in comfortable stages to reveal a panorama of the city, different views of the cathedral's interior and close-ups of the dome's 16th-century frescoes. Begun by Giorgio Vasari and finished by his pupil Federico Zuccari, it is the world's largest depiction of the Last Supper. (Brunelleschi's original wooden model of the cupola is displayed in the cathedral museum.) Look for Ghiberti's **bronze shrine** below the high altar, as well as his three stained-glass windows on the entrance wall. In the third bay on the north aisle is Paolo Uccello's statue-like equestrian painting of 15th-century English mercenary Sir John Hawkwood (a name unpronounceable for Italians – he is known as *Giovanni Acuto*).

The campanile

The octagonal 12th-century Romanesque **baptistery** (Mon–Wed and Fri 8.15–10.15am and 11.15am–6.30pm, Thu and Sat 8.15am–6.30pm, Sun 8.15am–1.30pm) of San Giovanni (St John) is celebrated as the oldest building in Florence and for the magnificent bas-reliefs of its three sets of **bronze doors**. The oldest, facing south and telling the story of John the Baptist, was designed by Andrea Pisano in 1330. A century later, Lorenzo Ghiberti won the competition to design the great north and east doors, devoted respectively to the Life of Jesus and to various scenes from the Old Testament. Michelangelo remarked that the latter, which are facing the Duomo, were good enough to adorn the entrance to heaven, and they have been known ever since as the *Doors of Paradise*. Among the losing candidates was Filippo Brunelleschi, who from then on devoted himself entirely to architecture.

Ghiberti's original bronze panels were removed from the baptistery after flood damage in 1966 and can now be admired in the glass-topped courtyard of the Museo dell'Opera del Duomo (www.museumflorence.com; Mon and Fri–Sat 9am–9pm, Tue–Thu and Sun 9am–7pm). The panels were restored and can be seen as a whole for the first time in over 30 years. The museum holds a wealth of other treasures from the Duomo and baptistery including originals

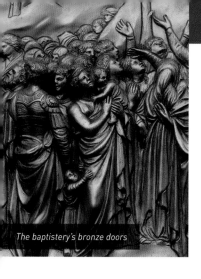
The baptistery's bronze doors

of Donatello sculpture and Michelangelo's unfinished *Pietà*. The dead Jesus in his mother's arms empha-sises the agony rather than the pathos portrayed by the *Pietà* in St Peter's in Rome. Michelangelo conceived the group for his tomb and represented himself in the figure of Nicodemus. Flaws in the marble so enraged the artist that he hurled a hammer at it, destroying Christ's left leg – the left arm has been restored, and the rather insipid Mary Magdalene was later added by a pupil.

The magnificent Byzantine-style **mosaics** inside the cupola include scenes from *The Creation, Life of St John* and a *Last Judgement*, and date from the 13th century.

The Medici Palace
The might of the Medici family can be sensed in their massive palazzo, northwest of the cathedral on Via Cavour, the 15th-century **Palazzo Medici-Riccardi** (www.palazzo-medici.it; Thu–Tue 9am–7pm). Now Florence's prefecture offices, the formidable edifice set the style for the city's Renaissance palaces. The ground floor had an open loggia at the corner for the family banking business. The upstairs chapel contains Benozzo Gozzoli's 15th-century **fresco**, *Journey of the Magi to Bethlehem*. It portrays the Medici clan led by Lorenzo the Magnificent in an allegory of an ecumenical council with Pope Pius II in Florence. The Medici family lived here until moving to the Palazzo Vecchio, then the Palazzo Pitti.

Around the corner is the family church of **San Lorenzo** (Mon–Sat 10am–5.30pm, Sun 1.30–5.30pm), designed by Brunelleschi before he worked on the Duomo's cupola. Inside, you will see the Medici family arms set in the floor in front of the altar. Brunelleschi is at his most elegant in the **Old Sacristy** at the end of the left transept (site of a few Medici tombs), decorated with four Donatello wall-medallions (the artist is buried in the left transept). Adjacent to the church is the Laurentian Library (*Biblioteca*; daily 9am–1pm) commissioned in 1524 and known for the graceful cloisters and monumental Michelangelo-designed stairway.

Adjoining the church but with a separate entrance in the back are the **Medici Chapels** (Cappelle Medicee; www.operamedicea laurenziana.it; Mon–Sat 10am–5pm, Sun 1.30–5.30pm, closed Sun Nov–Feb), monuments to the family dynasty. The **Princes' Chapel** (Cappella dei Principi) is a piece of 17th-century Baroque bombast in marble; the altar was only completed in 1939. The summit of Medici

⊙ WAR AND FLOOD

In the 20th century, the River Arno meant nothing but trouble. To slow the Allied advance in August 1944, the Germans blew up all of Florence's bridges except the Ponte Vecchio. And in case their enemy planned to drive vehicles across this ancient footbridge, they blocked approaches by destroying buildings within a radius of 200m/yds. On 4 November 1966, the river burst its banks and flooded the city, destroying and damaging more than 1,000 paintings and 500 sculptures as well as countless precious books and manuscripts in Florence's libraries. In Bargello's Michelangelo Hall, wall marks record the flood level at 3m (10ft) and higher. But in that golden Age of Aquarius, the 1960s' art-loving brothers and sisters poured into the city from all over the world to help with the rescue operation, spearheaded by Florence's own proud citizens.

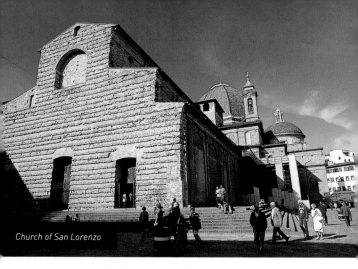

Church of San Lorenzo

power is found in Michelangelo's **New Sacristy** (Sagrestia Nuova), worked on from 1521 to 1534. Lorenzo the Magnificent and his brother Giuliano lie in simple tombs beneath the sculptor's *Madonna and Child*, flanked by lesser artists' statues of the family patron saints Cosmas and Damian. Michelangelo's greatest work here is for Lorenzo's grandson, Lorenzo the Duke of Urbino, portrayed as a pensive Roman soldier, and his son, Giuliano the Duke of Nemours.

The church of San Lorenzo is next to hundreds of stalls that make up the open-air **Mercato San Lorenzo**, one of Italy's largest tourist markets, offering bargains and interesting buys.

Fra Angelico Museum

It is an easy walk to Piazza San Marco and the Dominican monastery, which is now the **San Marco Museum** (Mon–Fri 8.15am–1.50pm, Sat and Sun 8.15am–4.50pm, closed 2nd and 4th Mon and 1st, 3rd and 5th Sun of the month). The museum is an evocative setting for a museum largely devoted to the paintings of Florentine-born Fra Angelico (1387–1455), who lived here as a monk. Off the cloister, with its ancient cedar tree, is the Pilgrims' Hospice (Ospizio dei Pelligrini), where some of his finest works are found, notably a *Descent from the Cross*. In the monks' cells upstairs, the frescoes of Beato (Blessed) Angelico were intended to be inspirational rather than decorative. His celebrated *Annunciation* faces the top of the stairs, while other outstanding works include the mystic *Transfiguration* in cell six and *Jesus Mocked* in cell seven. In the small refectory is the important Ghirlandaio mural of the *Last Supper*. The Prior's Quarters in the second dormitory (cells 12, 13 and 14) were the home of fire-and-brimstone preacher Girolamo Savonarola from 1481 until his death in 1498. You can see his portrait by Fra Bartolomeo and the famous picture of his burning at the stake in Piazza della Signoria.

As a museum conceived primarily for students of Florentine painting from the 13th to 16th centuries, the **Accademia Gallery** (Galleria dell'Accademia; www.galleriaaccademiafirenze.beniculturali.it; Tue–Sun 8.15am–6.50pm) at Via Ricasoli 60, ranks high on the list of things that must be seen. Its major interest is in the seven statues by Michelangelo. Six are unfinished – four *Prisoners* (also known as *The Slaves*), *St Matthew* and a *Pietà* – each a fascinating revelation of how Michelangelo released their power from the marble. The Accademia's highlight is the original David, which once stood in the Piazza della Signoria (now substituted by a life-size copy). It was carved by the artist from a discarded defective column of marble in 1504, when he was just 26.

In the Piazza Santissima Annunziata, Brunelleschi produced a pioneering example of the piazza as stage-set. In the 1440s he designed the gracefully arched loggia and the **Ospedale degli Innocenti** (www.museumsinflorence.com; Mon–Sat 8.30am–7pm, Sun 8.30am–2pm), the first hospital for foundlings in Europe; swaddled babes are the subject of Andrea della Robbia's roundels above the arches. Michelozzo's Santissima Annunziata church, together with the 17th-century fountains and equestrian statue of Grand Duke Ferdinando, preserve the harmonies of the master's overall design.

Across Via della Colonna is the entrance to the **Museo Archeologico** (www.archeotoscana.beniculturali.it; Mon 8.30am–2pm, Tue–Fri 8.30am–7pm, Sat–Sun 8.30am–2pm; free first Sun of the month). Its important collection of ancient Egyptian, Greek, Roman and Etruscan art offers an alternative to Renaissance overload.

Piazza della Signoria to Piazza Santa Croce

Flanked by some of the city's most stylish boutiques, this quarter's main street retains the commercial tradition of its medieval name, **Via de' Calzaiuoli** (Stocking- and Shoemakers' Street). It connects the Piazza Duomo with the Piazza della Signoria.

If the **Orsanmichele** (www.museumsinflorence.com; Tue–Sun 10am–5pm) looks more like a grain silo than a church, that is because it has been used as both. Originally a church, it was rebuilt in the late 13th century as a market and then as an open loggia, converting its Gothic arches to the present ground-floor windows and adding a granary upstairs. The fortress-like exterior is decorated with 14 niches for saints of the major guilds that commissioned the statues (replicas now stand in their place). Look for Ghiberti's bronze of the city's patron *St John* (east wall, on the Via de' Calzaiuoli); *St Matthew*, the bankers' tax-collector turned apostle (west); Donatello's *St George*, the armourers' dragon-killer (north); *St Mark*, whose vividly sculpted robes do credit to the linen-drapers he protects (south); and Nanni di Banco's outstanding conspiratorial group of *Four Crowned Martyrs* for the sculptors' own guild of stonemasons and woodworkers (north).

David's detractors

On first seeing *David*, most people would be inclined to agree with the novelist D. H. Lawrence, who called the statue 'the genius of Florence'. However, the 19th-century drama critic William Hazlitt disagreed, describing *David* as 'an awkward overgrown actor at one of our minor theatres, without his clothes'.

Piazza della Signoria is Florence's civic and social centre. Site of the stoic town hall (Palazzo Vecchio or della Signoria) since 1299, the square bustles in all seasons, not least because it leads to the richest of Italy's art museums, the Uffizi. At the south end of the square is the 14th-century **Loggia della Signoria** (or **dei Lanzi**), transformed from the city fathers' ceremonial grandstand into a guardroom for Swiss mercenary *Landsk-*

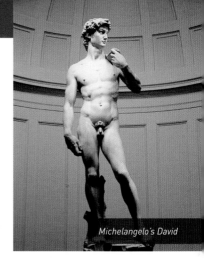

Michelangelo's David

nechte. It shelters Benvenuto Cellini's bronze masterpiece, *Perseus*, brandishing the severed head of Medusa. Also in the loggia, the spiralling *Rape of the Sabines* of Giambologna (the Flemish artist Jean de Boulogne) is another piece of dazzling virtuosity.

In a piazza that is an open-air sculpture gallery, more statuary graces the orator's platform along the Palazzo Vecchio's sober facade. To the left of its entrance is a copy of Donatello's *Marzocco*, Florence's heraldic lion, next to his bronze of *Judith and Holofernes*, which made the Medici uneasy with its theme of a tyrant decapitated. Getting little attention is Bandinelli's clumsy 16th-century *Hercules and Cacus*, standing in the shadow of Michelangelo's magnificent *David*; this life-size copy was placed here in 1873. A plaque (near the Baroque fountain) embedded in the piazza marks the spot where Savonarola was executed.

In contrast to the austere Gothic exterior of the **Palazzo Vecchio** (http://musefirenze.it; Apr–Sept daily 9am–11pm, until 2pm on Thu; Oct–Mar daily 9am–7pm, until 2pm on Thu) by Arnolfo di Cambio,

Vasari added ornate stucco and frescoes to the first inner courtyard for a Medici wedding in the 1560s. The palazzo was a Medici residence until they moved to the Palazzo Pitti. A copy of Verrocchio's bronze cherub tops the porphyry fountain in the centre. Upstairs, the **Salone dei Cinquecento** was built in 1495 for the short-lived Florentine Republic before serving as Duke Cosimo's throne room and, three centuries later, the chamber of Italy's first national parliament. The decor celebrates Florentine power – Vasari frescoes of victories over Siena and Pisa and Michelangelo's *Victory* statue. The second-floor **Sala dei Gigli** (Hall of the Lilies) is brilliantly decorated in blues and golds with vivid Ghirlandaio frescoes. It adjoins the **Chancery** (Cancelleria) where Niccolò Macchiavelli served as secretary to the Florentine Republic. Any world-weary thoughts inspired by the old cynic's portrait and bust are quickly dispelled by Verrocchio's cherub cuddling a dolphin like a baby doll. The excellent 'Secret Passageways' guided tours (daily 10 and 11.30am, 2.30 and 4pm, Thu 10 and 11.30am, tel: 055-276 8224 or book online) give small groups access to areas that are normally off limits. Highlights include the painted coffered ceiling of the Salone del Cinquecento and the medieval stairway of the Duke of Athens. In 2012 the soaring Tower of the Palazzo Vecchio, affording fine views, was opened to the public for the first time.

The Gucci Museum (www. guccimuseo.com; daily 10am–8pm, Fri until 11pm) on the square provides light relief from Renaissance

The Palazzo Vecchio

masterpieces. Gucci exhibits, such as zebra-skin suitcases, Oscar gowns or monogrammed flippers, are juxtaposed with contemporary art installations from the collection of French magnate, François Pinault. There is also a nice café and a restaurant.

Uffizi tickets

Queues at the Uffizi are common year-round, but tickets for a timed entrance can be booked in advance. Ask at your hotel, the tourist office or book online (for a small fee, at www.firenzemusei.it) as early as you can.

The Uffizi

The **Uffizi Museum** (www.uffizi.beniculturali.it; Tue–Sun 8.15am–6.50pm, last entry 30 mins before closing) of Italian and European painting stretches in a long U-shape from the Palazzo Vecchio down to the Arno river and back. Duke Cosimo had Vasari design it in 1560 as a series of government offices (uffizi), a mint for the city's florin and workshops for the Medici's craftsmen. Vasari's greatest architectural work, it is now the home of one of the world's most famous and important art galleries. The Uffizi has been undergoing a massive and painfully slow redevelopment since 1989 and the work is not yet complete. The Nuovo Uffizi (New Uffizi) project will double the number of paintings on show and allow twice as many visitors. Some elements of the project have not been without controversy, especially the design for a new modern exit by the Japanese architect Arata Isozaki. Two staircases with lifts have already been added to the museum to increase capacity, and several new rooms were opened including the Blue Rooms (dedicated to 16th and 17th century Spanish, French, Flemish and Dutch artists, including Rembrandt) and the Red Rooms with the great Medici family portraits by Bronzino and some superb works by Raphael. In 2014, the Green Rooms (no.33-34), which include Greek portraits and works that inspired Michelangelo, were added.

Stop for an occasional peek out of the window over the Arno and Ponte Vecchio and recharge your batteries at the museum's caffè above the Loggia dei Lanzi. It has lovely views of the piazza. Reorganisation makes it hazardous to specify room numbers, but the paintings are generally exhibited chronologically from the 13th to the 18th centuries. Here are some of the highlights:

Giotto breathes warm humanity into his *Madonna Enthroned* (1310), distinguishing it from the formal pictures of the subject by Cimabue and Duccio in the same room. Giotto's Madonna polyptych is also distinctive. Some 30 years later came the *Annunciation* triptych of Simone Martini, with Mary shying away from the archangel Gabriel.

Paolo Uccello shows a dream-like, almost surrealist obsession with his (unsolved) problems of perspective and merry-go-round horses in his *Battle of San Romano* (1456). It contrasts with the cool dignity of Piero della Francesca in his *Federigo da Montefeltro* and wife *Battista* (1465), portrayed against their Urbino landscape.

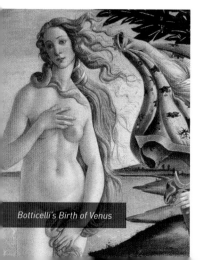
Botticelli's Birth of Venus

Some of the museum's most visited rooms are to come: in his graceful *Allegory of Spring* (1478) and the exquisite *Birth of Venus*, Botticelli achieves an enchanting mixture of sensuality and purity. His Flemish contemporary Hugo van der Goes is more down-to-earth in the realism of his triptych *Adoration of the Shepherds* (1478), which influenced Florentine painters such as Ghirlandaio. In the *Baptism of Christ* (1470) of Verrocchio, you can see the earliest identified work of his most famous pupil, Leonardo da Vinci – the background landscape and the angel on the left, beautiful enough to reduce his companion angel to wide-eyed jealousy. Leonardo's *Annunciation* (1472–7) of a few years later already shows his characteristic gentle tone and feeling for precise detail and the *Adoration of the Magi*, even as an underdrawing left unfinished by his departure for Milan (1481), reveals his power of psychological observation.

Northern European Rooms

The Northern European Rooms include a splendid *Portrait of His Father* (1490) by Albrecht Dürer; *Adam and Eve* (1528) by Lucas Cranach the Elder; *Richard Southwell* by Hans Holbein; and a moving *Mater Dolorosa* by Joos van Cleve. In the mystic *Holy Allegory* (1490) of Giovanni Bellini, we can appreciate the typical Venetian serenity even without understanding its symbols. Titian has a superbly sensual *Venus of Urbino* (1538), less Greek goddess than the prince's mistress she probably was and an equally disturbing *Flora* (1515; more works by Raphael and Titian can be found in the Palazzo Pitti). Some are also upset by the eroticism of Parmigianino's strange but undeniably graceful *Madonna with the Long Neck* (1534), a masterpiece of the sophisticated and subsequently decadent Mannerism that followed the High Renaissance.

There is an intriguing ambiguity to the half-naked peasant youth posing as a *Bacchus* for Caravaggio (1589), but nothing complicated about the straightforward and robust sexiness of the Rubens *Bacchanale*. Compare Caravaggio's mastery of *chiaroscuro* (the play of light and shadow) in the service of realism in his violent *Abraham and Isaac* (1590), with the more contemplative style of Rembrandt in the *Old Rabbi* (1658) and other portraits. The only work by Michelangelo in the Uffizi is the *Holy Family* or *Doni Tondo* (1503–4), his only known panel painting. Without Michelangelo's strength, or Leonardo's complexity, the third of Italy's three Renaissance giants, Raphael, brings his own powers of clarity and restraint to the *Madonna of the Goldfinch* (1505) and a *Self-Portrait* made when the artist was 23.

The Vasari corridor, an aerial walkway along the east side of the Ponte Vecchio and hung with the self-portraits of many great artists, is only accessible on a pre-booked tour (tel: 055 265 4321; Tue and Thu at 9 and 11.30am, Wed and Fri 2 and 4.30pm; groups of up to 20 people).

Close to the Uffizi, by the Arno, the Museo di Galileo (www.museogalileo.it; Wed–Mon 9.30am–6pm, Tue 9.30am–1pm) makes a welcome change after over-indulgence in the arts. The museum is home to telescopes designed and built by Galileo, beautifully engraved astrolabes and armillary spheres, fascinating 15th and 16th century maps and globes – and two fingers and a thumb of the great astronomer, which were removed from his corpse by admirers in the 18th century.

The Bargello, a prison-turned-art museum

Santa Croce

Designed in the late 13th century by Arnolfo di Cambio (architect of the Palazzo Vecchio and the Duomo) with a neo-Gothic facade added in 1863, the Franciscan church of **Santa Croce** (east of the Uffizi; Mon–Sat 9.30am–5.30pm, Sun 2–5.30pm), has an important series of **Giotto frescoes**. The pathos shines through the heavily restored paintings of St Francis in the Bardi Chapel (c.1320s), to the right of the apse and two St Johns in the Peruzzi Chapel next door. In a chapel in the left transept, the wooden *Crucifixion* by Donatello (1425) is in affecting naturalistic contrast to the Renaissance idealism of the time.

The church is also the last resting place of Galileo, Machiavelli, Ghiberti and composer Rossini. **Michelangelo's tomb** (right aisle, second bay) was designed by Vasari, with symbolic statues of Painting, Sculpture and Architecture mourning beneath a bust of the Florentine-born artist who died aged 89.

At the back of the cloister of Santa Croce's monastery adjoining the church, Brunelleschi's **Pazzi Chapel** (*Cappella dei Pazzi*) is a little gem of Renaissance elegance designed in 1443. Luca della Robbia's subdued glazed ceramic roundels depict the 12 Apostles and Four Evangelists. The most cherished treasure in the **Santa Croce Museum** is Cimabue's massive 13th-century *Crucifixion*, rescued and restored after the 1966 flood. It now hangs on a cable to be hoisted out of harm's way should another flood ever occur.

The First Town Hall

The ominous 13th-century fortress-like *palazzo* that houses the **Bargello Museum** (www.bargellomusei.beniculturali.it; Via del Proconsolo 4, daily 8.15am–1.50pm, closed 1st, 3rd and 5th Mon and 2nd and 4th Sun of the month; free first Sun of each month) was Florence's first town hall and prison under the jurisdiction of the police chief, or *Bargello*, before becoming the National Museum of Sculpture. The **Michelangelo Hall** (Sala Michelangelo) displays the master's drunken *Bacchus*, carved when he was only 22, and the much later bust of

Brutus. Among the Cellini bronzes is an imposing bust of his master, *Duke Cosimo*. The **General Council Hall** (Sala del Consiglio Generale) is dominated by Donatello, including his famous *David*, naked and restless in bronze (1450), and the stone *Marzocco* lion, the town's symbol, from the Palazzo Vecchio. You can also see the two bronze panels submitted for the Baptistery doors' competition in 1401. On the second floor is a Verrocchio *David* (c.1471), for which his 19-year-old pupil Leonardo da Vinci is believed to have been the model.

From the Mercato Nuovo to Santa Maria Novella

Start out from the centre, the heart of medieval Florence, on the street named after the drapers' guild, the **Via Calimala**. Just south of the caffè-ringed Piazza della Repubblica is the covered **Mercato Nuovo**, a 16th-century loggia where the bronze statue of a wild boar, *Il Porcellino*, is every Florentine child's favourite. If you rub its burnished snout and throw a coin in the fountain, your wish for a return trip to Florence is supposed to come true. The market was once called the Straw Market because of the straw products for which Florence was known. These items (bags, place mats) are now made in China, as are most tourist souvenirs on sale here. The mementoes pale in comparison to the open-air **Mercato San Lorenzo**, north of the Duomo, near the church of the same name. The nearby Central Market (www.mercatocentrale.it; daily 10am–midnight) has been given a thorough revamp and converted into a covered gastronomic and cultural centre.

West on the Via Porta Rossa is the 14th-century **Palazzo Davanzati** (tel: 055-238 8610; www.beniculturali.it; daily 8.15am–1.50pm, closed 1st, 3rd and 5th Mon and 2nd and 4th Sun of the month; upper floors by reservation only). Its stern, fortress-like exterior belies a truly luxurious interior, which gives a fascinating insight into life in medieval Florence.

The church of **Santa Trinità** has a late-16th-century Baroque facade with a Gothic interior. Ghirlandaio, master teacher of Leonardo da Vinci, decorated the Sassetti Chapel.

Florence's most elegant shops continue along the **Via de' Tornabuoni**. On the 15th-century **Palazzo Strozzi**, look out for the intricate wrought-iron lanterns; the massive *palazzo*, once a private residence, hosts blockbuster exhibitions three times a year. West of here is the **Via della Vigna Nuova**, where the overspill of Tornabuoni's most exclusive stores continues.

The 13th-century Dominican church of **Santa Maria Novella** (www. smn.it; Mon–Fri 9am–7pm, until 5.30pm in winter, Sat 9am–5.30pm, Sun 1–5pm, last entry 45 minutes before closing) – recognisable by its graceful facade in white, green and pink marble added by Leon Battista Alberti in 1470 – is the finest of Florence's monastic churches. Among its artistic treasures is one of the city's greatest paintings, Masaccio's *Trinity* (from around 1427; left aisle, third bay), which is famed for its early handling of perspective and depth. The church also has one of Italy's most delightful fresco cycles, by Ghirlandaio, of the lives of the Madonna and St John, which kept the master's entire workshop busy from 1485 to 1490. The Filippo Strozzi Chapel (right of the altar) is decorated with Filippino Lippi's frescoes of saints Philip and John. In the Gondi Chapel (left of the high altar) is the Brunelleschi *Crucifixion* (1410) while Giotto's serene *Crucifixion* (1290) is in the Sacristy (left transept).

You can escape the bustle of the piazza in the Dominicans' 14th-century **cloister** (Chiostro Verde), with Paolo Uccello's frescoes of the *Universal Deluge*. The **Spanish**

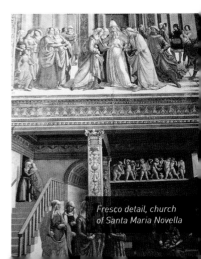

Fresco detail, church of Santa Maria Novella

Chapel (Cappellone degli Spagnoli) is covered by 14th-century frescoes by Andrea da Firenze. The cloisters are within the renovated museum, with an entrance on the station square.

North of Santa Maria Novella, spare a glance for the simple, clean-lined architecture of the **Stazione Centrale** (main railway station), built in 1935 during Mussolini's heyday but avoiding the bombastic pomposity of the Fascist regime.

Heading back down towards the river, have a drink in the plush neo-Renaissance bar or the panoramic terrace of the five-star Westin Excelsior (Piazza Ognissanti, tel: 055-27151), then cross the square to the church of the **Ognissanti** (All Saints' Church; Mon–Sat 7.15am–12.30pm and 4–8pm, Sun 9am–1pm and 4–8pm), built in the 13th century with a 1637 Baroque facade. Portrayed to the right of Mary in Ghirlandaio's *Madonna of Mercy* (right aisle, second bay) is the Florentine banker-navigator Amerigo Vespucci, who gave his name to the continent of America and whose family was a sponsor of this church. Botticelli is buried in a chapel (right transept). The highlight of the church is Domenico Ghirlandaio's huge fresco of the *Last Supper* (1480), which is through the cloister in the old refectory, the **Cenacolo** (Mon–Tue and Sat 9am–noon).

South of the Arno

There is nothing romantic about the murky waters of the River Arno, with broad, 19th-century *lungarni* embankments that protect it from flooding. Of the many bridges that cross it, two are noteworthy. The **Ponte Santa Trinità**, destroyed in 1944, has been rebuilt with the original 16th-century masonry scooped from the bottom of the river, including statues of the *Four Seasons*. Bartolomeo Ammanati's three lovely elliptical arches follow drawings by Michelangelo.

The **Ponte Vecchio**, intact since 1345, was Florence's first and, for centuries, its only, bridge. The shops with their back rooms overhanging the river were built from the 16th to the 19th centuries. Across the tops of these small former workshops, Vasari provided a covered corridor for Duke Cosimo to keep out of the rain when crossing from the Pitti Palace to the Uffizi. The duke didn't like the smell of the bridge's butcher shops and had them replaced with goldsmiths and jewellers, whose descendants offer you their high-quality wares today: this is some of Italy's finest window shopping. A bronze bust (1900) of Italy's celebrated goldsmith, Benvenuto Cellini, holds a position of honour in the middle of the bridge with a vantage point of lovely views.

In Renaissance times, the quarter south of the Arno, Florence's 'Left Bank', also known as Oltrarno, was an aristocratic preserve where the Medici held court. Today their sprawling **Pitti Palace** (www.uffizi.firenze.it) is home to four museums, and its heavy and graceless facade belies an ornate and colourful interior. Duke Cosimo I and his wife, Eleonora of Toledo, acquired the palace from the bankrupt Pitti merchant family in 1549.

The **Palatine Gallery** (Galleria Palatina) is the family art collection and the most important in Florence after the Uffizi. The richly

The Ponte Vecchio, Florence's first bridge

decorated salons on the first floor are named after the themes of their 17th-century frescoes – Venus, Hercules, Prometheus. Family pictures portray princesses, cardinals and popes.

The Medici's taste and means brought a considerable number of masterpieces. Titian displays his masterly use of colour and light in *The Concert* (Hall 32, Venus), a haunting portrait of *The Englishman* and bare-breasted *Magdalen* (Hall 31, Apollo). Rubens shows Venus restraining Mars in his vivid *Consequences of War* and portrays himself on the left of his *Four Philosophers* (Hall 26, Mars). Raphael is well represented by a stately *Veiled Woman* (Hall 25, Jupiter), a classic Madonna of the Chair and *Maddalena Doni* (Hall 24, Saturn), deliberately imitating the pose of Leonardo da Vinci's *Mona Lisa* and *Pregnant Women* (Hall 23, Iliad). Caravaggio contributes a typically disturbing canvas, an ugly *Sleeping Cupid* (Hall 25, Education of Jupiter). The **Royal Apartments** (Appartamenti Reale; same opening hours as the Palatine Gallery; gallery ticket valid for entry) are made up of 14 splendidly furnished rooms, which show a truly palatial life.

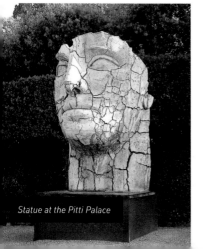
Statue at the Pitti Palace

On the next floor is the **Modern Art Gallery** (Galleria d'Arte Moderna), devoted to 19th- and 20th-century Italian art. Most notable is the work of the *Macchiaioli* school of Tuscan pre-Impressionists, who used to meet at the Caffè Michelangelo in Florence in the 1860s seeking freedom from academic art. Giorgio de Chirico and Eduardo de Pisis are among the more important of the 20th-century exhibitors.

The Pitti's next-most visited gallery, the **Treasury of the Grand Dukes** (Tesoro dei Granduchi**, formerly known as the Silver Museum**), occupies sumptuously decorated rooms that offset the Medici family's treasures – gold, silver, jewels, beautiful 16th- and 17th-century amber and ivory, crystal, porcelain and Baroque furniture. The **Costume and Fashion Museum** (Museo della Moda e del Costume) is a collection of traditional dress from the 18th–20th centuries. The nearby **Museo delle Porcellane** (Porcelain Museum) is also within the Boboli Gardens.

> ## Pitti Palace hours
>
> The Pitti Palace currently houses four museums: the Palatine Gallery and the Modern Art Gallery are both on the upper floors (both open Tue–Sun 8.15am–6.50pm; one ticket valid for entry to both), the Treasury of the Grand Dukes on the ground floor, and the Costume and Fashion Museum in the Palazzina della Meridiana building (both open daily 8.15am–4.30pm, until 6.30pm in summer; one ticket valid for entry to both). Combined tickets also allow entry to the Boboli Garden. .

Boboli Gardens

Take a rest in the shade of the cypresses, pines and holm oaks of the palace's **Boboli Gardens** (daily from 8.15am–4.30pm in winter, until 7.30pm in summer, closed 1st and last Mon of the month), which form a Renaissance and Baroque theme park dotted with loggias, cool fountains, grottoes with artificial stalactites and myriad statues of gods, nymphs and grotesques.

Directly behind the palace, the **Amphitheatre**, shaped like a Roman circus and with lovely views of the Palazzo Pitti and the city beyond, was the scene of the Medici's most extravagant fêtes and staged performances. In the middle of the nearby Pond of Neptune (Vasca del Nettuno), the burly sea god wields his trident in petrified parody of one of the Boboli's gardeners.

Adjacent to the Boboli Gardens are the Bardini Gardens. Restored to former glories, but little known, these peaceful gardens rise up in terraces towards Piazzale Michelangelo. They formerly belonged to Stefano Bardini, collector and antiquarian, who left his *palazzo* and his works of art to the city in 1923. This is now the Museo Bardini (Fri–Mon 11am–5pm), just by the Ponte Grazie. After the Pitti's overwhelming riches, the unadorned white facade of the nearby Augustinian church of **Santo Spirito** (in the Piazza Santo Spirito) is a sobering antidote. Brunelleschi's design was never completed but the interior of the church preserves the spatial clarity of his Corinthian colonnades. In the right transept is a strikingly theatrical Madonna Enthroned by Filippino Lippi.

The church of **Santa Maria del Carmine** (Cappella Brancacci; tel: 055-238 2195; Wed–Mon 10am–5pm, Sun, reservations advised) is an essential stop on any artistic pilgrimage to Florence. The church itself is an unprepossessing reconstruction after a devastating fire

Pitti Palace

of 1771, but the Brancacci Chapel (http://museicivici fiorentini.comune.fi.it) containing the great **Masaccio frescoes**, miraculously survived intact. Due to their popularity, visitors are only allowed 15 minutes to see them. The bright light of the early years of the Renaissance, the talented painter died at the age of 27 after only five years of promising creative activity (1423–1428), working with his teacher Masolino on scenes from Genesis and the life of St Peter. Compare Masolino's sweet and harmonious Adam and Eve in his *Original Sin* (chapel entrance, upper right) with Masaccio's agonising figures in the *Expulsion from the Garden of Eden*, opposite, to appreciate one of the early Renaissance's most dramatic statements. The chapel frescoes were completed in the 1480s by Filippino Lippi, who painted the side walls' lower panels.

> ### Sunset viewpoint
>
> For a last panoramic sunset view of the city, take a bus or taxi to the vast Piazzale Michelangelo (anchored by a second copy of his *David*). The lovely 11th-century church of San Miniato (up the hill behind the square; Sun 8.15am–7pm, Mon–Sat 9.30am–1pm and 3–7pm, until 8pm in summer; free) is Florence's oldest and one of its most beloved churches. Be there in late afternoon when a handful of resident monks chant timeless Gregorian vespers.

AROUND TUSCANY (TOSCANA)

The original territory of the ancient Etruscans, Tuscany has always been independent-minded, even aloof, in its attitude to Rome and the other regions. For the serious Italophile, its beauty and riches deserve weeks, months, even years of attention, but no first visit is complete without at least a brief foray here. After a side-trip from Florence to Fiesole, we range further afield – west to Pisa and Lucca before turning south through the hills of Chianti to Siena.

Villa Medici in Fiesole

Fiesole

Just 8km (5 miles) northeast of Florence the road winds up a wooded cypress-studded hillside, revealing at each bend ever-changing views of the gardens and historical villas of **Fiesole** ❹ and the monuments of the great Renaissance city below. Drivers can negotiate the winding old side road **Via Vecchia Fiesolana** for glimpses of villas half-hidden among the cypresses and olive trees. The town centre, Piazza Mino da Fiesole, is the starting-point for some exhilarating hill walks, the most immediate being the steep paved lane leading from the square up to the small **San Francesco** convent.

Only fragments remain of the former Etruscan stronghold in Fiesole itself, but there are extensive Roman ruins, including the **Teatro Romano** (www.museidifiesole.it; Wed–Mon Nov–Feb 10am–3pm, daily Mar and Oct 10am–6pm, Apr–Sept until 7pm), which dates from the 1st century BC and still in use for the popular summer arts festival. Within this **Zona Archeologica** are the Museo Archeologico (same hours as the theatre) and Museo Bandini (Fri–Sun Nov–Feb 10am–3pm, until 6pm Mar and Oct, until 7pm Apr–Sept).

Pisa

In its heyday from the 11th to the 13th centuries, **Pisa 5** created a powerful maritime empire down the Tyrrhenian coast and in Corsica, Sardinia, Sicily, Syria, Palestine and Egypt. Its riches and prestige called for a legacy, providing the funds for the gleaming white marble complex of religious edifices known as the **Campo dei Miracoli** (Field of Miracles), of which its leaning bell tower is a national icon. Visitors with little time to spare see the square, admire the tilting tower and leave town.

This serene set of buildings in an emerald green square, also known as the **Piazza del Duomo**, celebrates the whole cycle of life, from baptistery, cathedral and campanile (the Leaning Tower) to the monumental cemetery of the Campo Santo. The **Duomo** (www.opapisa.it; daily 10am–6pm, until 8pm in summer) was begun in 1063 during the Golden Age, to honour Pisa's victory over the Saracens in Sicily. With Oriental and Byzantine decorative elements reflecting the Pisan Republic's overseas interests, its four-tiered arcaded facade over three porches is a masterpiece of delicacy. Architect Buscheto did not hesitate to write in Latin (in the far left arch) 'This marble church has no equal'. Inside, there was no reason either for local Giovanni Pisano to show false modesty about his sculpted 14th-century **marble pulpit** (left aisle), the cathedral's masterpiece.

Thanks to its unstable subsoil, the **Leaning Tower** (Torre Pendente; tel: 050-560 547; www.opapisa.it; daily Apr–Sept 8.30am–8pm, later in high season, Oct 9am–7pm, Nov–Feb 9am–6pm, Mar times vary; advanced reservation advisable) has always tilted. Begun after the Duomo in 1173, it started to lean when only three of its eight storeys had been completed. The overhang increased over time and by the late 20th century it was 4.5m (15ft) out of alignment. The tower was closed in 1990, while engineers sought a remedy. It was finally decided that soil should be extracted from the foundations on the opposite side to the lean and by early 2001 the top of the tower had been brought back 45cm (18ins), a 10 percent reduction in inclination.

The Leaning Tower

Each tour lasts 30 minutes and the number of visitors is strictly controlled. Note that no children under 8 years old are allowed, and 8–18-year-olds must be accompanied by an adult.

The lovely **Baptistery** (Apr–Sept daily 8am–8pm, Mar 9am–6pm, Oct 9am–7pm, Nov–Feb 9am–6pm), is topped by a traditional statue of John the Baptist. Left of the baptismal font and altar is Pisa's greatest work of sculpture, a hexagonal **marble pulpit** by Nicola Pisano, father of Giovanni who designed the cathedral pulpit.

Note the Gothic tabernacle enclosing a *Madonna and Saints* in the 13th-century cloistered cemetery of the **Camposanto** (Holy Ground, believed to be filled with sacred dirt brought from the Holy Land during the Crusades; same hours as the Baptistery). The north gallery of the cloister has a **fresco** of the *Triumph of Death* (1360).

Lucca

The 'sights' of **Lucca ❻** take scarcely a day to see, but the seductive tranquillity within its perfectly preserved ramparts is irresistible. Things were not always so peaceful here. In the stormy 15th and 16th centuries, Lucca's prosperous silk merchants preserved the peace by intercepting enemy armies and paying them to bypass the town. It has been particularly rich in musicians, notably Boccherini and Puccini, and hosts a series of music festivals in summer.

Begin with a stroll or bike ride on the tree-shaded pathway atop the 16th–17th-century brick **ramparts**, along the Passeggiata delle

Mura, for an excellent overall view of the traffic-free *centro storico* contained within the walls. Begun in 1060, the **Duomo di San Martino** (www.museocattedralelucca.it; Mon–Sat 9.30am–7pm, Sun 9–10am and noon–7pm; Nov–mid-Mar Mon–Fri 9.30am–5pm, Sat until 6.45pm, Sun 1.30am–5pm) has a Pisan-style three-storey facade with a *Descent from the Cross* carved by Nicola Pisano over the north door. Its prized possessions are two: the haunting **Volto Santo** (Holy Face), a wooden crucifix said to have been carved by Nicodemus and with alleged miraculous powers; and the graceful white marble **tomb of Ilaria del Carretto Guinigi**, carved in 1408 by the master Sienese sculptor Jacopo della Quercia, in the former sacristy.

Northwest of the cathedral is the town's other beloved church, **San Michele in Foro** (daily 7.40am–noon and 3–6pm, 5pm in winter), on the site of the Roman Forum. Begun in 1143, its arcaded facade varies the patterns of its four tiers of columns in pink, green, black or white marble. With a pair of binoculars, you should be able to spot, on the third tier of arches (third from the right), busts of Risorgimento heroes Garibaldi and Cavour.

To capture something of the town's medieval character, explore the **Via Guinigi**, with smart 14th-century palaces, and the towered houses of **Via Fillungo**, leading to the Roman amphitheatre, now the Piazza del Mercato. Nearby, the facade of the church of **San Frediano** has a 13th-century mosaic of the *Ascension of Christ*. In the interior (fourth chapel on the left aisle), look for Jacopo della Quercia's marble altar (1422).

Chianti

The best introduction to the Tuscan hill country is a tour of the famous **vineyards** that grace its southern-oriented slopes. The grapes that qualify as *Chianti Classico*, distinguished by a coveted black rooster label, grow in the region between Florence and Siena, most of them along the ancient Via Chiantigiana, which is route SR222. The liveliest, most colourful time is during the autumn grape harvest, *la vendemmia*, but tasting – and buying – goes on at many of the Chianti vineyards all year round.

Start out at San Casciano in Val di Pesa, 17km (11 miles) south of Florence, with a bonus for art-lovers of a Simone Martini *Crucifixion* and other Sienese works in the church of La Misericordia. Southeast across to route SR222, you find vineyards interspersed with equally renowned olive groves as you approach Greve in Chianti, a characteristic town that is the major wine centre for the area. The wine route continues through **Castellina** with its 15th-century castle and ancient town gate. Continue on to the hilltop town of **Radda**, where you will find good restaurants; and to **Gaiole in Chianti**, one of the best centres for tasting and a place to linger.

San Gimignano

The haunting silhouette and well-preserved centre make **San Gimignano** ❼ the most magical of Tuscany's hill towns. There were once 76 towers – erected as symbols of mercantile power and prestige – until the town's Florentine conquerors ordered them to be dismantled in the 14th century. Only 14 remain. The most important are clustered around three adjoining **piazzas**: the triangular Piazza della Cisterna named after the city's 13th-century well, surrounded by elegant palaces; the Piazza del Duomo, grouping church and town hall as the seat of civic and religious power; and the Piazza delle Erbe marketplace with twin Salvucci towers.

Best view

The most photogenic view of San Gimignano is from the north, on the road from Certaldo, the home and last resting place of Boccaccio, author of *The Decameron*.

The 13th-century town hall, **Palazzo del Popolo**, houses the **Museo Civico** and **Pinacoteca** (daily Apr–Sep 9am–7pm, Oct 9.30am–5.30pm, Nov–Mar 11am–5.30pm). The latter includes a *Crucifixion* by Coppo di Marcovaldo and a Taddeo di Bartolo painting of

The towers of the hill town San Gimignano

St Gimignano, in which you can see what the towers of the medieval city looked like. The Palazzo's Torre Grossa, the only climbable tower in San Gimignano, offers great views.

The 12th-century Romanesque **Collegiata** (Apr–Oct Mon–Fri 10am–7.30pm, Sat 10am–5.30pm, Sun 12.30–7.30pm, Nov–Mar Mon–Sat 10am–5pm, Sun 12.30–5pm) is known as the town's duomo, although it is not officially a cathedral. Along the right aisle are dramatic frescoes of New Testament scenes. The Ghirlandaio **frescoes** in the Santa Fina Chapel (at the end of the right aisle) form a series of social portraits (1475) dedicated to the young patron saint of San Gimignano. By the east wall, flanking the church entrance, are statues of Mary and the Archangel Gabriel by Jacopo della Quercia.

To view Tuscany at its most poetic, climb up to the ruins of the **Rocca** citadel, the town's highest point and a good picnic spot.

Volterra

Fortified **Volterra** ❽, perched on a hill, exerts a sober charm, with the 13th-century stone edifices of the **Piazza dei Priori** and adjacent Piazza San Giovanni. The Palazzo dei Priori (1208) is the oldest of Tuscany's typical town halls, with a two-tiered tower, battlements and mullioned windows. It stands opposite the massive triple-arched **Palazzo Pretorio**, medieval police headquarters. The two squares are separated by the 12th-century cathedral and 13th-century octagonal baptistery. The latter's baptismal font has basreliefs by Andrea Sansovino. Away from the centre, trace the town's beginnings in the **Museo Etrusco Guarnacci** (Via Don Minzoni 15; daily mid-Mar–Oct 9am–7pm, Nov–mid-Mar 10am–4.30pm). The collection includes 6th-century BC sculpted stone, alabaster and terracotta funeral urns. Volterra is known for its alabaster, as a glimpse in any shop window will confirm.

Siena

A time-locked city of rich russet browns and weathered ochres, **Siena** ❾ is as perfectly medieval as grey-stone Florence is a Renaissance showcase, yet contrasts with its centuries-old rival to the north are striking and inevitable. Whereas the nucleus of Florence was built to a strict Roman city plan of straight streets intersecting at right angles, Siena has all the Tuscan hill-town's haphazard organic forms, straggling up and down a forked ridge of three hilltops. Closed to traffic (and free of taxis), it is not for the weak of knee.

While Florentine art developed its formidable intellectual and emotional power, the tone of Sienese painting – Simone Martini, the Lorenzettis, even the Mannerist Sodoma – remained gentle and delicate, bathed in the light and colour of its surrounding countryside. But as its obstinately independent spirit has shown, even after the Florentine conquest of 1555 – a spirit epitomised by its lusty Palio tournament – the town was not without vigour. Like an open-air museum, Siena is still a very dignified lived-in town, with fashionable restaurants and boutiques, a vibrant local pride nurtured by a rich historic legacy.

At its heart is the sloping, fan-shaped **Piazza del Campo**, site of the old Roman forum and arena of the town's famous annual Palio horse race (see page 102). The unique piazza's red-brick herring-bone paving is divided by nine marble strips for the nine patrician clans that ruled the city at the end of the 13th century.

The painterly impact of the 'burnt sienna' glows from the arcaded Gothic **Palazzo Pubblico**, with its grand 102m (335ft) **Torre del Mangia** (daily mid-Mar–Oct 10am–7pm, Nov–mid-Mar until 4pm). Climb to its first tier at 88m (288ft) for a magnificent view of the city and countryside beyond. The loggia at the tower's base is a chapel (Cappella di Piazza) marking the city's deliverance from the plague of 1348. Note that there are 503 steps in total, and that visitors are limited to 30 at a time so be prepared to queue.

The Palazzo Pubblico's ground floor houses the offices of the town hall, but its upstairs chambers, frescoed by the city's fore-most artists, have been transformed into a **Museo Civico** (Municipal

Siena, a perfect medieval city

Museum; www.comune.siena.it; daily Mar–Oct 10am–7pm, Nov–Feb 10am–6pm; combined ticket for the museum and the tower). The **Sala del Mappamondo** (named after a lost map of the Sienese world painted by Ambrogio Lorenzetti to trace the city's international banking interests) has two great frescoes by the Siena-born master Simone Martini. To the left is the stately *Maestà* (Madonna Enthroned; 1315) and to the right, *Guidoriccio da Fogliano* (1328, but its authenticity has been disputed), depicting the Sienese captain's ride to a historic victory at Montemassi; in the nicely detailed Tuscan landscape, notice the little Chianti vineyard in the military encampment. In the **Sala della Pace** (Hall of Peace, council chamber of the Nine Patricians), the full force of Siena's civic pride strikes home in the impressive allegorical frescoes (1337–9) by another local master, Ambrogio Lorenzetti. One wall is devoted to *Bad Government*, a gloomy portrait of Tyranny; the other two to Siena's own enlightened *Good Government*, full of fascinating detail – roof-builders, shoe shop, school, outdoor tavern, ladies dancing in the street – and hunters riding out to the countryside.

⊘ RIDING FOR THE PALIO

The Palio horse race, held on 2 July (7.45pm) and 16 August (7pm), is part of a traditional pageant dating to before the 15th century. Colourful Renaissance-costumed pages and men-at-arms put on a procession and show of flag-throwing with emblems – eagle, snail, porcupine, goose and others – of the 17 parishes *(contrade)* of the city and surrounding communes. Ten of them compete in the climactic breakneck bareback horse race round the Campo for which a painted silk standard, the Palio, is the prize. The race lasts about a minute and a half. To avoid the crush of spectators in the square, reserve a seat in a stand or a place on a balcony well in advance. Contact Palio Viaggi, tel: 05-7728 0828.

Siena's bareback Palio horse race

Southwest of the Campo, the **Duomo** (www.operaduomo.siena.it, Mar–Oct 10.30am–7pm, Nov–Feb 10.30am–5.30pm) built from the 12th–14th centuries, is for many the greatest of Italy's – possibly all of Europe's – Gothic cathedrals. For some, it is a tasteless iced cake. John Ruskin, for example, dismissed it as 'over-striped...a piece of costly confectionery and faithless vanity'. The interior continues the bands of black-and-white marble that decorate the exterior. Elaborately **inlaid marble paving** – with large sections regularly covered for protection – covers the floor with 56 pictures of biblical and allegorical themes, done over two centuries by some 40 artists. The early 16th-century **Cardinal Piccolomini Library** (Libreria Piccolomini), off the left aisle, is decorated by Pinturicchio's vivid, action-packed frescoes of the life of Pope Pius II (the locally born Piccolomini cardinal himself became pope, Pius III, but lasted only 10 days). In the left transept is a magnificent octagonal 13th-century pulpit carved by Nicola Pisano, in which the damned are being eaten alive in the *Last Judgement*. In 2013 the cathedral opened its rooftops to tourists for the first time, offering breathtaking views down into the cathedral and over the rooftops of the city.

In the **Cathedral Museum** (Museo dell'Opera del Duomo; same times as Duomo) the focal point is the *Maestà* (Enthroned Madonna, 1308) by local master painter Duccio. Simone Martini's *Miracles of St Agostino Novello* and Pietro Lorenzetti's *Birth of Mary* are not to be missed.

Opposite the Duomo, the **Ospedale di Santa Maria della Scala** (www.santamariadellascala.com; mid-daily 10.30am–8.30pm) is a large cultural complex, converted from one of the oldest hospitals in Europe. The Pilgrims' Hall frescoes chart the history of the former Pilgrims' Hospital. Upper floors are devoted to major temporary exhibitions while the underground passageways and chambers are home to the archaeological museum, with Etruscan, and Roman treasures.

The importance of Siena's 13th- and 14th-century school of art is illustrated in the Palazzo Buonsignori's **National Art Gallery** (Pinacoteca Nazionale; www.pinacotecanazionale.siena.it; Tue–Sat 8.15am–7.15pm, Mon and Sun 9am–1pm). Besides the works of the 14th-century masters Duccio, Pietro and Ambrogio Lorenzetti, as well as Simone Martini, you can see Siena's 16th-century Mannerists: Beccafumi's dreamy *Birth of Mary* and a decorative *Christ at the Column* by Sodoma.

Montepulciano and Monte Argentario

South of Siena is a little-trammelled niche of Tuscany and some of the region's most attractive hill towns with excellent local wines. **Montepulciano ⑩** (famous for its superb Vino Nobile di Montepulciano), perched 610m (2,000ft) above sea level, is known as 'The Pearl of the 16th Century'. A stroll along the Via di Gracciano and Via Ricci to see the town's Renaissance palazzi will explain why.

Piazza Grande, the highest point in town, is the site of the graceful town well, decorated with griffins and lions. The 13th-century Gothic **Palazzo Comunale** (Town Hall) is a particularly imposing expression of civic dignity. From the top of its tower (Mon–Sat

Montepulciano, bathed in a russet glow at sunset

10am–6pm) there are views of the whole province. In the austere 16th–17th-century **Duomo** (daily 9am–12.30pm) see Taddeo di Bartolo's fine triptych on the high altar. Antonio da Sangallo the Elder, architect of many of the town's palazzi, built his masterpiece, the 16th-century church of **San Biagio**, southwest of town, a gem of High Renaissance architecture hidden at the end of a cypress-lined road with views of the Chiana valley. The nearby towns of **Montalcino** (known for its Brunello wines) and **Pienza** promise small-town distractions and culinary pleasures.

If you are taking the coast road to or from Rome during warm-weather months, stop off at the fashionable seaside resorts on the pine-forested peninsula of Montepulciano beside the town of **Orbetello**. The sandy beaches and yachting harbours of **Port' Ercole** and **Porto Santo Stefano** are favourite weekend destinations for well-heeled Romans, but they are quieter during the week. The pretty island of **Giglio** hit the news headlines in 2012 when a cruiser ran aground here. Elba, also in the Tuscan archipelago, is best known as the island of Napoleon's retreat.

Orvieto's magnificent Gothic cathedral

UMBRIA

Umbria is renowned for its great artistic treasures and the dreamy rolling green landscapes that inspired them. The area was dominated in the past by the papacy, which conquered the Lombard dukes of Spoleto in the Middle Ages, Perugia in the 16th century, and held sway until the unification of Italy.

Orvieto

Half the pleasure of **Orvieto** ⓫, a lovely town dramatically perched on a rocky precipice, is a first glimpse from afar. For a good view, approach it from the southwest, on route SS71 from Lake Bolsena, or look across from the medieval abbey La Badia (now a hotel, www. labadiahotel.it) 8km (5 miles) south of town.

Connoisseurs come for its white wine, but it is the **Duomo** (www. opsm.it; daily Mar and Oct 9.30am–6pm, Apr–Sep until 7pm, Nov–Feb 9.30am–1pm and 2.30–7pm, Sun Nov–Feb 2.30–4.30pm, Mar–Oct 1–5.30pm), a magnificent Gothic building, that attracts art-lovers. More than 100 architects worked on the church between 1290 and 1600. The highlight is the gleaming **facade** with four slender spired pilasters and a rose-window above the beautifully scrolled porches. At the base of the two northern pilasters are Lorenzo Maitani's marvellous marble **bas-relief** scenes from the Old Testament and the Last Judgement.

Grey and white bands of marble give the interior a spacious simplicity. Off the right transept, the **San Brizio Chapel** (Cappella Nuova; same hours as Duomo) is famous for Fra Angelico's 1447 frescoes *Christ in Glory* covering the ceiling and Luca Signorelli's glorious cycle *The Last Judgement* (*c*.1500) on the walls. To the left, Signorelli portrays himself and Fra Angelico as bystanders in the vivid *Preaching of the Antichrist* (identified here with Savonarola). On the right, the nude figures in the *Resurrection of the Dead* are less convincing, echoing da Vinci's comparison to 'sacks of nuts'.

To cool off, explore the **Pozzo di San Patrizio** (daily May–Aug 9am–7.45pm, Mar–Apr and Sept–Oct until 6.45pm, Nov–Feb 10am–4.45pm), a 16th-century well that is dug 63m (206ft) into the volcanic rock on the northeast edge of the precipice. Lit by 72 windows, two spiral staircases of 248 steps go down to water level. The town sits on a labyrinth of tunnels, caves and storerooms carved into the tufa begun by the Etruscans and elaborated by the Romans. Guided visits explore Orvieto's history (tel: 0763 343 768).

Spoleto

The greatest attractions in hill town **Spoleto ⑫**, 50km (30 miles) southeast of Orvieto,

Umbria & Marche Earthquakes

In 2016, two major earthquakes devastated Umbria and Marche. The first struck on August 24, killing nearly 300 people and leaving the town of Amatrice in ruins. The second one, which occurred barely two months later, destroyed the beautiful 14th-century Basilica of St Benedict in the town of Norcia, leaving as many as 3,000 people homeless in the process. Fortunately, there were no fatalities caused by the second earthquake.

is the summer Festival dei Due Mondi (Festival of Two Worlds), an extravaganza of theatre, music and art, but the town's beautiful natural setting amid wooded hills also makes it a base for country hikes. Especially popular is the oak forest (and monastery) on Monteluco, favoured by St Francis and St Bernardino of Siena.

An important Roman outpost with an amphitheatre, Spoleto also has a sober Romanesque **cathedral** (daily 8.30am–12.30pm, 3.30–7pm; until 5pm in winter) in the medieval Upper Town. Its 17th-century additions are decorated with damaged but still graceful Fra Filippo Lippi frescoes (1469). The tomb for the painter-monk who seduced Sister Lucrezia (the model for many of his Madonnas) was designed by Filippino Lippi, the son of Filippo and Lucrezia.

Assisi

The enduring appeal of St Francis (1182–1226) has turned **Assisi** ⑬, his native pink-hued town, into Italy's major pilgrimage destination,

⊙ ST FRANCIS OF ASSISI

The spoiled son of a rich family, Francesco di Bernardone was known for his profligate ways. But a sojourn in a Perugia jail at 23, followed by a severe illness, sobered him up. After a vision in the Chapel of San Damiano, he vowed a life of poverty in the service of the Church. He nursed lepers, converted bandits and travelled to Spain, Morocco, Egypt and Palestine. But it was his impact on a troubled Italian population that mattered most to a Church beleaguered by heresy. Thousands responded to the simple eloquence of his preaching. They told how the example of his gentle life had tamed wild wolves and taught swallows to sing more sweetly. The new Pope, elected in 2013, chose the name of St Francis (never before used in papal history) after St Francis of Assisi as a way to symbolize the need for the church to be 'of the poor, for the poor'.

second only to Rome. Its basilica, like the peaceful medieval town centre, has been beautifully preserved and the centuries-old pilgrim trade manages (sometimes just barely) to avoid the unashamed commercialism that blights other religious shrines.

The **Basilica of San Francesco** (www.sanfrancescoassisi.org; daily Lower Church 6am–6.50pm in summer, until 6pm in winter; Upper Church from 8.30am–6.50pm, until 6pm in winter; closed Sun am for services) is two churches, one above the other, built on top of the saint's tomb in the crypt. The epicentre of the 1997 earthquake was located to the east, in the Marche. However, several priceless frescoes were severely damaged or destroyed, notably invaluable works by Cimabue (1226–1337); featured on a portion of the Upper Church's vaulted ceiling, they plunged to the floor during the quakes. The **Lower Basilica** was begun in 1228, the year of Francis's canonisation, two years after his death. The frescoes were painted in the 14th century, but a Renaissance porch now precedes the Gothic side entrance. Simone Martini decorated the **St Martin Chapel** (Cappella di San Martino, first left) with fine frescoes, including an aristocratic Jesus appearing in St Martin's dream. Stairs in the nave lead to the crypt and St Francis's simple tomb, rediscovered in 1818, after it had been hidden from plunderers.

The superb frescoes of the life of Jesus in the **St Mary Magdalen Chapel** and of St Francis's vows of poverty, chastity and obedience above the high altar are attributed to Giotto (1307). In the right transept, Cimabue's **portrait of St Francis** shows him to the right of the Madonna. In the left transept is Lorenzetti's *Descent from the Cross*. In the **Upper Basilica** Cimabue's works in the apse and left transept have blackened because of the oxidized white lead in his paints, yet the crowd's anguish in his *Crucifixion* is palpable.

In the nave, the faithful are exalted by one of the most grandiose series of **frescoes** in Christendom and, sadly, some of the most damaged in the 1997 earthquake. Generally accepted as the work of a young Giotto, the Life of *St Francis* (1296–1304) is celebrated in 28 scenes along the lower tier (from the right transept), while 32 frescoes in the upper tier illustrate scenes from the Bible.

The Historic Town

Visit the historic heart of Assisi along the **Via San Francesco**, with its 15th-century Pilgrims' Hostel (Oratorio dei Pellegrini) at No. 11 with frescoes attributed to Perugino. The **Piazza del Comune** forms the town centre, where medieval palazzi are grouped around the Roman forum. The church of **Santa Maria sopra Minerva** was built on the site of a Roman temple. A small art museum (**Pinacoteca**) (daily 10.30am–1pm and 2–5pm, until 7pm in summer) is across the square.

The 11th-century church of **San Damiano** (daily 10am–12.30pm, 2–6pm, winter until 4.30pm) is a pleasant 1.5km (1-mile) stroll from the Porta Nuova and is a point of pilgrimage for those interested in the wooden crucifix that spoke to a 27-year-old St Francis in 1209 (the crucifix is now on show in the Basilica di St Chiara). Also worth the 4.5km (2-mile) trip is the **Eremo delle Carceri** (www.eremodellecarceri.it), a hermitage founded by St Francis and now a convent.

Perugia

Dominating the Umbrian countryside from its 494m (1,600ft) hill, **Perugia** ⑭ is emphatically more secular and more profane than its Umbrian neighbour Assisi. In medieval times Perugia was said to have the most warlike people in the whole country and in 1265 it was the birthplace of the Flagellants. But the imposing weight of its past is lightened by the lively student population of the two universities and its popularity as the site of one of Europe's best jazz festivals each July. Perugia's antiquity is symbolised on the north side of town by the **Arco Etrusco** (Etruscan – and partly Roman – triumphal arch) that was incorporated into its medieval ramparts.

In Perugia's picturesque town centre is the formidable **Palazzo dei Priori** (town hall). Nicola Pisano carved the 13th-century **Fontana Maggiore** (Great Fountain), a favourite rendezvous in the shadow of the 14th-century cathedral. The fourth floor of the town hall (entrance on Corso Vannucci) contains the **Galleria Nazionale**

Fontana Maggiore in Perugia's town centre

dell'Umbria (www.artiumbria.beniculturali.it; Tue–Sun 8.30am–7.30pm), with a splendid collection of 13th–18th-century Umbrian and Tuscan paintings. It includes a Fra Angelico triptych and Piero della Francesca's *Annunciation* and *Madonna with Angels*. But Umbria's pride and joy is the work of Perugia-born Pietro Vanucci, or Perugino (1445–1523). Next door on Corso Vannucci is the **Collegio del Cambio** (www.collegiodelcambio.it; Mon–Sat 9am–12.30pm and 2.30–5.30pm, Sun 9am–1pm), the 15th-century hall and chapel of the bankers' guild where the **Audience Hall** (Sala dell'Udienza) is covered with Perugino frescoes, seen as his masterpiece.

Gubbio

Some 40km (25 miles) north of Perugia, this beautifully situated hill town is not easy to get to and its steep cobbled streets are hard to navigate. But for anyone who cherishes the tranquillity of an unspoilt medieval atmosphere, Gubbio is a delight. The brick-paved **Piazza della Signoria** is the centre stage of 'the city of stone'. Its 14th-century crenellated **Palazzo dei Consoli** (daily 10am–1pm, 3–6pm, Nov–Mar 10am–1pm, 2.30–5.30pm) is one of the grandest civic edifices in Italy and the bell tower gives a magnificent panorama. Lifts hewn into the rocks take you to the cathedral and the Renaissance courtyard of the 15th-century Palazzo Ducale. In summer an open *funivia* (cable-car) takes you to the basilica of Sant'Ubaldo, Gubbio's patron saint. Walk from there to the 12th-century fortress of **La Rocca** for superb views of the Appennines.

THE NORTHEAST

Throughout Italy's history, its northeast regions have linked the country to the exotic world of Byzantium and the Orient through Venice and its Repubblica Serena and to the Alpine countries north of the Dolomites, while the plains of Emilia-Romagna from Ravenna to Parma provided an anchor to the heartland of the Po Valley.

The Grand Canal and Rialto Bridge, Venice

The result is a rich variety of distinctive cities and colourful hinterland. Elegant Palladian villas grace the Veneto mainland from Venice to Padua and Vicenza. The glories of Verona extend from its grand Roman arena to the palaces of medieval and Renaissance families whose intrigues and love stories inspired Shakespeare. In Emilia-Romagna, the pride and creativity of the great city-states is still much in evidence in the monuments and museums of Bologna, Ferrara and Parma. Stretch your muscles in the Dolomites with first-class winter sports and summer hiking, or soak up sun and sea in the Adriatic resorts around Rimini.

VENICE (VENEZIA)

The incomparable palazzi, canals and lagoons of **Venice** ⑮ claim a place apart in our collective imagination. Today it remains a dream-world more than ever, its myth more powerful than the harsh reality. Even when it threatens to disintegrate into nightmare at times of winter floods, Carnival shenanigans, or summer hordes, visitors can take refuge in a caffè once frequented by Casanova or in a

Ca' Pesaro

back alley and continue their dream uninterrupted. One of the city's many blessings is that there remain so many quiet and beautiful corners, hidden away in the narrow streets, which have changed little with time. Another obvious bonus, impossible to overemphasise, is the absence of cars; the simple joy of wandering around a town relieved of traffic noise and fumes, of standing on a little humpbacked pedestrian bridge far from the Grand Canal and hearing only the water lapping against the moss-covered walls, or the occasional swish of a sleek gondola that appears out of nowhere. Staying here forever is most likely to cross your mind.

Try to avoid high summer months, but whatever time of year you go, don't try to see all of Venice in one day. Without the time to meander and explore those hidden corners, you risk not seeing much more than Piazza San Marco and understanding little of the city's inherent charm.

Give yourself a minimum of three days, time to get lost. The city has more than enough sights to see, but you can taste much of its pleasures before setting foot inside the museums, churches and monuments.

Grand Canal (Canal Grande)

From the railway station or the car park of Piazzale Roma, begin with a *vaporetto* waterbus along the **Grand Canal**, Venice's unique and stunning main 'street'. Use this wonderful first contact with the city as your introductory (and inexpensive) tour. Vaporetto No. 1 takes you from Piazzale Roma to the historic centre of town, Piazza San Marco. Save your gondola ride – yes, it is touristy and expensive but not to be missed – for when you have settled in.

Along the Grand Canal's 3.8km (more than 2 miles), varying in width from 30 to 70m (100 to 230ft), are the old trading headquarters and warehouses of its distant commercial heyday. Known locally as *ca'* (short for *casa*, or house) as well as *palazzo*, the marble, brick and white-limestone palaces range over 600 years from Venetian-Byzantine to Renaissance, Baroque and neoclassical, but most of them are exotically 14th- and 15th-century Gothic, Venice's 'trademark' in architectural styles. Their sea-resistant limestone foundations stand on massive pinewood stilts driven 8m (26ft) into the lagoon bed.

The magnificent Renaissance **Palazzo Vendramin-Calergi**, where Richard Wagner died in 1883, is home to the city's casino and a museum dedicated to the famous composer (open Tue and Sat mornings, Thu afternoon, booking essential, tel: 041 276 0407). The gilt has gone from the freshly restored facade of the 15th-century Ca' d'Oro (see page 131), but it's still the most beautiful and best preserved of the city's Gothic palaces. Renovated by the world-famous architect Rem Koolhaas, **Fondaco dei Tedeschi** was once the trading centre of Czechs, Hungarians and Austrians as well as the Germans of its name, and is now is a luxury T Galleria department store (www.dfs. com) with shops offering the best Italian products (food, beverages and fashion). Just beyond, the shop-lined white marble **Rialto Bridge** arches

When to visit

Visit Venice in May or October if you can – the crowds at Easter and in June to September can be horrible. Venice at Christmas has become fashionable and Carnival commercial. In the winter months, Venice is dank and cold but has a mystical beauty.

the canal at its narrowest point. The prefecture puts its bureaucrats in the fine Renaissance **Palazzo Corner** (or Ca' Grande), while gondoliers claim Othello's Desdemona lived in the lovely late-Gothic **Palazzo Contarini-Fasan**.

The 700-year-old **Fondaco dei Turchi** was a warehouse used by the merchants of Constantinople, now the **Natural History Museum** (http://msn.visitmuve.it; Tue–Fri 9am–5pm, Sat–Sun 10am–6pm). It stands next to the plain brick, 15th-century **Megio** wheat granary, decorated by battlements and the republic's seal of St Mark's lion. The imposing 17th-century **Ca' Pesaro** houses the **Modern Art Museum** (see page 129) (http://capesaro.visitmuve. it; Tue–Sun 10am–5pm). Come back early in the morning to enjoy the 20th-century, neo-Gothic **Pescheria** (fish market) and adjoining produce market. The university has a department in the handsome 15th-century Gothic **Ca' Foscari**. The **Ca' Rezzonico** (www. carezzonico.visitmuve.it; Wed–Mon Apr–Oct 10am–6pm, Nov–Mar 10am–5pm) is a fine specimen of the 18th-century Venetian art, for which it is now a museum. Beyond the wooden Accademia Bridge and the **Accademia Art Gallery** (www.gallerieaccademia.org), the

⊙ GOING, GOING, GONDOLA

The fleet of 10,000 gondolas of a century ago has dwindled to a few hundred, while the prices have gone in the opposite direction. Apart from commuters taking cross-canal ferry gondolas, Venetians leave the sleek and slender black craft to the tourists. Still handing on the business from father to son, the gondoliers in their straw hats and sailors' jumpers or striped T-shirts are as cheerful and witty as any other taxi-driver. Sadly, they don't sing as often or as well as they used to. Exorbitant yes, but how will you explain to grandchildren, after the last of the gondolas have disappeared, that you visited Venice and never experienced one?

St Mark's, at the heart of Venice

perspective is completed by the magnificent Baroque church of **Santa Maria della Salute**, which marks the arrival at (or departure from) Piazza San Marco.

Around Piazza San Marco

Building space on the water being what it is, Venice has only one real piazza (all others are called *campi*), but in comparison any other contender would have died of shame anyway. Gloriously open to sky and sea, **Piazza San Marco** – to locals, just 'the Piazza' – embodies the whole compass of Venetian history and adventure. Its airy arcades reach out to the 900-year-old basilica and turn a corner past the soaring brick campanile to the piazzetta and landing stage of St Mark's basin (*Il Bacino*), historic gateway to the Adriatic and distant ports beyond. For centuries, the odysseys of victorious commanders and commercial ventures of local merchants began and ended here.

This is where the 1,000-year-old Repubblica Serena fell to Napoleon in 1797. While he was busy removing the four ancient bronze horses from the basilica's facade (since returned) along with other art treasures to ship back to Paris, he was said to remark that the Piazza San Marco was 'the world's most beautiful salon'. He closed off the piazza's west end with the Ala Napoleonica (Napoleonic Wing), through which you now enter the **Museo Correr** (http://correr.visitmuve.it), devoted to Venetian history and paintings.

The north and south arms of the square, the 16th-century **Procuratie Vecchie** and the 17th-century **Procuratie Nuove**, were the residences of the republic's most senior officials. They are now lined with Murano glass and souvenir shops, exclusive jewellery and lace shops and, most important for weary or hungry travellers, elegant 18th-century caffès. During the Imperial Austrian rule, the enemy frequented **Quadri** on the north side, while Italian patriots met only at **Florian**, opposite. To catch the basilica and square bathed in moonlight is a magical experience.

The glittering facade of the **Basilica di San Marco** (www.basilica sanmarco.it; Mon–Sat 9.30am–5pm, Sun 2–4pm, free on Sun)

The bronze horses in Museo Marciano

forms an exotic backdrop, illuminating Venice's unique role at the crossroads of Eastern and Western culture. What began in AD830 as the Doges' chapel for the remains of the evangelist Mark, the republic's patron saint, was rebuilt in the 11th century as a grandiose Byzantine-Oriental basilica influenced by the Hagia Sofia in Constantinople. Greek mosaicists were brought in to decorate the arches and domes. Five Romanesque portals correspond to the five Islamic-style domes covering the church's Greek-cross ground plan. With its five mosque-like domes, it is the most sumptuously exotic and Orientally inspired church ever built in the Roman Catholic world.

The first portal on the left is the only one decorated with an original 13th-century mosaic, depicting the *Transfer of St Mark's Body*, smuggled out of Alexandria in Egypt. Mosaics also show the basilica with the famous bronze horses brought from Constantinople after the Crusade of 1204 (the ones over the main entrance are copies; since their restoration, the originals have been kept in the Museo Marciano – see page 120).

The Church of Gold

There is a soft glow in the gilded interior from the **mosaics**, illuminated by high stained-glass windows and reflected in the patina of the inlaid-marble flooring. Entire books have been written about the original mosaics on the five domes and the great barrel vaults separating them, dating from the 11th–15th centuries. Among the best are the 12th-century Pentecost dome in the nave and the central dome's 13th-century *Ascension*. Others have been heavily restored or replaced, not with true mosaics, but with reproductions in coloured stone of drawings by such artists as Bellini, Mantegna and Tintoretto. The whole is worthy of its nickname, 'church of gold'.

The imposing **high altar** stands over St Mark's tomb. Behind it is the basilica's greatest treasure, the **Pala d'Oro** (Golden

Altarpiece; Mon–Sat 9.45am–4pm, Sunday 2–4pm), dating back 1,000 years and bejewelled in the 14th century. Guides will tell you that its 255 enamelled panels were encrusted by master Venetian and Byzantine artisans with close to 2,000 precious stones, including pearls, garnets, sapphires, emeralds and rubies. It requires an entrance charge, as does the **Tesoro** (Treasury), a collection of the Crusaders' plunder. To the left of the high altar is a small chapel of the 10th-century *Madonna di Nicopeia*, a bejewelled icon from Constantinople; it is said to have healing powers and is a runner-up as Venice's protective patron, after St Mark.

Steep stairs to the right of the main entrance lead to the small **Museo Marciano (**daily 10am–5pm), where you can see the original four tethered **bronze horses**, dating from the 2nd or 3rd century AD and a privileged close-up of the basilica's mosaic ceilings from the open galleries. From the outdoor **Loggia dei Cavalli**, you get an excellent view over the Piazza San Marco.

On the north side of the piazza is the restored **Torre dell'Orologio** (Clock Tower; tel: 8480-82000; two tours in English daily, by appointment, tickets online at www.vivaticket.it). Its clock mechanism, all gilt and polychrome enamel, keeps perfect time, activating statues of two green bronze Moors that hammer out the hour. For centuries, the clock tower has been every Venetian's favourite rendezvous point, an arched ground-level entranceway leading to the Merceria, a zigzagging boutique-lined street that cuts through this ancient quarter north to the Rialto Bridge.

The piazza's **Campanile** (Bell Tower; daily Nov–Mar 9.30am–3.45pm, Apr–mid-Jun 9am–7pm, mid-Jun–Aug 8.30am–9.30pm, Sept until 7.45pm, Oct 9.30am–5.30pm), at 99m (324ft), is the highest structure in the city, with its belfry, lighthouse, weather vane and gun turret. Emperor Frederick III rode his horse up its spiral ramp (tourists can opt for the lift). Criminals were suspended from it in wooden cages. In 1902, the campanile cracked and collapsed unexpectedly. Ten years later, on its 1,000th anniversary, it was rebuilt using much of the original brick and rescuing one of its five historic bells that is still used today: *'com'era, dov'era'* ('as it was, where it was'). Its collapse crushed Jacopo Sansovino's beautiful 16th-century Loggetta, equally lovingly restored as the entrance to the campanile's lift.

A gondolier

The two tall **columns** facing out over St Mark's Basin were brought from Constantinople in the 12th century. They are topped by statues of St Mark's winged lion and the city's first patron saint, Theodore (replaced by St Mark), with his dragon.

The Doge's Palace

On the waterfront sits the **Doge's Palace** (Palazzo Ducale; www. palazzoducale.visitmuve.it; daily Apr–Oct 8.30am–7pm, Nov–Mar 8.30am–5.30pm, last entry one hour before closing), for 900 years the focus of Venice's power and pomp, evoked in the imposing elegance of its delicate pink marble and white limestone facades with their airy arcades and loggias. Erected over an older Byzantine-style castle, the present 14th–15th-century Flamboyant Gothic building fronts the *piazzetta* and the basin. The palace is one of the city's top attractions so expect long queues. If visiting other museums consider purchasing a Museums of San Marco's Square Pass or a Museum Pass (for 12 museums) both of which can be used to avoid the queues (see Doge's Palace website).

The principal entrance to the Palazzo was the **Porta della Carta** (Gate of the Paper), where the doge posted his decrees and scribes gathered). The Gothic sculpture shows the doge kneeling before St Mark's lion. The current entrance is under the portico on the lagoon side.

In the inner courtyard, the **Scala dei Giganti** staircase is so named for Sansovino's giant statues of Neptune and Mars. Visitors take the golden **Scala d'Oro** past the doge's opulent private apartments to the spectacularly decorated council chambers on the third floor. Here, as in most of the city's palaces and churches, the walls are decorated with painted panels and canvases by Venetian masters rather than frescoes, which are too easily damaged by the Venetian climate. Look out for Veronese's *Rape of Europa* and Tintoretto's *Bacchus and Ariadne* and *Vulcan's Forge* in the **Anticollegio**: a masterly allegorical series by Veronese glorifying Venice in the **Sala del Collegio**, where foreign ambassadors were received; and weapons and suits of armour in the **Armoury** (Sala d'Armi).

A highlight of the palace tour, back down on the second floor, is the huge **Sala del Maggior Consiglio** (Great Council Hall), where

⊙ IT'S A DOGE'S LIFE

The doges saw their authority wax and wane from absolute monarch to powerless figurehead. Subject to the changing powers of the republic's oligarchic council, many were murdered, executed for treason, or ritually blinded – the traditional punishment for a disgraced ruler. Though elected by the council, many created virtual dynasties. When the revered Giustiniani family was reduced by battle and plague in the 12th century to one last monk, he was hauled out of his monastery on the Lido and persuaded to sire nine boys and three girls to continue the line, before being allowed to return to his vows of chastity.

ordinary citizens presented their complaints in person in the democratic days before the oligarchy reserved it for their secret deliberations. The last doge presented his abdication to Napoleon here. Of the 76 doges portrayed, one is blacked out, Marino Faliero, beheaded for treason in 1355. Tintoretto's *Paradise* adorns the entrance wall above the doge's throne. Said to be the world's largest oil painting, 22 x 7m (72 x 23ft), it was

The magnificent Scala d'Oro inside the Doge's Palace

done, with the help of his son Domenico, when the artist was 70. Look for the brilliant colours of Veronese's oval ceiling painting of *Venice Crowned by Victory*.

The Bridge of Sighs and the Prisons

For those hoping to go from the sublime to the sinister, the palace **prisons**, neat and tidy today along their narrow corridor, become all too romantic with the 17th-century Baroque **Bridge of Sighs** (Ponte dei Sospiri). The celebrated passage linked the Ducal palace with the prisons, and those on their way to the torture chambers, were supposedly moved to sigh at their last sight of *'Le Serenissima'* (The Serene City). Original graffiti can be seen in the prisons, one of which held Casanova for 15 months in 1755, before he escaped.

The guided tours to the lesser-known areas of the palace are highly recommended – *Itinerari Segreti* (Secret Itineraries) – in English (pre-book on tel: 041 4273 0892 or at www.vivaticket.it; daily 9.55am, 10.45am and 11.35am).

The waterfront **Riva degli Schiavoni** (Quay of the Slavs) begins at the Ducal Palace and is named after the Dalmatian merchants who unloaded their goods here. The ghosts of Dickens, Wagner and Proust wander around the lobby of the venerable **Danieli**, a former doge's residence and one of Italy's most romantic hotels. The lobby bar offers a moment of rest for the weary.

Probably nowhere is there so much spectacular painting on view in such a tiny space as in the **Scuola di San Giorgio degli Schiavoni** (Mon 2.45–6pm, Tue–Sat 9.15am–1pm, 2.45–6pm, Sun 9.15am–1pm). This building was the confraternity guildhall of the wealthy *schiavoni* merchants who commissioned Vittore Carpaccio to decorate their hall. His nine pictures, completed between 1502 and 1508, cover the walls of the ground-floor chapel. Note the ornate wooden ceiling. It is one of a number of *scuole* (literally, 'schools' or confraternities) unique to the days of the Venetian Republic.

Just four minutes by vaporetto from the *piazzetta*, on its own little

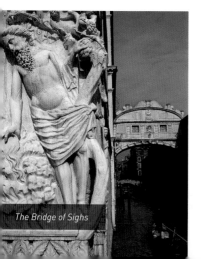

The Bridge of Sighs

island, is the church of **San Giorgio Maggiore** (Apr–Oct 9am–7pm, Nov–Mar 8.30am–6pm, visits suspended during mass on Sun). Its campanile offers the best views of the city and lagoon. The 16th-century church is a rare ecclesiastical building by Andrea Palladio, the master Renaissance architect from nearby Vicenza whose classic designs have dominated aristocratic residential architecture throughout North America and Europe. His customary Corinthian-columned elegance prevails here, extended from the facade to an airy interior. Two superb paintings by an elderly Tintoretto flank the main altar, *Gathering of the Manna* and an otherworldly *Last Supper*, in which Jesus administers communion while servants bustle to clear up the dishes. The resident monks still sing Mass in Gregorian chant every Sunday. A lift ascends to the top of the bell tower for superb panoramic views.

Around the Accademia

With justifiable pride, the rambling **Galleria dell'Accademia** (Accademia Gallery; tel: 041-522 2247; www.gallerieaccademia.it; Mon 8.15am–1pm, Tue–Sun 8.15am–8.15pm, last admission 45 minutes before closing) is devoted almost exclusively to the artistic legacy of the master artists of Venice and the Veneto. Works range from the 14th century of the republic's emerging glory to the 18th century of its gentle decadence. One of Italy's most important art museums, showcasing the world's finest collection of Venetian art, it offers the chance to see just how little Venice has changed over the centuries. Here are a few of its most representative highlights:

Room 1: Dedicated to Byzantine and Gothic artworks including the 14th-century *Coronation of the Madonna* of Paolo Veneziano, first of the city's great masters, and glowing with characteristic Venetian colour and texture.

Room 2: Giovanni Bellini, youngest and most gifted member of the painter family, brings gentle humanity to his *Enthroned Madonna with Job and St Sebastian* (1485).

Room 4: Andrea Mantegna (a brother-in-law of the Bellini family) shows why *St George*, the dragon-killer, became the most appropriate patron saint for England.

Room 5: Giorgione's *Tempest* (1505) is one of the museum's most cherished, most mysterious treasures – a girl calmly nursing her child in a landscape prickling with the electricity of the approaching storm. This room contains the most celebrated works.

Tintoretto's Miracle of St Mark, in the Accademia

Room 10: this is the most important of Renaissance rooms. Titian's *Pietà*, a vibrant last work completed by pupil Palma il Giovane, was originally intended for his tomb in the Frari church (see page 129). Veronese's *Feast in the House of Levi* was meant to be the *Last Supper*, until the Holy Inquisition complained about its 'buffoons, drunkards, dwarfs, Germans and similar vulgarities'. Tintoretto gives full play to his dark sense of drama in the *Miracle of St Mark*.

Room 17: Canaletto's immensely popular 18th-century *vedute* (views) of Venice were aristocratic precursors of modern postcards. In such fine works as *Island of San Giorgio Maggiore*, Francesco Guardi managed to achieve both poetry and melancholy.

Room 20: Gentile Bellini breathes little life into his *Procession on San Marco* (1496), but it remains one of the museum's most fascinating 'photographs' of Renaissance Venice.

Room 21: Vittore Carpaccio depicts in nine canvases the bizarre *Story of St Ursula*, a British princess, said to have led 11,000 virgins on a pilgrimage to Rome, all of whom were raped and slaughtered by the Huns on their way back.

Peggy Guggenheim Collection

To the east of the Accademia along the Grand Canal, a breath of the 20th century awaits at the **Peggy Guggenheim Collection** of modern art in the **Palazzo Venier dei Leoni** (www.guggenheim-venice. it; Wed–Mon 10am–6pm). Home of the American heiress until her death in 1979, this unfinished 18th-century palace provides a delightful canal-side setting for one of the world's most comprehensive collections of modern art. Picasso, Duchamp, Magritte, Kandinsky, Klee, Chagall, Dalí, Bacon and Sutherland are all represented here, but it is known above all for its works by Jackson Pollock, Mark Rothko and Robert Motherwell. In the garden are sculptures by Giacometti, Henry Moore and the collector's husband, Max Ernst. Guggenheim and her dogs are buried here.

Where the Grand Canal empties into the lagoon stands the imposing church of **Santa Maria della Salute** (http://basilica salutevenezia.it; Mon–Sat 9.30am–5.30pm, Sun 9.30am–noon and 3–5.30pm). Called *La Salute* by the Venetians, Santa Maria is the masterpiece of Baldassare Longhena, built to mark the city's deliverance from a plague in 1630. For a Baroque edifice, the interior is rather sober, even chaste. One of Tintoretto's best, the *Marriage at Cana*, is opposite the entrance, while three vivid Titian canvases decorate the chancel: *Cain and Abel*, *Abraham Sacrificing Isaac* and *David and Goliath*, their drama heightened by the perspective *di sotto in su* (looking up from below).

To the west of the Accademia, the 18th-century **Ca' Rezzonico** (www.carezzonico.visitmuve.it; Wed–Mon 10am–5pm), is now a museum of 18th-century life, **Museo del Settecento Veneziano**, dedicated to those swan-song years of Venice's Most Serene Republic. When the last of the wealthy Rezzonico family disappeared, Elizabeth Barrett and Robert Browning bought the *palazzo* and the poet died in here in 1889. The extravagant ballroom and soaring allegorical frescoes such as Giambattista Tiepolo's *Merit between Virtue and Nobility* in the 'Throne Room' and others, more wistful, by Guardi, all catch the tone of a declining Venice and the frivolous lives of the rich. Opposite the Ca' Rezzonico is **Palazzo Grassi** (www.palazzograssi.it; Wed–Mon 10am–7pm, last entry 6pm), bought by the French businessman François Pinault to show-case his stunning collection of modern art.

At the tip of the peninsula the Punta della Dogana (same hours and website as Palazzo Grassi) exhibits further works from Pinault's collection. The superbly sited former Customs House was converted in 2009 by Japanese architect Tadao Ando into a contemporary art gallery (Wed–Mon 10am–7pm, last entry 6pm).

The Scuole of Venice

Venice was home to a number of *scuole* – not 'schools' at all but secular confraternities similar to today's Rotarians or Lions. North of Ca' Rezzonico, the **Scuola Grande di San Rocco** (www.scuola grandesanrocco.org; daily 9.30am–5.30pm) is Venice's richest

Santa Maria della Salute

confraternity, in a fine 16th-century chapter house next to its own church. Local master Tintoretto (1518–94) won a competition to create some 50 paintings (the largest collection of his work) over 23 years. In the Sala Grande is the high drama of *Moses Striking Water from the Rock* and a fascinating *Temptation of Christ*, with Satan portrayed as a beautiful youth. Tiepolo and Titian are interlopers here, the latter with a solitary but remarkable easel painting of the *Annunciation*. Tintoretto's chiaroscuro masterpiece is the grandiose *Crucifixion* in the Sala dell'Albergo.

Nearby is the brick and white-marble Gothic Franciscan church, the **Frari** (www.basilicadeifrari.it; Mon–Sat 9am–6pm, Sun 1–6pm), the largest and greatest of all of the Venetian Gothic churches, celebrated for the high altar adorned with Titian's jubilant *Assumption of the Virgin*. The master's only painting on such a massive scale is a triumph of primary reds, blues and yellows. His other work here is the *Madonna di Ca' Pesaro* (left nave). Titian's monumental tomb is in the right aisle. Venetian composer Monteverdi's tomb is in a chapel left of the altar. Donatello sculpted a fine polychrome wood *St John the Baptist* for his compatriots' **Florentine Chapel**, to the right of the altar.

Back on the Grand Canal: Longhena's Baroque **Ca' Pesaro** is the town's Modern Art Museum (www.capesaro.visitmuve.it; Tue–Sun 10am–6pm, winter until 5pm), devoted principally to a small collection of purchases from the Venice Biennale exhibitions. Italian artists – Futurists Giovanni Fattori and Telemaco Signorini and the Ferrara trio of Filippo de Pisis, Carlo Carrà and Giorgio de Chirico – are well represented; less so other Europeans, although there are works by Matisse, Klee, Chagall, Kandinsky and Ernst. The top floor is home to the Oriental Museum (same hours as Modern Art Museum).

Around the Rialto

The Rialto is the ancient commercial heart of the city, named after the 9th-century settlement on *Rivo Alto*, the high bank. Here, cargo from

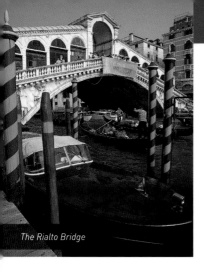
The Rialto Bridge

faraway ports was unloaded from the republic's galleons. The merchants headed for the banks, the sailors to the brothels. Today, the action is in the food markets and boutiques on the Grand Canal's west bank. The **Pescheria** (fish market) bustles early in the morning (Tue–Sat), while the **Erberia** (fruit and vegetables) is open until late afternoon. Hidden among it is the 11th-century church of **San Giacomo di Rialto** – San Giacometto to local people.

The 16th-century **Rialto Bridge**, one of four that cross the Grand Canal, is an architectural icon designed by Antonio da Ponte for a competition entered by Michelangelo, Palladio and Sansovino. It is still one of the liveliest spots in town.

Northeast of the bridge, past the Fondaco dei Tedeschi post office, seek out the little 15th-century church of **Santa Maria dei Miracoli** (Mon–Sat 10.30am–4pm). Its refined facade of inlaid coloured marble and intricately carved friezes has won it the name of 'golden jewel box' *(scrigno d'oro)*. The church is a favourite with Venetian brides.

Santi Giovanni e Paolo

It is worth carefully mapping out your visit to the **Campo Santi Giovanni e Paolo**. Follow the Calle Larga Giacinto Gallina to the humpbacked Ponte del Cavallo bridge for the all-important first view of the piazza's magnificent **equestrian statue** of the *condottiere* Bartolomeo Colleoni, by Andrea Verrocchio. Colleoni left his fortune to Venice on the understanding that his monument would be on Piazza San Marco. Once dead, he had to settle for this spot in front of the Scuola of San Marco, a clever Venetian solution. The piazza's main attraction is the 13th-century Gothic church of **Santi Giovanni e Paolo** (www.basilicasantigiovanniepaolo.it; Mon–Sat 9am–6pm, Sun noon–6pm), known to Venetians as San Zanipolo. Built by Dominicans, it was the doges' funeral church and there are many masterpieces among some 25 vast tombs.

Returning to the Grand Canal, you will find the glorious *palazzo* **Ca' d'Oro** (www.cadoro.org; Mon 8.15am–2pm, Tue–Sun 8.15am–7.15pm). Completed in 1440, its Gothic style bewitches you into imagining the long-gone gilt of its facade, from which it earned its name 'Palace of Gold'. Treasures of Ca' d'Oro's **Galleria Franchetti** of Renaissance art include Titian's *Venus at the Mirror* and Mantegna's *St Sebastian*.

Jewish Ghetto

The old **Jewish Ghetto** (northeast of the railway station) is particularly peaceful and reveals a fascinating page of Venetian history. It was the former site of an abandoned iron foundry – *ghetto* in old Venetian dialect – that lent its name to future enclaves throughout Europe. In 1516, some 900 Jews (rising to a peak of nearly 5,000 by the mid-17th century) were confined to what was then a remote and isolated island. They built the six- and eight-storey tenements you see today, twice as high as those permitted elsewhere, with some floors no more than 2m (6ft) high. Tours to six still-active 16th-century synagogues are offered by the **Museo Ebraico** (www.museoebraico.it; Sun–Fri 10am–7pm, winter until 5.30pm) in the Campo del Ghetto Nuovo.

The Islands

On the island of the **Giudecca**, you will find another Palladio-designed church, the **Redentore** (Mon 10.30am–4pm, Tue–Sat 10.30am–4.30pm). The grace of its form is best viewed from across

Colourful houses on the island of Burano

the canal, because the dome disappears at closer quarters behind its elongated nave. The Giudecca is a quiet residential refuge popular with artists.

Out in the lagoon, Venetians have been making glass on the island of **Murano** since 1292, when the hazardous furnaces were moved away from the city centre. Today, its factories and shops are tourist traps, but the **Museo del Vetro** (Glass Museum; http://museo vetro.visitmuve.it; daily 10am–5pm, Apr–Nov until 6pm) is worth a look. The 12th-century Venetian-Byzantine church of **Santa Maria e San Donato** (www.sandonatomurano.it; Mon–Sat 9am–6pm, Sun 12.30–6pm) is a quiet spot.

The island of **Burano** is a simple fishing village and a tranquil haven, though the women making lace on the doorsteps of their colourful houses and artists on the quay are all but history. Much of the lace that is hawked is machine-made in China. The **Scuola Museo del Merletto** (Piazza Galuppi 187; http://museomerletto.visit muve.it; Tue–Sun 10am–6pm, winter until 5pm) is devoted to the art of lacemaking.

The overgrown island of **Torcello**, beyond Burano, is one of the lagoon's oldest inhabited spots, prosperous until emptied by a malaria epidemic. Its cathedral, **Santa Maria dell' Assunta** (daily 10.30am–6pm, winter until 5pm), founded in the 7th century and rebuilt in 1008, is a splendid Venetian-Byzantine church.

With sandy beaches and smart hotels, the **Lido** is as restful as any fashionable seaside resort though cars come as something of a shock after Venice. A few public beaches are the principle draw in summer but avoid Sundays when all the Venetians come to cool off in the waters of the Adriatic. Film fans and celebrities flock here during the Venice Film Festival in late August/early September.

THE VENETO: THE VENETIAN MAINLAND

The Venetian mainland reflects some of the *Serenissima's* artistic and architectural glories. Most of the cities remained under its domination until the 15th century, yet retained much of their individuality. An *autostrada* and easy train service link Venice to Padua, Vicenza and Verona for those in a hurry, but others should take the charming back roads; this is one of Italy's principal wine growing regions.

The Brenta Canal

When Venetian aristocrats gave up the high seas for a more leisurely life on the land, they built Palladian Renaissance villas and Baroque country houses on the banks of the Brenta Canal between Venice and Padua.

Follow the canal along the pretty country road (route SS11) to Padua (Padova). First stop, off a side road to Fusina at Mira (about 20km/12 miles from Venice), is Palladio's **La Malcontenta** (1571), also known as **Villa Foscari** (tel: 041-547 0012; www.la malcontenta.com; Apr–Oct Tue and Sat 9am–noon; other times by appointment), to which a flighty Venetian countess was once sent to pine malcontentedly. The villa, with a classical portico to catch

Brenta by boat

A romantic way to visit villas on the Brenta Canal is by burchiello, a modern version of the rowing barge that took the gentry, Casanova and Lord Byron to their trysts and parties in the country. The full-day tour includes a return bus trip from Padua. Details on half and full-day cruises from March to October are available from the tourist office or at www.ilburchiello.it.

the summer breezes, was the Renaissance architect's 'visiting card' for scores of commissions, copied worldwide, especially on the cotton plantations of America's Deep South. At nearby Oriago, the Palladian style can be seen in **Villa Gradenigo** and at Mira, in the 18th-century **Villa Widmann**. The influence is clear even in the most spectacular of the Brenta villas, at **Stra ⑯**, with the opulent **Villa Pisani** (www.villapisani.beni culturali.it; Apr–Sept Tue– Sun 9am–7pm, Oct–Mar until 4pm). Built for the Pisani doges in 1756, with 200 rooms, Tiepolo frescoes in the ballroom and a vast park with pond, labyrinth and stables, it was purchased by Napoleon in 1807 and subsequently hosted Tsars, Habsburg emperors and, for their first meeting in 1934, Hitler and Mussolini.

Padua (Padova)

Padua (Padova) ⑰, this proud university town – Galileo taught physics here from 1592 to 1610 – was a major centre of the Risorgimento reunification movement. Something of the old spirit remains at the handsome neoclassical **Caffè Pedrocchi**, the activists' meeting place on a little square off bustling Piazza Cavour.

North along the Corso Garibaldi is Padua's undisputed draw, the 14th-century **Scrovegni Chapel** (tel: 049-201 0020; www.cappella degliscrovegni.it; daily 9am–7pm). To see the frescoes here you must book at least three days in advance, or 24 hours before with a credit card. The chapel is also known, due to its site among ruins of a Roman amphitheatre, as the Arena Chapel. As a penance for his father's usury, the patrician Enrico Scrovegni built the simple little hall in 1303 specifically for the great Giotto frescoes. Beautifully preserved, these are considered some of the most important artworks of the early Renaissance. In 38 pictures arranged in three rows under a starry heavenly blue vault, Giotto tells the story of Mary and Jesus, portrayed by the *Kiss of Judas*, the *Crucifixion* and the *Lamentation*. A monumental *Last Judgement* covers the entrance wall.

The entrance to Piazza del Santo, south of the city centre, is guarded by Donatello's **statue of Gattamelata**, the 15th-century Venetian condottiere Erasmo da Narni. Behind him is Padua's site of pilgrimage, the 13th- and 14th-century **Basilica di Sant'Antonio** (daily 6.20am–6.45pm), built in honour of the city's protector, the Franciscan monk known simply as Il Santo, who died in Padua in 1231. The tomb of the patron saint of lost items is covered with photos, flowers and notes left by pilgrims.

Vicenza

Vicenza  is the hometown of Andrea Palladio (1508–80), the most important architect of the High Renaissance. At its centre, **Piazza dei Signori** is graced by Palladio's first public work, the **Basilica Palladiana** (1549), a gathering place for the law courts and assembly hall of the Gothic Palazzo della Ragione that it encases with a colonnade and

Giotto frescoes, Scrovegni

Palladio's opinion

'Basilica Palladiana ranks among the most noble and most beautiful edifices since ancient times, not only for its grandeur and ornaments, but also its materials.'
– Palladio's modest opinion of his own work.

loggia. Inside is a museum of Palladio's designs.

The main commercial street is **Corso Andrea Palladio**, lined with elegant mansions by the master and his disciples (converted to banks, shops and caffès); his simple home was No. 163. The 15th-century **Palazzo da Schio** (No. 147) is also known as Ca'd'Oro, after the Venetian Gothic palace. Palladio's greatest opus is where the Corso widens into the Piazza Matteotti, giving him freedom for the airy **Palazzo Chiericati**. Its Pinacoteca (Art Gallery; www.museicivicivicenza.it; Tue–Sun 9am–5pm, until 6pm in summer) has works by Tintoretto, Veronese and Tiepolo.

Across the piazza in a little garden, the audacious **Teatro Olimpico** (www.teatrolimpicovicenza.it; Tue–Sun 9am–5pm, summer 10am–6pm) is Palladio's last work, completed by his protégé Vincenzo Scamozzi in 1584. Facing an amphitheatre auditorium are Classical Roman statuary and columns that look far deeper than their 4m (14ft), a permanent stage trompe l'oeil 'curtain' depicting the ancient streets of Thebes. It was the first covered theatre in Europe and is still used for concerts and other events.

A half hour walk from town or short bus ride (No 8) will bring you to Palladio's most celebrated building, the hilltop **Villa Rotonda**, also known as **Villa Capra** (www.villalarotonda.it; gardens mid-Mar–early Nov Tue–Sun 10am–noon, 3–6pm (2.30–5pm in winter); villa Wed and Sat only 10am–noon, 3–6pm). Designed as a belvedere for Cardinal Capra in 1567, it is an exquisite piece of applied geometry, a domed rotunda set in a square surrounded on all four sides by simple Ionic-columned porticoes. From here it is a 10-minute walk to the Palladian-inspired **Villa Valmarana**

ai Nani (www.villavalmarana.com; Mar–Oct Tue, Thu and Sun 10am–12.30, 3–6pm, Sat–Sun 10am–4pm, Nov–Mar Sat–Sun 10am–12.30 and 2–4pm, other days upon request), notable for its Tiepolo frescoes.

Verona

Shakespeare's 'Fair Verona' of Romeo and Juliet fame was first a favourite of ancient Roman emperors and the 'barbarian' rulers who followed. **Verona** ⓳ likes to be known as *la Degna*, the Dignified, but it also has a lively, well-to-do ambience, stimulated by the presence of the River Adige that flows down from the Dolomites.

The hub of city life is the Piazza Bra, with the town hall on its south side and the **Roman Arena** (www.arena.it; Tue–Sun 8.30am–7.30pm, Mon 1.30–7.30pm; July–Aug usually closes at 4pm), dating from AD 100, to the north. Only four of its outer arches survived an 1183 earthquake undamaged, but the inner arcade of 74 arches is intact. The amphitheatre's 22,000 seats sell out months in advance for open-air productions of the best-known operas, such as *Aida*.

Along the north side of the Piazza Bra, the **Liston**, a people-watcher's delight lined with smart caffès and fine restaurants, is the street for the Veronese bourgeoisie's popular evening stroll (*passeggiata*). It leads to the boutiques, galleries and antiques shops of the equally fashionable Via Mazzini. Turn right at the end down Via

Statue of Juliet

Cappello for the 13th-century *palazzo* that the local tourist authorities will have you believe was **Juliet's House** (Casa di Giulietta Cappelletti; Tue–Sun 8.30am–7.30pm, Mon 1.30–7.30pm), complete with balcony. The **Piazza delle Erbe** along the ancient elongated Roman forum makes the prettiest of marketplaces and the adjoining, elegant **Piazza dei Signori** (also known as Piazza Dante) is ringed by crenellated *palazzi* and the historical Antico Caffé Dante. The 14th-century **Arche Scaligeri** (Scaligeri Tombs) just beyond are some of the most elaborate Gothic funerary monuments in Italy.

West of Piazza Bra, the brick 14th-century **Castelvecchio** (Tue–Sun 8.30am–7.30pm, Mon 1.30–7.30pm) fortress on the Adige houses an art museum. Its collections are principally of the Venetian school, notably Mantegna's *Holy Family*, a Giovanni Bellini *Madonna* and Lorenzo Lotto's *Portrait of a Man*.

The handsome 9th–12th-century basilica of **San Zeno Maggiore** (www.basilicasanzeno.it; Sun 12.30–6pm, until 5pm in winter,

The dramatic Dolomites

Mon–Sat 8.30am–6pm summer, winter 10am–1pm and 1.30–5pm), dedicated to the city's patron saint, is Verona's most visited church. The simple interior is illuminated by the magnificent Mantegna triptych (1459) on the high altar.

THE DOLOMITES

The landscape of Italy's eastern Alps is a mixture of rich green Alpine meadows with jagged white limestone and rose-coloured granite peaks. Summer hiking in the largely German-speaking region of Alto Adige (Austrian South Tyrol till 1918) is a delight. Well-marked paths lead to farmhouses and rustic mountain restaurants where you can try the local cured ham *(Speck)* or spinach dumplings *(Spinatknödl)* as a change from pasta.

BOLZANO (BOZEN)

South Tyrol's historic capital, **Bolzano** ⓴, makes a good base for walking. It has a 14th-century Gothic **church** with a characteristically Austrian polychrome tiled roof. The **Museo Archeologico** (www.iceman.it; Tue–Sun 10am–6pm, daily July–Aug and Dec) has a fascinating collection including the mummified body of Ötzi, found by chance in the Ötzaler Alps in 1991 and estimated to be over 5,000 years old. Head northeast of town to the **Renon** (Ritten) plateau for views of the Dolomite peaks, reached by cableway and funicular.

Cortina d'Ampezzo

The most upmarket of Italian winter sports resorts, chic **Cortina d'Ampezzo** ㉑ has elegant hotels, smart boutiques and a buzzing nightlife. In a sunny, sheltered basin high in the Boite valley of the eastern Dolomites, Cortina provides excellent skiing facilities and is also a favourite with summer hikers, many of whom come for guided treks in stunning scenery. Known as the Queen of the Dolomites, it is one of Europe's most beautiful alpine resorts.

A series of three cable-cars run up to **Tofana** at 3,243m (10,640ft), from where there is a variety of walking (and skiing) trails linked by more than 50 mountain refuges/huts.

EMILIA-ROMAGNA

These two regions were united at the time of the 19th-century Risorgimento, with Emilia following the Apennines from Bologna to Piacenza, while Romagna covers the eastern area of Ravenna and the popular Adriatic resorts around Rimini down to Cattolica.

Rimini

The Adriatic coast, of which **Rimini ㉒** is the chief resort, has wide sandy beaches, at some points stretching 300m (1,000ft) from the water's edge back to the dunes. Its lively hotels, beach clubs and myriad discos make Rimini a favourite playground for sun-seekers (Germans, Scandinavians and Eastern Europeans arrive in droves) while in off-season months it is a sleepy place.

Inland, on the other side of the railway, is the old city that was Ariminium to the Romans. The 27 BC **triumphal arch** (Arco d'Augusto), ornamented with medieval battlements, stands at the junction of the imperial highways from ancient Rome: Via Flaminia and Via Emilia (which gave the region its name). The **Ponte di Tiberio** bridge built over the Marecchia river in AD 14–21 is still in use.

The unfinished 15th-century **Tempio Malatestiano** (daily 9am–noon and 3.30–6.30pm) is a Renaissance design of Leon Battista Alberti, incorporating elements of the Arco d'Augusto in the facade. More pagan temple than

Fellini's Rimini

Film director Federico Fellini, born in Rimini in 1920, immortalised the area in the 1970s with his Oscar-winning *Amarcord*. The Grand, the famous 'old lady' of Adriatic hotels, is beautifully located in the park named after Fellini.

church, it served as a mausoleum for the cultivated but cruel tyrant, Sigismondo Malatesta and his wife, Isotta degli Atti.

South of Rimini are the resorts of **Riccione** and the quieter **Cattolica**. To the north is **Cesenatico**, which is notable for its colourful fishing port.

On the beach at Rimini

Ravenna

The beautifully preserved mosaic decorations of Ravenna's churches, some 1,500 years old, come as an exciting revelation. They stand at the summit of the art as originally practised by the Byzantines and are the finest in Europe.

Ravenna ㉓, now some 10km (6 miles) from the sea, was once a flourishing port and the capital of the Western Roman Empire after the fall of Rome. Honorius, last emperor of Rome, made it his capital in 404, but it was the Emperor Justinian in 540 who left his mark of Byzantine culture on the town.

You will see something of the town's Venetian-dominated era on the graceful **Piazza del Popolo**, bordered by the 17th-century Palazzo Comunale. Next to the church of San Francesco, in a building from 1780, is the **tomb of Dante**, who died here, in exile, in 1321, with a fellow poet's epitaph: 'Here I lie buried, Dante, exiled from my birthplace, son of Florence, that loveless mother.'

The oldest, most striking of the Byzantine monuments, located in the northern corner of the city centre, is the 5th-century **Mausoleum of Galla Placidia** (www.ravennamosaici.it; daily 9am–5pm, until 7pm in summer). Three sarcophagi stand in the cross-shaped chapel. The deep blue, gold and crimson mosaics on the vaults and arches depict *St Laurence*, *the Apostles* and the *Good Shepherd Feeding His Sheep* (over the entrance).

In the same grounds is the three-storey brick basilica of **San Vitale** (same opening times as Galla Placidia), consecrated in 547. The octagonal construction provides the interior with seven *exedrae*, or recesses, the eighth being the choir and apse. The Old Testament scenes, such as *Abraham Sacrificing Isaac*, are more lively than the rigidly formal Emperor Justinian and Empress Theodora, with their court retinue and Christ between two angels, St Vitalis and, far right, Bishop Ecclesius holding a model of the church. These are the finest series of Byzantine mosaics outside Istanbul. The cloisters house a National Museum of Roman, early Christian and Byzantine Sculpture.

East of the city centre, the early 6th-century church of **Sant' Apollinare Nuovo** (same opening times as the Mausoleum of Galla

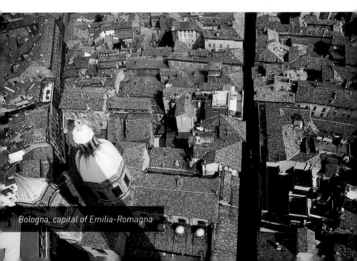

Bologna, capital of Emilia-Romagna

Placidia, see page 141) was built by the Christian Ostrogoth king, Theodoric. In the nave, the church's Byzantine mosaics show, on the left, Ravenna's fortified port of Classis, from which a procession of 22 virgins follows the three Magi with gifts for Jesus; on the right, from Theodoric's palace, 26 male martyrs march towards Christ.

Bologna

The capital of Emilia-Romagna, **Bologna** ㉔ is a thriving town with a certain patrician atmosphere to its beautifully preserved historic centre lined by 35km (22 miles) of loggias (arcade-covered pavements). It is famous as the home of Europe's oldest university, established in the 10th century on the foundation of a renowned law school dating back to the 5th century, at the end of the Roman Empire. The town's revered age-old place in Italian gastronomy compares with that of Lyon in France.

On the west flank of the **Piazza Maggiore**, the massive medieval **Palazzo Comunale** with a Renaissance porch is an expression of Bologna's civic power. The 14th-century basilica of **San Petronio** (daily 8.30am–6.30pm) ranks among the most imposing of Italy's Gothic churches. It has a fine **central portal** with reliefs of Old Testament scenes on its pilasters, sculpted by Siena-born master Jacopo della Quercia. Adam's pose in the **Creation** scene (top left) inspired the Michelangelo figure reaching out to God on the Sistine Chapel ceiling.

In the adjoining square, the 16th-century **Neptune Fountain** is one of the town's most popular symbols, for which Giambologna sculpted the immodest sea god surrounded by nymphs and cherubs.

A medieval atmosphere clings to the houses in the streets behind the Metropolitana Cathedral to the north. At the end of the Via Rizzoli, the two **leaning towers** are all that remain of a whole forest of more than 200 medieval status-symbols. The Torre degli Asinelli (daily Apr–Sept 9am–7pm, Oct–Mar until 5pm), 98m (320ft), is the taller, with 498 steps to its rooftop. Built in 1109, it leans more than 2m (7.5ft), less than its twin, Torre Giselda (currently closed to the public).

You will find the city's characteristic arcaded palazzi along the Via Zamboni leading past the university to the **Pinacoteca Nazionale** (Tue and Wed 9am–1.30pm, Thu–Sun 2–7pm). The gallery's fine collection is devoted largely to the Bologna school, most notably the Baroque paintings of Guido Reni and the Carracci family.

South of the city centre, the founder of the Dominican order is buried in the basilica of **San Domenico** (Mon–Fri 9.30am–noon, 3.30–6pm, Sat until 5pm, Sun 3.30–5pm), built in the 13th century with Baroque modifications. The monk died in Bologna in 1221, and his **tomb** was designed later by Nicola Pisano, with works by Nicolò dell'Arca and the 20-year-old Michelangelo (he did the saints Petronius and Proculus and the angel on the right).

Ferrara

A half-hour's drive from Bologna on the *autostrada* takes you to **Ferrara ㉕**, the stronghold of the high-living d'Este dukes – archetypally scheming, murderous, lovable Renaissance villains who ruled from 1200 to 1600. In their formidable **Castello Estense** (Jan–Feb and Oct–Dec Tue–Sun 9.30am–5.30pm, Mar–Sept daily 9.30am–5.30pm), a 14th-century moated fortress that is this lovely town's centrepiece, guides tell delightfully dubious tales of what went on in the dungeons.

You get a sense of the dukes' grandeur among the Renaissance palazzi of the **Corso Ercole I d'Este**, part of an ambitious 15th-century urban expansion, *Addizione Erculea*. The d'Estes' **Palazzo dei Diamanti** has 12,000 stones sculpted in the shape of a diamond on its walls and houses the **Pinacoteca Nazionale** (Tue–Wed 8.30am–2pm, Thu until 7pm, Fri–Sun 1.30–7pm), with notable works of the Ferrara masters Cosmè Tura, Ercole de' Roberti and Garofalo and prints by Andrec Mategne. It also hosts exhibitions.

The triple-gabled 12th-century **Cathedral** (Mon–Sat 7.30am–noon, 3.30–6pm, Sun until 7pm) still has its loggia of shops attached to the south wall. The cathedral museum exhibits two major works by

Frescoes in Parma Cathedral

Ferrara's 15th-century master Cosmè Tura, *St George* and the *Annunciation*, and sculptures by Jacopo della Quercia.

Parma

The home of two famous painters, Correggio and Parmigianino, and birthplace of the conductor Arturo Toscanini, **Parma** ㉖ has much more to offer than just great cheese and ham. The **Piazza del Duomo** forms a harmonious space for the graceful baptistery, begun in 1196, and the austere nobility of the 12th-century **Cathedral** (www.piazzaduomoparma.com; daily 10am–7pm), with its 13th-century campanile. Inside, on the ceiling of the central octagonal dome, are Correggio's greatest masterpieces, his **frescoes** of the *Assumption of the Virgin* (1530). Also acclaimed is Benedetto Antelami's *Deposition (Descent from the Cross)*. The 13th-century pink Verona marble **Baptistery** (Mar–Oct daily 10am–6.30pm, Nov–Feb until 4.30pm) has superbly sculpted doors by Antelami, who also carved most of the 12 statues of the months inside.

Behind the cathedral, the 16th-century Renaissance church of **San Giovanni Evangelista** (Mon–Sat 8.30–11.45am, 3–5.30pm, Sun 3–5.30pm) also has in its dome a fine Correggio fresco of the *Vision of St John on Patmos*. Look for the Parmigianino frescoes in the first, second and fourth chapels on the left aisle.

In the lovely Benedictine **Monasterio di San Paolo** (Via Melloni; Tue–Fri 8.30am–2pm, Sat 8.30am–6pm, Sun Apr–May 8.30am–2pm) is a private dining room (Camera di Correggio), which the unconventional abbess, Giovanna da Piacenza, commissioned Correggio to decorate in

1519 (his first work) with a feast for the senses, including mischievous *putti* and a view of Chastity as symbolised by the goddess Diana.

The Palazzo della Pilotta, on Piazzale della Pace, is home to the **Galleria Nazionale**, housing work by Correggio and Parmigianino, and to the Biblioteca Palatina, the Museo Archeologico and the Teatro Farnese, a Palladian theatre with a revolving stage (all Tue–Sat 8.30am–7pm, Sun 8.30am–2pm).

THE NORTHWEST

Lombardy, Piedmont and the Ligurian coast make up the country's most prosperous region. Industry and commerce have made the fortune of its three great cities – Milan, Turin and Genoa. If the last has drawn on the riches of the seas, Milan and Turin – in close contact with France and Germany just across the Alps – have had the added underpinning of flourishing agriculture in their Po Valley hinterland. The early lords of this constant economic expansion also called on the greatest artists from Italy and beyond, from Leonardo da Vinci to Jan Van Eyck. The region has won world recognition in the vanguard of the arts, of modern design in clothes and furniture, not forgetting the automobile and communications industries.

For relaxation, the Italian Riviera east and west of Genoa alternates a rugged coastline with the occasional fine sandy beach. Hugging the slopes of Mont Blanc (Monte Bianco), Courmayeur is one of Italy's oldest and most picturesque ski resorts. To the north and east of Milan are the romantic lakes of Como, Maggiore and Garda.

MILAN

Quite happy to leave the embroiled politics of national government to Rome, **Milano** ㉗ prides itself on being the country's economic, cultural and design capital. This is Italy at its most fashionable, self-assured and sophisticated. It is also home to Europe's largest and most sumptuous Gothic church (the Duomo), La Scala opera house

The grandiose facade of Milan's Duomo

and Leonardo da Vinci's *Last Supper*. The city underwent a €15 million infrastructure upgrade for the EXPO World Fair in 2015.

Nowhere does a cathedral more distinctly dominate a major city centre. Almost non-stop throughout the day, but especially in the evening during the *passeggiata* (evening stroll), the **Piazza del Duomo** is one of the liveliest squares in Europe. It is dominated by the **Duomo** (www.duomomilano.it; daily 8am–7pm). The most grandiose of Italy's flamboyant Gothic cathedrals, it was begun in 1386 by the ruling Visconti family and involved teams of Italian, French, Flemish and German architects and sculptors. For the best view of the its rich facade, completed in 1813, and a bristling silhouette of marble pinnacles and statues, stand in the courtyard of the **Palazzo Reale** south of the cathedral. The *palazzo* houses the Cathedral Museum, which displays fine examples of sculpture from the facade. Inside the cathedral, the vast interior is divided by 52 soaring columns and **stained-glass windows**, from the 15th century to the present day.

Give yourself plenty of time for a spectacular walk on the **roof** (daily 9am–7pm, summer Thu–Sun until 9pm). The lift entrance

Galleria Vittorio Emanuele

(signposted) is accessed via the north (left) transept; alternatively, climb all 250 steps. Wander high above the city turmoil under the flying buttresses and around the statues (3,400 in all) and forest of pinnacles (135) for unbeatable views of the city.

Leading north from the Piazza del Duomo is the huge cross-shaped shopping arcade, **Galleria Vittorio Emanuele**, an impressive steel-and-glass monument to the expansive commercial spirit of the 19th century and a prototype for the modern shopping mall. Caffès, restaurants, bookshops and top designer boutiques can be found here.

The Galleria provides a sheltered passage from the Duomo to another holy entity, the revered 18th-century **La Scala** theatre, high temple of opera. The **Opera House Museum** (Museo Teatrale alla Scala; www.teatroallascala.org; daily 9am–5.30pm) traces the fascinating history of opera and theatre in the city, with memorabilia of composers including Verdi, Bellini and Donizetti on show, as well as temporary exhibitions. You can also see the refurbished theatre from a box unless there is a rehearsal or production on-stage.

Milan's most prestigious retail quarter is the Quadrilatero d'Oro, bordered by Via Montenapoleone, Via Manzoni, Via Spiga and Via Sant'Andrea. All the big designer names are here, occupying beautifully preserved palazzi. Prices are sky-high, but it is worth coming just to window-shop at the gallery-like boutiques, and to see the impeccably-clad Milanese who frequent them.

Around Castello Sforzesco

The massive brick fortress, the **Castello Sforzesco** (www.milanocastello.it; grounds Tue–Sun 7am–7.30pm, winter until 6pm), situated northwest of the city centre, was built by the Visconti and rebuilt in its present form in the 15th century by Duke Francesco Sforza. The bulk of the solid square structure stands around a vast courtyard, Piazza d'Armiles. Beyond, in the handsome old residential quarters of the Corte Ducale, is the entrance to the Castello Sforzesco Musei Civici, a series of small **art museums** (Tue–Sun 9am-5.30pm) devoted to sculpture, painting (the Pinacoteca), ceramics, furniture and archaeology. In collections that include works by Giovanni Bellini, Mantegna, Titian, Correggio and Tintoretto, pride of place goes to Michelangelo's last work (at the age of 89), the Rondanini *Pietà* (1564). He worked on it until six days before his death, chiselling a strange throwback to medieval sculpture for his last tussle with the recalcitrant stone. Now, restored to its former gleaming white marble, the masterpiece is displayed in the separate **Rondanini Museum** (http://rondanini.milanocastello.it).

Tip: A three-day Turism Museum Card (www.comune.milano.it/cultura) costs just €12 and grants the holder entry to all civic museums in Milan, including those in Sforza Castle.

The Last Supper

Even without Leonardo da Vinci's masterpiece in the adjoining refectory, the church of **Santa Maria delle Grazie** (Piazza Santa Maria delle Grazie; http://legraziemilano.it; Mon–Sat 7am–noon, 4–7.30pm Sun and holidays

La Scala tickets

Plan well ahead for performances at La Scala. For information on the various different ways of purchasing tickets go to www.teatroallascala.org, where you can buy online. You can also use the automated telephone booking service, tel: 02-860 775. Alternatively, go to www.milanopera-tickets.com.

7.30am–12.30pm, 4–9pm), southwest of the Castello, would be worth a visit as a jewel of Renaissance architecture. Adding to an earlier Gothic design, Donato Bramante – Pope Julius II's chief architect in Rome – fashioned a magnificent red brick and white stone chancel *(tribuna)* in 1492. The graceful lines of the rectangular choir and 16-sided cupola are best viewed from Bramante's cloister, built on the north side. Inside, stand in the choir to appreciate the dome's full majesty.

Leonardo da Vinci's ***The Last Supper*** (*Il Cenacolo*; tickets by reservation only tel: 02-9280 0360 or www.vivaticket.it; http://legrazie milano.it; Tue–Sun 8.15am–6.45pm, operators speak English) has been lovingly resuscitated in the Dominican refectory to the left of the church. The completion in 1999 of a laborious 20-year restoration

⊙ POSTMORTEM OF A MASTERPIECE

The main culprit in the disintegration of the *Last Supper* was its creator, Leonardo da Vinci himself. For this summit of his life's work, he did not want the restrictions of painting frescoes onto damp plaster. A fresco, painted section by section without modification once dry, would deny him the chance to add the overall shadowy *sfumato* effect that gave his paintings depth and subtlety. Nor would the sustained effort demanded by a fresco's damp plaster permit him, as was his habit, to leave the painting when inspiration deserted him, to go to work on something else.

Leonardo chose to use a tempera with oil and varnish on a dry surface. Deterioration was already noted in 1517, when Leonardo was still alive. By the time fellow artist Giorgio Vasari saw it a generation later, there was 'nothing visible but a muddle of blots'. It is a miracle that 400 more years of dust and smog have left anything at all, much of it finally rectified by a decades-long restoration, completed in 1999.

helped to remove centuries of deterioration and clumsy restoration since it was completed in 1497. It unveiled the enormous psychological impact in Leonardo's depiction of the trauma for each of the disciples when Jesus declares, 'One of you will betray me'. As a result of the painstaking recovery of the 'real' Leonardo, we can now see that Philip (third to the right) has an expression of acute grief rather than the

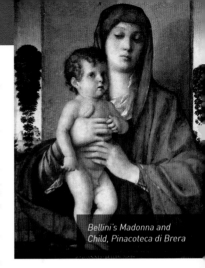

Bellini's Madonna and Child, Pinacoteca di Brera

simpering pathos left by 'restorers', who presumed to improve on the original.

For another aspect of Leonardo da Vinci's talents, visit the **Science Museum** (Museo della Scienza e della Tecnologia Leonardo da Vinci; www.museoscienza.org; Tue–Fri 9.30am–5pm, Sat and Sun 9.30am–6.30pm), in a former Benedictine monastery on nearby Via San Vittore. One gallery is reserved for Leonardo's inventions, displayed as models constructed from his notebooks. You will see his aircraft, a machine for making screws, hydraulic timber-cutter, revolving bridge, various machine-tools and a system of map-making by aerial views.

At the eastern end of Via San Vittore, the imposing church of **Sant' Ambrogio** (Mon–Sat 10am–noon, 2.30–6pm, Sun 3–5pm) is the city's most revered sanctuary, built from the 9th–12th centuries. It stands on foundations that date to the time of St Ambrose (340–97), first bishop and patron saint of Milan, a founding father of the Church; his remains are on view in the crypt. Its five-bayed facade set the standard for the Lombard Romanesque style.

The Brera and Other Museums

The handsome 17th-century palace of the Jesuits contains the **Pinacoteca di Brera** (http://pinacotecabrera.org; Tue–Sun 8.30am–7.15pm, Thu until 10.15pm), one of Italy's foremost museums of medieval and Renaissance art, concentrating on the master artists of northern Italy. A bronze statue of Napoleon stands in its arcaded courtyard. He was responsible for turning the Brera into a national gallery with confiscations from the Church and recalcitrant nobles. Among the highlights are: a Pietà and two Madonnas by Giovanni Bellini; Tintoretto's *Discovery of St Mark's Body*; Mantegna's *Dead Christ*; the *Montefeltro Altarpiece* by Piero della Francesca; and Raphael's *Marriage of the Virgin*. Non-Italian artists include El Greco, Rubens, Van Dyck and Rembrandt. In the modern collection, look out for Modigliani, Boccioni, de Chirico and de Pisis.

Brera is Milan's 'Greenwich Village'. It has been re-gentrified in the last decades and offers cutting-edge style and character in its trendy boutiques, stylish caffès and reputable art galleries.

The **Pinacoteca Ambrosiana** (Piazza Pio XI; www.ambrosiana.eu; Tue–Sun 10am–6pm) is housed in the restored 17th-century palace and library of Cardinal Federigo Borromeo. Its principal treasure, though of contested provenance, is Leonardo da Vinci's luminous *Portrait of a Musician* (1485). You can see his pervasive influence on Milanese artists in the decorative paintings of Bernardino Luini and a fine *Portrait of a Young Woman* by Ambrogio de Predis. Caravaggio's only still life, *Basket of Fruit*, is here.

The **Poldi-Pezzoli Museum** (Via Manzoni 12; www.museopoldi pezzoli.it; Wed–Mon 10am–6pm) is a small, formerly private collection displayed in its original home, dedicated to the city in 1881. The prize pieces include Piero della Francesca's *San Nicola da Tolentino*, Mantegna's *Madonna and Child*, a Botticelli *Madonna* and Pietro del Pollaiuolo's *Portrait of a Young Woman*. There are also decorative art items on show, such as clocks, sundials, glass and furniture.

The rather eccentric **Bagatti Valsecchi Museum** (Via Santo Spirito 10; http://museobagattivalsecchi.org; Tue–Sun 1–5.45pm) is housed in a delightful neo-Renaissance *palazzo*. The Bagatti Valsecchi brothers spent most of the late 19th century collecting antiques from all over Italy, and also commissioned period-style furnishings for their own home. The resulting museum is a collector's paradise.

AROUND LOMBARDY

The central part of the Po Valley is only a fraction of the Italian lands conquered by the Lombards when they crossed the Alps from Eastern Europe in the early Middle Ages. But it proved to be the most fruitful, all too tempting to the acquisitive appetites of France, Spain and rival Italian duchies and city-states such as Venice, which pushed its Serene Republic as far west as Bergamo. Natural fertility was enhanced by Europe's most advanced systems of irrigation, still operating in the medieval canals that you will see on your way

Village scene in Lombardy

south to Pavia. Lombardy's rice, wheat and corn are the basis of the nation's risotto, pasta and polenta. Italy's Lake District at the foot of the Lombardy Alps – its major lakes are Como, Garda and Maggiore – is the perfect setting for romantics.

Pavia

The Lombards' first capital, **Pavia** ㉘ is now a redbrick university town. Its main attraction, the **Charterhouse** or **Certosa di Pavia** (www.certosadipavia.com; Apr–Sept 8.30am–noon and 2.30–6pm, Oct–Mar until 5pm), is 10km (6 miles) north of the city, a half-hour drive from Milan. Built by Gian Galeazzo Visconti, Duke of Milan, as his family's burial chapel, the Carthusian monastery's 15th-century church is a high point in the transition from Gothic to Renaissance. The multi-coloured marble facade is striking, with its religious statues above the medallion reliefs of Roman emperors. The massive Gothic interior is lightened by coloured paving and groin-vaulting. Among the chapels given Baroque touches in the late 16th century is an exquisite Perugino altarpiece of *God the Father*. In the right transept is the Visconti tomb and a door leading to a small terracotta cloister, with a fine view of the church's octagonal tower. Since 1947, Cistercians have taken over from the Carthusians and continue to manufacture Certosa's Chartreuse liqueur and soaps, sold in an adjoining shop.

Bergamo

Rising out of the plain of the Po Valley on a steep little hill, 47km (29 miles) east of Milan, is the delightful town of **Bergamo** ㉙. The **Città Bassa** at the foot of the hill is an attractive, modern town full of shops, hotels and restaurants known for a risotto dish. **Piazza Matteotti** is the hub of a lively caffè scene, with the **Teatro Donizetti** and a monument to the composer who was born here in 1797 – accompanied by the naked lady he is said always to have needed for inspiration. Just behind the Citadella the **Museo Donizettiano**

(June–Sept Tue–Sun 9.30am–1pm, 2.30–6pm, Oct–May Tue–Fri 9.30am–1pm, Sat–Sun 9.30–1pm and 2.30–6pm), displays his piano, furniture and portraits.

One of the region's finest galleries, **Pinacoteca dell'Accademia Carrara** (www.lacarrara.it; Wed–Mon 10am–7pm), has an important Mantegna *Madonna and Child* and interesting works by Lotto (a Venetian master who lived here for many years), Bellini, Raphael, Titian and foreign masters. Opposite, the **Galleria d'Arte Moderna e Contemporanea** (or GAMeC; www.gamec.it) hosts temporary exhibitions by contemporary artists.

Venetian ramparts protect the historic **Città Alta** on the hill, the older section of town linked to the Città Bassa by funicular. The gracious **Piazza Vecchia** is surrounded by Renaissance edifices, notably the **Palazzo della Ragione** (Tue–Sun 10am–9pm, Sat 10am–11pm; winter Tue–Fri 9.30am–5.30pm, Sat–Sun 10am–6pm). The glass lift of the Torre Civica or Campanone (Belltower, Tue–Fri 9.30am–1pm and 2.30–6pm, Sat and Sun 9.30am–8pm, Nov–Mar Tue–Fri 9.30am–1pm, 2.30–6pm, Sat and Sun 9.30–6pm) whisks you up to the top of the tower for fine views of the city. The belltower still chimes some 180 times every evening at 10pm in memory of the curfew under the Venetians. The town's oldest building is the 12th-century basilica of **Santa Maria Maggiore** (winter Mon–Sat 9am–12.30pm, 2.30-5pm, Sun 9am–1pm and 3–6pm; summer Mon–Fri

Detail of Santa Maria Maggiore

9am–12.30pm, 2.30–6pm, Sat–Sun 9am–7pm, except Sunday services). Adjacent to the church the **Colleoni Chapel** (Tue–Sun 9am–12.30pm, 2–6.30pm, winter until 4.30pm), is a masterpiece of early Lombard Renaissance with a multi-coloured marble facade and ceiling frescoes by Tiepolo. It was built as a mausoleum for Bartolomeo Colleoni, a rich Venetian *condottiere* (mercenary).

THE LAKE DISTRICT

There are five major lakes in the Lake District, each with its own character. A playground of the rich, it has ravishing scenery and, in spite of its proximity to the Alps, a moderate climate.

Lake Garda (Lago di Garda)

Gaspare Bertolotti, regarded as the originator of the violin, is supposed to have based his design on the west shore of **Lake Garda** ③. But Italy's largest and easternmost lake is shaped more like a banjo, 52km (32 miles) from the rugged cliffs of the neck down to its broad 'sound box', 18km (11 miles) across, surrounded by rolling green hills and gardens. The lake has bewitched lovelorn Roman poets, writers, artists and not a few modern celebrities. Graced with vineyards (notably Bardolino), lemon trees, olive groves and cedars, it has mild winters and mellow summers.

At the south end of the lake, boat cruises start out from Peschiera, Sirmione and Desenzano, recommended for its dramatic view of the mountains. Begin your road tour out on the narrow **Sirmione** promontory. This former fishing village and renowned spa is the most popular of Garda's towns and the central alleyways can become impossibly crowded. There is an excellent view of the lake from the tower of the 13th-century moated castle, the **Rocca Scaligera** (www.roccascaligerasirmione.beniculturali.it). Crowning the rocky top of the peninsula are the Grotte di Catullo (Grottoes of Catullus; www.grottedicatullo.beniculturali.it; Tue–Sat 8.30am–7.30pm, Sun until 6.30pm, the site until 4.30pm and the museum

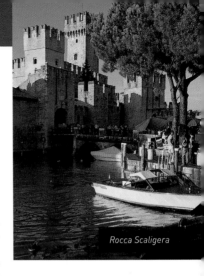
Rocca Scaligera

until 7.30pm in winter), the evocative ruins of one of northern Italy's finest Roman patrician villas.

The winding **Gardesana Occidentale**, which cuts through the cliffs of the west shore, is a spectacular drive. **Gardone Riviera** is much appreciated for its parks, Heller Botanical Gardens and as a base for walks back into the hills. Above the resort, in Gardone di Sopra, is a 20th-century 'folly', **Il Vittoriale** (www.vittoriale.it; grounds and museum daily Apr–Oct 9am–8pm, Mon from 10am, Nov–Mar Tue–Sun 9am–4pm, last entry one hour before closing), the bizarre hillside residence of Gabriele D'Annunzio – poet, adventurer and Fascist – who died here in 1936. Gardens of laurel and cypress lead up to a hilltop mausoleum of the writer's sarcophagus flanked by those of his disciples. It overlooks the prow of a patrol boat D'Annunzio commanded in World War I, the *Puglia*.

Lake Como (Lago di Como)

Embraced by green wooded escarpments and backed by the snow-capped Alps, **Lake Como** ㉛ was favoured by some of England's most romantic 19th-century poets – Wordsworth, Shelley and Byron – and has a wistful atmosphere that appeals to the Milanese (it's less than an hour from Milan). As at Garda, a mild climate nurtures luxuriant vegetation in the villa gardens and parks.

The lake dramatically divides into two arms on either side of the jewel of **Bellagio**, which juts out on a promontory. Up on the heights

Lake Como waterfront at Varenna

above the town, the elegant 18th-century **Villa Serbelloni** (Mar–Oct Tue–Sun guided tours 11am and 3.30pm) stands in the middle of a lovely park of roses, camellias, magnolias and pomegranates. Run by the Rockefeller Foundation, its famous gardens can only be visited by guided tour. Don't confuse the Villa Serbelloni with the luxury lake-front hotel of the same name.

The lake's southwest arm is the most attractive for excursions. From **Lezzeno**, take a boat cruise to see the grottoes and look out for the waterfall at Nesso. **Como** itself is a combination of historic city and commercial centre, famous for its silk production. The handsome Gothic-Renaissance cathedral, the **Duomo** (www.cattedraledicomo.it; Mon–Sat 7.30am–7.30pm, Sun until 9.30pm, museum Mon–Sat 9.30am–5.30pm, Sun 1–4.30pm) is crowned by a superb Baroque dome added in 1744 by Turin's Filippo Juvarra. It stands next to the arcaded and half-timbered Broletto, the 13th-century seat of municipal government.

The western shores of the lake are lined with gracious villas nestling in perfumed gardens. At **Cernobbio**, the 16th-century Villa d'Este is a palatial 5-star hotel (http://www.grandluxuryhotels. com), one of Europe's most special. Between the genteel resort towns (and ferry stops) of Tremezzo and Cadenabbia, you will find one of the lake's most beautiful and famous residences, the 18th-century **Villa Carlotta** (www.villacarlotta.it; Apr–mid Oct daily 9am–6pm, Mar and second half of Oct 10am–5pm, Nov until 4pm). There is a marvellous view of the lake from its terraced gardens, much visited for the display of camellias, rhododendrons and azaleas in late April and May.

Lake Maggiore

The northern, more blustery end of **Lake Maggiore ㉜**, the second largest after Garda, is in Switzerland, but the Italian side shares the other lakes' mellow climate known to the Romans as *Lacus Verbanus* (beneficent). The resort towns offer excellent opportunities for relaxation and sports, but for short visits you will get a better idea of the lake aboard a half-day boat cruise.

Stresa is Maggiore's principal resort. The lakeside promenade, Lungolago, is famous for its flowers and bewitching view of the lake's islands. Take the cable car to the 1,491m (4,892ft) peak of the **Mottarone** for an exhilarating view of the Lombardy lakes, the Alps and the Po valley and stop half way up for the Giardino Alpinia (Alpine Garden; http://giardinobotanicoalpinia.altervista.org), which displays over 2,000 varieties of mountain plants.

The most popular boat trip from Stresa is to the **Borromean Islands** (Isole Borromee; www.isoleborromee.it), celebrated for their *palazzi* and gardens. They are still the property of the Borromeo family that provided Milan with its greatest cardinals. The 17th-century *palazzo* on **Isola Bella** (daily late Mar–late Oct 9am–5.30pm) has a lavish interior, full of gilt, stuccowork and marble statues. The terraced gardens are one of the finest ensembles of the Italian formal style. View the lake from the uppermost 10 terraces, by the unicorn statue that is the Borromeo family emblem.

Isola dei Pescatori (also known as Isola Superiore) is a peaceful fishing village with narrow streets, while **Isola Madre** (same hours as Isola Bella) has another palace and luxuriant gardens.

PIEDMONT (PIEMONTE)

This region of the fertile upper basin of the Po river lies in the foothills *(pied monts)* between the Apennines and the Alps at the French and Swiss borders. From the fall of the Roman Empire to the 19th century, it stood outside the mainstream of Italian history. Its royal House of Savoy walked a diplomatic tightrope between France, Switzerland, Spain and the German emperors until the fall of Napoleon. The new nationalism led Piedmont into the Italian orbit at the head of the Risorgimento movement, and the House of Savoy served as Italy's reigning royal family from 1861 to 1946, with Turin briefly capital of the newly unified Italy in 1861.

Turin (Torino)

Best known for its industry, most notably the giant Fiat and Pirelli works, **Turin ㉝**, the Piedmontese capital, is far from being a dismal factory town. Classical and Baroque palaces and monuments give the main streets and squares a dignity and panache buoyed by the city's economic prosperity. The tone is set by the formal elegance of the **Piazza Castello**, dominated by Filippo Juvarra's richly articulated Baroque facade for the **Palazzo Madama** (www. palazzomadamatorino.it;Wed–Mon 10am–6pm). The medieval castle received its new name when transformed in the 17th century into the royal residence of Vittorio Amedeo I's widow, Maria Cristina of France, nicknamed 'Madama Reale'. It houses the **Civic Museum of Ancient Art** (Museo Civico d'Arte Antica).

Across the square is the former royal chapel, the 17th-century church of **San Lorenzo** (http://eng.sanlorenzo.torino.it; Mon–Sat 7.30am–noon, 4–7pm, Sun 9am–1pm, 3–7.30pm), designed by Turin's great Baroque architect, Fra Guarino Guarini. Philosopher and mathematician as well as priest, he has created an intricate interior surrounding the octagonal space. A replica of the shroud of Turin (see page 161) is on show here.

The **Royal Palace** (Palazzo Reale; www.ilpalazzorealedi torino.it; Tue–Sun 8.30am–7.30pm, free first Sun of the month) was the Baroque home of the Savoy princes from the mid-1600s to 1865. After strolling through one lavish room after another, visit the wing that houses the **Armoury** (Armeria Reale), one of the most comprehensive in Italy, then relax behind the palace in the **Royal Gardens** (Giardini Reali, Tue–Sun 9am–7pm).

Turin's Mole Antoniella

The Turin Shroud

The late 15th-century **Cathedral** (Duomo di San Giovanni Battista; www.duomoditorino.it; Mon–Sat 7am–12.30pm and 3–7pm, Sun 8am–12.30pm and 3–7pm) cherishes one of Italy's most celebrated (and controversial) relics, the **shroud** said to have wrapped Jesus after his descent from the cross, taking the imprint of his face and body. Sometimes enshrined in the **Chapel of the Holy Shroud** (Cappella della Santa Sindone, www.sindone.org), it was brought to Turin in the 17th century after a journey 200 years earlier from Jerusalem to France via Cyprus. Measuring 4.1 by 1.4m (13 by 5ft), the sheet is kept in an iron-lined silver casket in a marble urn behind bulletproof glass on the left-hand transept of the cathedral. The shroud can only be seen on rare occasions (the last chance was in 2015).

Many people dispute the modern scientific tests that have proven it to be a medieval fabrication, but crowds of the faithful and the curious still visit its black marble chapel, a masterpiece of Guarini's high baroque. It was restored after a 1997 fire when it came close to being completely destroyed. The **Museo della Sindone** (Via S. Domenico 28; daily 8am–7pm) covers the history of scientific tests carried out on the cloth over the years.

However, the pride of Turin is not in one monument but in its royal palaces, Baroque castles and churches, harmonious piazzas and sweeping boulevards that grace the city centre, covered by 18km (11 miles) of elegant, colonnaded walkways. For the Torinesi, the city's heart is the elegant arcaded **Via Roma**, which is lined by the most exclusive shops and designer names. The Piazza Carignano was the city's political centre in the 19th century, and its *palazzo* was the seat of Italy's first parliament from 1861 to 1864. Nearby are some of the city's most important and fascinating museums and galleries, including the Egyptian Museum. The Piazza San Carlo, known as the city's 'drawing room', is home to beautiful Baroque palaces, churches, elegant historic caffès and prestigious clothes shops.

The Turin shroud

The city's enduring symbol, the **Mole Antoniella**, from the top of which there are stunning views, houses the **Museo Nazionale del Cinema** (www.museocinema.it; Wed–Mon 9am–8pm, Sat until 11pm). The Italian film industry began in Turin in 1904, and this museum traces cinematic history from magic lanterns to cutting-edge technology.

Northeast of the piazza, in the Palazzo dell'Accademia delle Scienze, is the **Egyptian Museum** (Museo Egizio; www.museoegizio.it; Mon 9am–2pm, Tue–Sun 9am–6.30pm), second only to the one in Cairo. The Savoy collection of more than 30,000 items is on display, while the second floor's excellent **Galleria Sabauda** (Savoy Gallery; Wed–Thu 2–7.30pm, Fri—Sun and Tue 8.30am–2pm) has an important collection of Italian and European art.

Italy's automobile history – Fiat, Alfa Romeo, Bugatti and Ferrari – is celebrated at the **Museo dell'Automobile** (Corso Unità d'Italia 40; www.museoauto.it; Mon 10am–2pm, Tue 2–7pm, Wed, Thur, Sun 10am–7pm, Fri–Sat 10am–9pm), south of the city centre beside the Po river. It is near the Lingotto, a Fiat factory transformed into a modern complex of concert halls, shops and hotels by architect Renzo Piano in 2002. On the top floor the Pinacoteca Giovanni e Marella Agnelli (www.pinacoteca-agnelli.it; Tue–Sun 10am–7pm) has an exquisite collection of 25 masterpieces, Manet, Renoir, Matisse and Picasso among them, from the private collection of the late Fiat magnate, Giovanni Agnelli, and his wife, Marella.

Alpine Mountains and the Valle d'Aosta

Skiing is the main sport in Piedmont and the Valle d'Aosta. The so-called **Via Lattea**, or 'Milky Way' area, covers some 400km (250 miles) of linked runs and 90 ski lifts. **Sestriere** was the first purpose-built Alpine ski resort, created by Giovanni Agnelli, the head of Fiat. In the Valle d'Aosta, the pretty and chic town **Courmayeur** is framed by Mont Blanc (Monte Bianco) from where there are lovely walks, mountain climbing and good skiing in winter. On the northern side of the area the peaks of the Matterhorn (Monte Cervino) gaze down over **BreuilCervinia**, one of Italy's first ski resorts and still a very popular winter destination. In the south of the region is Italy's first national park, the **Parco Nazionale del Gran Paradiso**, a haven of wildlife and beautiful scenery.

Aosta ❸, the town from which the valley takes its name, was named after Emperor Augustus who created one of his mini-Romes in the centre of the valley. This attractive mountain town is encircled by the Alps and still has many Roman remains.

One of the most spectacular trips in Italy, with amazing views towards Mont Blanc, is the **cable-car ride** from La Palud, north of Courmayeur, to Point Helbronner, at 3,462m (11,358ft), and Aiguille du Midi, at 3,842m (12,606ft), to Chamonix in France.

ITALIAN RIVIERA

The Ligurian coast that holidaymakers have dubbed the Italian Riviera has an ancient history of piracy and commerce that is not always easy to differentiate. The great port city of Genoa made the Mediterranean more or less safe for respectable traders and the rest of the coast finally settled down to some quiet fishing, sailing and harmless traffic in postcards and suntan lotion.

The picturesque coast to the east of Genoa is known as the Riviera di Levante (Riviera of the Rising Sun), while the coast to the west is the Riviera di Ponente (Riviera of the Setting Sun).

Genoa (Genova)

Hemmed in between the Apennines and the sea, **Genoa** ❸ turned its back on Italy to seek its fortune on the high seas.

In the medieval Old City, the **Cathedral** (Cattedrale di San Lorenzo; daily 8am–noon, 3–7pm), was founded in 1118 and given its dazzling Gothic facade in the early 14th century. The dark and somewhat gloomy interior is enlivened by some richly decorated chapels. The underground **Museo del Tesoro** (www.museidigenova.it; Mon–Sat 9am–noon, 3–6pm) is a repository of precious relics, including the Sacro Catino, a green glass bowl, said to have been the one that Jesus drank from at the Last

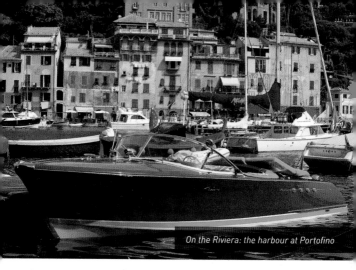

On the Riviera: the harbour at Portofino

Supper. Also here is the mid-15th-century processional casket for the ashes of St John the Baptist, which is carried through the streets on 24 June each year.

Nearby **Piazza San Matteo** was the home of the august Doria family, navigators and merchants who helped build Genoa's commercial empire. Their grey-and-white-striped arcade houses (Nos 15–17), were built from the 13th to the 15th centuries. The church of **San Matteo** has the same grey-and-white facade. Its crypt holds the tomb of Andrea Doria, a 16th-century admiral and city ruler.

At Via Garibaldi 11, **Palazzo Bianco** (winter Tue–Fri 9am–6.30pm, Sat–Sun from 9.30am, summer Tue–Fri 9am–7pm, Sat–Sun 10am–7.30pm) makes a sumptuous setting for the city's most notable art collection (consisting mostly of Genoese paintings). The 17th-century Baroque **Palazzo Rosso** (same hours as Palazzo Bianco) includes works by Veronese, Titian, Caravaggio, Dürer and Rubens.

With 28km (17 miles) of docks, Italy's biggest port remains the key to the city's identity. **Porto Antico** (Old Port), once fallen into

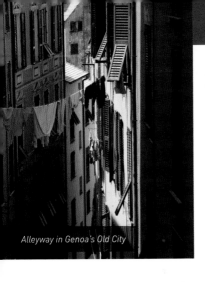

Alleyway in Genoa's Old City

disuse and dilapidation, was transformed by Genoa-born architect Renzo Piano and is the tourist hub of the city. The number one attraction is the **Acquario** (Aquarium; www.acquariodigenova.it; daily 8.30am–9pm, last entrance 7pm) the largest in Italy, with species ranging from sharks and manatees to penguins and jellyfish. Other seafront attractions are the **Biosfera** (www.biosferagenova.it), a futuristic glass sphere of tropical plants and butterflies, **the Bigo** (The Crane), a spider-like structure that takes you up 650ft for panoramic views and the **Galata Museo del Mare** (Galata Museum of the Sea; www.galatamuseodelmare.it; daily Mar–Oct 10am–7.30pm, Nov–Feb Tue–Fri 10am–6pm, Sat–Sun 10am–7.30pm, last entry 1 hour before closing), a maritime museum that charts the city's rich and varied seafaring history.

Riviera di Levante

Along the mostly rugged Riviera di Levante east of Genoa, by far the prettiest spot is tiny **Portofino** ③⑥. Seemingly more fishing and sailing harbour than resort, it contains some fine and extremely exclusive hotels and private villas, set back in the forest-covered hills. From the colourfully painted houses clustered around the postage stamp-sized harbour, avoid the many day-trippers by setting out on a paved cliff walk. Pass the yellow-painted church of San Giorgio to the **Lighthouse** (Faro) at the end of the government-protected Promontory Monte Portofino for a superb view along the coast. The cliffs are clothed in a profusion of exotic vegetation, with occasional glimpses of private homes framed by cypresses, palm trees and cascades of brilliant bougainvillea. Boat excursions will take you to other beautifully secluded villages, such as the historic monastery of **San Fruttuoso**, reachable only by boat or a two-hour walk, and delightful **Camogli**. On foot, you can also visit the charming little fishing hamlet of **San Rocco** and take a 40-minute walk over to Punta Chiappa, looking out over the whole Riviera.

Nearby, **Santa Margherita Ligure** is a lively resort town full of caffès, boutiques and good hotels, with a palm-lined waterfront esplanade and seafood-serving trattorias. It absorbs the tourism that neighbouring Portofino cannot accommodate. Just down the coast, the family resort of **Sestri Levante** has fine sandy beaches.

A favourite boat trip from Santa Margherita is to a cluster of former fishing villages called the **Cinque Terre** ③ – cliff-clinging hamlets hugging a stretch of coastline reminiscent of the Mediterranean of 100 years ago. They are linked by a network of ancient cliffside mule paths that provide some of Italy's loveliest treks.

Riviera di Ponente

The **Riviera di Ponente** ③, west of Genoa towards the French border, is an almost continuous chain of family resorts. A faded resort of earlier times, dignified **San Remo** has a well-heeled casino and elegant promenade along the Corso Imperatrice. For time away from the beach, explore the narrow, winding medieval streets of the hilltop **La Pigna** quarter, leading up to the 17th-century sanctuary of Madonna della Costa.

The quieter resort of **Bordighera** is particularly proud of the palm trees along the Lungomare Argentina promenade. **Alassio** completes this coast's trio of major resorts, justifiably proud of its gardens nurtured by a particularly mild winter. An excursion east leads to the quiet medieval town of **Albenga**.

THE SOUTH

One of the great joys of the south is the extent to which it is still virgin land for the majority of Italy's visitors. It has its perennial favourites: the sister islands of Capri and Ischia in the Bay of Naples, the ruins of Pompeii, the resorts of the singularly beautiful Amalfi coast and the island of Sicily. Otherwise, southern Italy is overlooked by tourists almost as much as it has been by the national government since reunification.

Less prosperous than the north, although benefiting from EU funds, it doesn't offer the same wealth of tourist facilities. Monuments and museums have suffered from earthquakes and civic neglect. But things are improving, with restoration of historic buildings and a wider choice of accommodation. For many, the chief pleasure of the south, or Mezzogiorno, is the people, who are friendly, outgoing and gregarious.

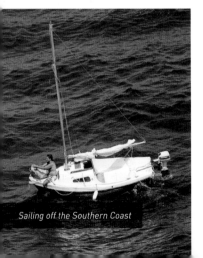
Sailing off the Southern Coast

NAPLES (NÁPOLI)

The very idea of this teeming, undisciplined and gritty town once intimidated the faint-hearted, but times are changing in this history-rich city of which the Neapolitans are rightly proud. For adventurous travellers looking for an introduction to the south, the rewards are rich. Indeed, two of Naples' museums are among Europe's most important, but they play second fiddle to the colourful and chaotic street life.

In the outdoor theatre that is Italy, Naples' unabashed melodrama can be seen everywhere: around the port, the popular quarters of Spaccanapoli, even the more bourgeois neighbourhoods of Vomero and Posillipo. You will want to spend hours in the restaurants – this is where pizza began.

The face of **Naples** ③⑨ has been made and remade by its many earthquakes. Many churches, palaces and museums still show signs of ongoing reconstruction and restoration after the devastating quake of 1980. The revival has not been helped by the increasing prevalence of the Camorra, Campania's powerful Mafia, who were exposed in Roberto Saviano's book, *Gamorrah*, and the eponymous film.

The Port and Spaccanapoli

Traffic roars down the broad Corso Umberto I towards the pivotal **Piazza Municipio** to serve the docks or spin off into the commercial district behind Santa Lucia, the teeming historic centre of Spaccanapoli, or the residential districts of Vomero and Posillipo. Towering over the long rectangular square on its south side is the massive **Castel Nuovo** (Mon–Sat 9am–7pm) with its dry moat. The 13th-century fortress of Naples' French ruler Charles d'Anjou, it was rebuilt in the 15th century as a palace for the Spanish kings of Aragon. Entrance to what is now administrative offices and a communal library is between two towers on the west side through a two-storey Renaissance **Triumphal Arch**, crowned by a statue of St Michael.

South of the Piazza Municipio, the Via San Carlo curves round to the 19th-century steel-and-glass shopping arcade of **Galleria Umberto I**, opposite the great neoclassical temple of Neapolitan *bel canto*, the restored **Teatro di San Carlo** opera house (www.teatro sancarlo.it). Built in 1737 and rebuilt in 1816, it was once under the musical direction of Gioacchino Rossini (1815–22) and has excellent acoustics. The monumental **Piazza del Plebiscito** was laid out by Joachim Murat, King of Naples, who occupied the Spaniards'

Palazzo Reale (Thu–Tue 9am–8pm) on the east side of the piazza. The rooms are decorated and furnished with the Baroque pomp of the 17th and 18th centuries and reconstructed following Allied bomb damage in 1943. The *palazzo*'s sumptuous royal apartments are the draw, but it also holds temporary exhibits.

Just south of here, the old popular harbour district of **Santa Lucia** is lined with elegant hotels and restaurants, many overlooking the formidable medieval **Castel dell'Ovo** (Egg Castle; www.castel-dell-ovo.com; Mon–Sat 9am–7.30pm, winter until 6.30pm, Sun 9am–2pm; free) on an islet, with a handful of outdoor trattorias and caffès that enjoy a unique setting. The waterfront walk at sunset offers timeless views of the bay and Mount Vesuvius, with the addition of a gleaming-white luxury cruise ship or two. At the workaday zone of Mergellina at the western end of the harbour, fishermen bring their morning catch into Porto Sannazaro.

Leading north from Piazza del Plebiscito, the Neapolitans' favourite shopping street of **Via Toledo** separates the town hall (Municipio) and the broad commercial streets going down to the harbour from a chequerboard of narrow alleys to the west. This 16th-century Spanish neighbourhood, a mass of dilapidated working-class housing, is a great opportunity for watching everyday life. Via Toledo leads to the old historic heart of **Spaccanapoli** (around a Roman road that divides Naples into upper and lower districts). In an area stretching from the traffic-jammed Piazza Dante, between Via San Biagio dei Librai and Via Tribunali and over to the Porta Capuana, the popular image of old Naples survives. Laundry hangs across the narrow streets, gossip flies between balconies, and ropes haul up baskets of vegetables, letters and even pet cats.

Dangerous driving

The cautious tell you not to drive in Naples, where one-way signs are meaningless, parking is impossible, traffic is relentless and red and green lights can be purely decorative. They are right.

View over Naples' port and harbour towards Mount Vesuvius

Santa Chiara

For a sense of the historic neighbourhood's old splendour, start on **Piazza Gesù Nuovo**, with the extravagant Baroque Immacolata column (Guglia) in the centre. Architectural exuberance continues inside the Jesuit church. But the jewel, on the south corner of the square, is the 14th-century Gothic **Santa Chiara** (www.monasterodi santachiara.eu; daily 7.30am–1pm, 4.30–8pm), built for the wife of Robert the Wise d'Anjou and retrieved from its 18th-century Baroque additions and 1943 firebombing. The rose window and elegant porch survive and the French Gothic interior is beautifully restored. Vaults include the **sculpted tombs** of Marie de Valois (on the right) and Robert the Wise d'Anjou (d. 1343; behind the high altar). Next to the church are the lovely 14th-century **cloisters** (Chiostro delle Clarisse; daily Mon–Sat 9.30am–5.30pm, Sun 10am–2.30pm), converted in 1742 into a country garden of shaded walkways and Capodimonte tiles – a delightful haven and one of the city's most charming spots.

Take the Via Tribunali to the Franciscan church of **San Lorenzo Maggiore** (Mon–Sat 9.30am–5.30pm, Sun 9.30am–1.30pm). Its

Baroque facade, incorporating a 14th-century marble porch, was added after the earthquake of 1731. Inside is a sober French Gothic chancel.

The three original 14th-century portals of the **Cathedral** (Via Duomo 147; daily 9am–noon and 4.30–6.30pm) are overpowered by the 19th-century neo-Gothic facade. It contains Naples' earliest-known Christian sanctuary, the 4th-century **Basilica of Santa Restituta**, in which the original Roman columns survived the 1688 earthquake. At the end of the right nave is the 5th-century domed baptistery, one of the oldest buildings in Europe, with some original mosaics intact. The cathedral's richly Baroque **Chapel of San Gennaro** is the highlight. Its altar contains two phials of blood from Naples' patron saint, and three times a year (the first Sunday of May, 19 September and 16 December) it is said to liquefy, or 'boil'. When it fails, disaster befalls Naples. The last time it is said not to have liquefied was in 1980, the year of the great earthquake.

Archaeological Museum

The roguish image of the city makes it easy to forget its glorious past. Luckily, two truly magnificent museums preserve the region's treasures from the ravages of earthquake and theft. Constructed in the 16th-century as a cavalry barracks, the **Archaeological Museum** (Museo Archeologico Nazionale; Wed–Mon 9am–7.30pm) is a feast of southern Italy's Greek, Etruscan and Roman past. All visits to Pompeii and Herculaneum should begin or end here, since the world-famous collections display not only the

A secret gallery

The Archaeological Museum's Gabinetto Segreto (Secret Gallery) displays a collection of mosaics and paintings, many of which have never before seen because of their erotic (some would say 'pornographic') nature.

Mosaic of a chained dog, from Pompeii

paintings and mosaics buried there by Mount Vesuvius nearly 2,000 years ago, but a host of other sculptures from the region's villas and temples.

The ground floor is devoted to **sculpture**, including many Roman copies of classics from Greece's Golden Age in the 5th century BC, which are our only access to these lost masterpieces. The most famous is the *Doryphorus* (Spear-carrier) of Polycletus, second in fame among Greek sculptors only to Phidias. Also on display is the **Farnese Bull** (*Toro Farnese*), the largest Classical sculpture ever discovered, hewn from a single marble block.

Most popular are the stunning **Herculaneum bronzes** and **Pompeii mosaics** on the mezzanine floor. The lively mosaics from Pompeii's patrician villas make a striking contrast with the rigid formality of church mosaics elsewhere in Italy. They include *Clients Consulting a Sorceress, Strolling Musicians*, vivid little friezes of an octopus, a chained dog, a cat catching a quail and the huge exciting mural of Alexander driving Darius of Persia from the battlefield at Issus in 333 BC. The **paintings** here are the best preserved of any from Roman antiquity – frescoes in brilliant blues, greens and the inimitable Pompeii reds. The most celebrated is the sophisticated portrait of *Paquius Proculus and his Wife*. Also look for the elegant *Hercules and Telephus* and four delicate portraits of women, including *Artimedes and the Flower Gatherer*.

The Capodimonte Museum

The **Capodimonte Museum** (www.museocapodimonte.beniculturali. it; Thu–Tue 8.30am–6.30pm) is housed in a beautifully restored 18th-century hilltop palace, the **Palazzo Reale di Capodimonte**. The grounds offer a welcome rest before and after a visit to the exceptional collection of Italian and European paintings. Highlights include Giovanni Bellini's gentle *Transfiguration of Christ* standing serenely between Moses and Elijah; Mantegna's *Portrait of a Boy*; and Michelangelo's drawing of *Three Soldiers* for his Vatican fresco of *St Peter's Crucifixion*. The stark realism you will see in Caravaggio's *Flagellation* and the *Seven Works of Mercy* launched a whole Neapolitan school of 'Caravaggeschi' shown here.

Vomero and Posillipo

Much of Naples' middle class looks out over the city from the hilltop Vomero neighbourhood. On the southeast edge of the hill just below the massive Castel Sant' Elmo, the elegant Baroque charterhouse **Certosa di San Martino**, now home to the **Museo Nazionale di San**

Palazzo Reale di Capodimonte

Martino (www.coopculture.it; Thu–Tue 8.30am–7.30pm), offers a soothing haven of tranquillity in its cloisters and monastery gardens – and unbeatable views. The monastery's museum traces the kingdom of Naples' long history in costumes, sculpture, paintings and prints. A popular exhibition in the museum shows four centuries of the unique Neapolitan speciality of hand-crafted Nativity characters, known as *presepi*.

CAMPANIA

The fertile region around Naples, between the Tyrrhenian coast and the western slopes of the Apennines, was colonised by the Etruscans and Greeks. Since time immemorial, the volcanic soil has produced a profusion of olives, walnuts, grapes, oranges, lemons and figs. The succession of authoritarian rulers from the Middle Ages to the 18th century – Norman and Angevin French, German emperors and the Spanish – kept in place a feudal system that has left the region with a greater social and economic divide than that of the north. Village festivals and processions bear witness to the heavy rural attachment to religion and even pagan superstition harking back to ancient times. The international jet set has long frequented the idyllic islands in the Bay of Naples and the resorts of the Amalfi coast. In easy reach of Naples' museums are the archaeological remains of Pompeii and Herculaneum, the Vesuvius volcano and, further down the coast, the Greek temples of Paestum.

Capri

Ferries or hydrofoils leave from Naples, Sorrento and Positano (and Amalfi in the summer months only) for this fabled island, **Capri** ④, 10 sq km (4 sq miles) in size. With walled villas surrounded by gardens, mountainous terrain and a dramatic craggy coastline, this beautiful island manages to cater to the boisterous fun of day-trippers and package tourists while providing quiet hideaways for

Capri's Marina Grande

pure hedonism. Winters here are marvellously mild and deserted, but even during the peak summer months you can seek out the island's many enchanted corners away from the crowds. Evenings are immeasurably calmer, when local people venture out to reclaim the caffès and restaurants until the cool small hours, and restore some of the charm and seduction for which Capri has been famous since the times of the ancient Roman emperors.

At the main harbour of Capri's **Marina Grande**, take the funicular railway up to the main town of **Capri**. Here, souvenir shops, pricey boutiques and bar-caffès cluster around the pretty 17th-century domed church of **Santo Stefano** in the Piazzetta (officially the Piazza Umberto I). Many day-trippers see little more than this. You can hire a taxi for the day – not cheap, but negotiable. Escape down the little road south of town to the peaceful shady cloisters of the 14th-century **Certosa di San Giacomo**, or go in the direction of Via Camerelle that eventually leads to the famous Punta Tragara lookout and the **Faraglioni**. These rocky islets, carved into fantastic shapes, are a symbol of the island's natural beauty.

Dominating the western (and larger) side of the island, the quieter and only slightly less crowded hillside town of **Anacapri** derives a sleepy charm from its white villas along narrow lanes flowering with bougainvillea. A short walk from Piazza della Vittoria takes you to **Villa San Michele** (www.villasanmichele.eu; May–Sept daily 9am–6pm; shorter hours in winter), home of Swedish doctor-writer Axel Munthe (d. 1949). The house is a mixture of Baroque furniture and Roman antiquities, but the main attraction is the garden, with dramatic views across the island and the bay. Back at the piazza, take the *seggovia* chair-lift for a view of the island and some of the mainland on your way to the terraced gardens of **Monte Solaro**, at 589m (1,933ft), Capri's highest point.

The island's most popular excursion – prettiest by boat from Marina Grande, but also possible by road northwest of Anacapri – is to the celebrated marine cave, the **Blue Grotto** (Grotta Azzurra), most effective (and most crowded) at noon. The sun shining through the water turns the light inside the cave a brilliant, unearthly blue and objects on the white sand sea bed gleam like silver. The cave, 54m (177ft) long, 15m (49ft) high and 30m (98ft) wide, is believed to have been a *nymphaeum*, a kind of watery boudoir for the Emperor Tiberius, who retired to Capri in the 1st century AD and built a villa directly above. The ruins of Tiberius' **Villa Jovis** (Jupiter's Villa; 9am–4.15pm) sprawl across an eastern promontory. Come for the fabulous view from the 297m (974ft) Salto di Tiberio (Tiberius' Leap), the last pleasure enjoyed by the emperor's enemies before being hurled over the edge.

Ischia

Lying at the western end of the Bay of Naples – reached by ferry or hydrofoil from Naples and Pozzuoli – the island of **Ischia** ⓐ is almost as popular with tourists in summer as its little sister Capri, thanks to thermal springs and spas, fine sandy beaches, facilities for water sports and naturism. Casamicciola Terme and Lacco

Colonnade around the Forum, Pompeii

Ameno are among the smarter spa resorts. One of the best beaches is the **Lido dei Maronti** near the picturesque fishing village of Sant' Angelo. Nature lovers can hike (or go on a hired donkey) up the extinct volcano of **Mount Epomeo**, at 788m (2,585ft), starting from Fontana; there are unforgettable views of the island and the Bay of Naples.

Pompeii

The everyday reality of Roman life comes alive in the bakeries, wine shops, groceries and brothels of **Pompeii** ㊷, a town of 25,000, thought to have been founded in the 8th century BC. A cataclysmic eruption of Mount Vesuvius wiped out the flourishing town, along with neighbouring Herculaneum, on 24 August AD79, burying it under 7m (23ft) of ash. It remained entombed until 1594, when building work led to its discovery, but excavation did not begin until the mid-1700s.

The road from the main gate that led to the sea (Porta Marina; tel: 081-857 5111/347; www.pompeiisites.org; Apr–Oct daily

9am–7.30pm, Nov–Mar daily 8.30am–5.30pm, last entry 90 mins before closure) passes on the right of the basilica, law courts and stock exchange to reach the **Forum**, the centre of town and its main public meeting place directly facing Mount Vesuvius. Imagine a vast square looking something like Venice's Piazza San Marco, with two-storey porticoes running along three sides and the six-columned **Temple to Jupiter** flanked by ceremonial arches at the north end. After earlier earthquake damage, the temple was used as the *Capitolium* and city treasury. You can see plinths from the square's statues of local and national celebrities and the white base of the orator's platform. In the northeast corner is the large, originally covered, market *(macellum)*, while in the southwest corner is the **Basilica**, the largest building in Pompeii.

On the **Via dell'Abbondanza** running east from the Forum, ancient graffiti is daubed in red on the walls of the houses and shops. Election slogans, insults, and obscene drawings – the tradition continued today has a long history. Prominent phallus signs often indicate a house of ill repute, with an arrow pointing upstairs to where the action was, although sometimes these were just a shopkeeper's good luck symbols. Notice the oil and wine jars in

⊘ THE LOST WORLD

Unlike the predominantly aristocratic Herculaneum, ancient Pompeii's population of 25,000 was a mixture of patricians, nouveaux riches merchants, small shopkeepers, artisans and slaves. They made their money from commerce in wool and wine. The typical patrician house had two storeys, with servants and lodgers living upstairs. The family's living and sleeping quarters surrounded a first courtyard or atrium. Opposite the entrance was a main living room *(tablinum)* backing onto the dining room *(triclinium)*. This looked onto another courtyard or Greek-style porticoed garden *(peristylium)*.

the shops, the bakers' ovens and flour-grinding mills shaped like giant cotton reels.

At the **Stabian Baths** (*Thermae Stabianae*), Pompeii's largest, you can see the men's and women's facilities – changing rooms, with clothes niches and three baths: cold, lukewarm and hot (*frigidarium*, *tepidarium* and *calidarium*). The 2nd-century BC **Teatro Grande** seated 5,000 spectators. Behind the stage was the Gladiators' Barracks, where 63 skeletons were found. Weapons and armour, along with Pompeii's more fragile works of art, are exhibited at Naples' Archaeological Museum.

Pompeii's Finest Villas

At the far end of Via dell'Abbondanza are two of the town's best villas. The **House of Loreius Tiburtinus** has a beautiful peristyle garden of fountains, water channels and cascades, one of them with paintings of *Narcissus* and *Pyramus and Thisbe*. The **House of Julia Felix**, big enough to have been perhaps a luxury hotel, has its own bathhouse and a handsome portico of slender marble columns around the peristyle. Just to the south is the great **Amphitheatre** (*Anfiteatro*), the oldest surviving in Italy dating back to 80 BC, with a fine view over the town from its upper tiers.

North of the Forum area are two of Pompeii's most important sites. The restored **House of the Vettii** was owned by two wealthy merchant brothers, whose

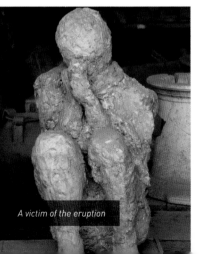
A victim of the eruption

large home is one of the best preserved and elaborately decorated. Outside the main site to the north, the **Villa of Mysteries** (Villa dei Misteri) is Pompeii's other most cherished artistic treasure. The 'mysteries' are those depicted in a vast fresco of a young woman's initiation into the cult of Dionysius, of Greek origin. Archaeologists, who are still unsure of what was involved, suggest that the gorgeously painted scenes of dancing satyrs, flagellation and a woman kneeling before a sacred phallus, indicate rites that the town preferred to keep at a decorous distance. This suburban villa was most likely the home of a priestess. To this day the fresco's brilliant and little faded background of intense red is called 'Pompeiian red'.

The collapse of the House of Gladiators in 2010 refuelled debate on whether the government is doing enough to maintain what is one of the world's most important archaeological sites. As a result, a major renovation programme of the site has been started.

Vesuvius (Vesuvio)

The old Roman name of Europe's most famous volcano means 'Unextinguished' – it is the only active volcano on the European mainland (there are others on the islands of Sicily and Stromboli). **Vesuvius** **43** rises to 1,281m (4,203ft), having gained 79m (259ft) in the eruption of 1944 and subsequent smaller ones. Barring risks from 'unscheduled activity,' you can go as far as the 600m (1,960ft) wide crater. Exploiting the fertile volcanic soil, some vineyards still produce the esteemed *Lacryma Christi* white wine. The **Eremo Observatory** halfway up the mountain has been studying eruptions since 1845 and has an impressive display of relief plans, seismographs and geological specimens spewed out of the volcano.

Aware that one million people are sitting on a time bomb and that a major eruption is a matter of when, and not if, the Italian authorities have offered incentives for families to relocate. However, the take-up has been minimal so far.

Stunningly well-preserved fresco in Herculaneum

Herculaneum (Ercolano)

Some 7km (4.5 miles) from Vesuvius, **Herculaneum ④** (www.pompeii
sites.org; Apr–Oct daily 8.30am–7.30pm, until 5pm Nov–Mar) is
smaller and less renowned than Pompeii, but its compactness and
better-preserved state give a more immediate sense of the shape
and ambience of a Roman town. While Pompeii was incinerated by
volcanic cinders, a lethal 20m (65ft) tide of ash and mud swamped
Herculaneum, hardening and covering the houses in a protective
crust that kept upper storeys and even some of the woodwork intact.
Rediscovered by well-diggers in the 18th century, the town is still
being excavated, a delicate business as much of it is covered by the
modern city of Ercolano. The three main streets dividing the town
(Cardine III, IV and V) have kerbed pavements, lined with two-storey
houses with balconies and overhanging roofs for shade. Most visited
are the **Baths** *(Terme)*, which are in excellent condition, well-equipped
and practically laid out with separate areas for men and women.

At the southern end of Cardine V, the patrician **House of the
Deer** *(Casa dei Cervi)* is named after its frescoes of two stags being

attacked by hounds. In one of the rooms off the garden is a statue of a shockingly drunken Hercules, alleged founder of the ancient town. In the middle of Cardine IV, the **House of Charred Furniture** (*Casa del Mobilio Carbonizzato*) has a uniquely preserved latticed divan bed and small table. Next door, the **House of Neptune** has lost its upstairs facade, but the ground floor wine shop with its narrow-necked amphoras on the shelves looks open for business. The inner courtyard has a lovely green-and-blue mosaic of Neptune with his wife Amphitrite.

The grandest of the villas, the **House of the Bicentenary** (excavated 200 years after the first 'dig' in 1738) stands on Avenue Decumanus Maximus on the northeast edge of town. It has splendid marble paving and, etched in the wall of one of the smaller rooms, a cross regarded by some as one of the oldest Christian relics.

Like Pompeii the site is under continuous restoration. If you want it all brought to life, visit the **Museo Archeologico Virtuale** (MAV, www.museomav.it), a multisensory tour of the past with computerized recreations of the streets, squares and villas and a 3D film on a 26m screen reproducing the eruption of Vesuvius, complete with vibrating platform.

Sorrento and the Amalfi Coast

The coast curving along the southern arm of the Bay of Naples round the Sorrento Peninsula to Salerno is one of the most romantic and dramatic drives in Europe. The sinuous white-knuckle coastal road and its sheer drop of rugged cliffs and Falbero ravines can tame even the most audacious Italian driver. In former times, only brigands and pirates ventured out here, their ruined redoubts and look-out towers still dotting the hillsides and promontories. Now, road-side look-outs tempt travellers and aspiring photographers onto jutting crags high above terraces of orange and lemon groves, vineyards, and walnut and almond trees.

Surrounded on three sides by ravines above the sea, the pretty tree-shaded resort of **Sorrento** 45 still retains something of its old-fashioned air and is a popular base for boat and car excursions along the coast and peninsula. Its local craftsmen are famous for their inlaid woodwork called *intarsia*. Compare their modern, sadly more commercialised wares with their forefathers' Baroque furniture shown at the **Museo Correale** (www.museocorreale.it; Tue–Sat 9.30am–6.30pm, Sun 9.30am–1.30pm) in an 18th-century *palazzo* at the east end of town; the museum's porcelain collection is also worth a look.

Small, fashionable **Positano** spills down its hillside in a spectacular cascade of gleaming, bougainvillea-covered whitewashed houses, dotted with gardens of oranges and lemons and terraces of colourful hand-painted tiles. The pebbly beach is lined with canvas umbrella-shaded chairs and fishing boats, and flanked by pizzerias and restaurants that stay open late into the night. In the little church

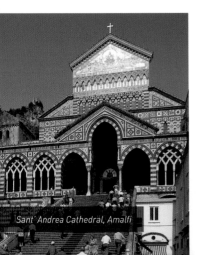

Sant' Andrea Cathedral, Amalfi

of **Santa Maria Assunta**, with a characteristic majolica-tiled dome, don't miss the 13th-century Byzantine-style altar painting. A wealthy international crowd keeps the four- and five-star hotels busy. With only two roads to speak of, most travel is by foot up and down its endless flights of steps.

The other lively resort, **Amalfi**, was once a powerful rival to the maritime republics of Pisa and Genoa, with trading posts in the 10th and 11th centuries

Amalfi's spectacular setting

in Palestine, Egypt, Cyprus, Byzantium and Tunis. Its two roles come together in the **Piazza del Duomo**, where open-air caffès and ice-cream parlours sit at the foot of a monumental staircase to the Arab-Norman **Campanile** and polychrome mosaic facade of the Romanesque **Sant'Andrea Cathedral** (summer daily 9am–9pm, 10am–5pm in winter), built as a symbol of the republic's glory. It was begun in the 9th century, its massive bronze doors crafted in Constantinople, and added to in the 11th century; the facade was added in the 13th, when the remains of St Andrew the Apostle were brought to its crypt from Constantinople. The ornate facade was rebuilt in the 19th century. The interlacing Arab-Norman arches of the 13th-century cloister, **Chiostro del Paradiso** (Cloister of Paradise), make a handsome setting for the summer recitals of chamber music.

Take a trip to nearby Conca dei Marini to view the stalactites of the **Grotta dello Smeraldo** (Emerald Grotto, daily 9am–4pm), where the waters are as brilliantly emerald green as those of Capri's Grotta Azzurra are blue.

Ravello

Set back on a high ridge 362m (1,184ft) above and behind Amalfi is the tiny and peaceful village of **Ravello**, once a hideout for Romans fleeing the Huns and Visigoths. Today Ravello is a delightful resort of stunningly situated, modest and elegant hotels and villas. Directly off the main square, which is anchored by its imposing Romanesque **Cathedral**, built in 1076, is the **Villa Rufolo** (www.villarufolo.it; daily 9am–5pm) with its mysterious polychrome-arcaded arabesque cloister. Its hanging gardens of exotic flowers and palm trees and mesmerising views were the inspiration for Richard Wagner in 1880 for his last opera, Parsifal. They are the perfect location for outdoor classical concerts in summer. Reached by a rambling footpath is the 1904 **Villa Cimbrone** (www.villacimbrone.com; gardens daily 9am–sunset), now the location of luxurious hotel with a Michelin-starred restaurant. Its surrounding fragrant gardens also command a marvellous, vertigo-inducing view of the craggy coastline and azure blue of the Gulf of Salerno. The view from here is the most photographed on the entire Amalfi coast.

Paestum

Italy has no more magnificent testimony of its many Greek colonies than this complex of wonderfully preserved **Doric temples**. **Paestum** ⓪, a 40-minute drive south from Salerno, dating back to the 5th and 6th centuries BC. Standing alone in fields leading to the sea, their buff-stone columns take on a wonderful golden glow at sunset. Four temples loom over the forum and residential quarters. In pre-Roman times the town was known as Poseidonia, after the Greek god of the sea (whom the Romans knew as Neptune). After the town was abandoned to malaria and Arab invaders in the 9th century, the monuments disappeared under wild vegetation until their rediscovery 900 years later.

The most spectacular temple, directly opposite the entrance to the site (www.infopaestum.it; daily 8.30am–7pm), is the 5th-century

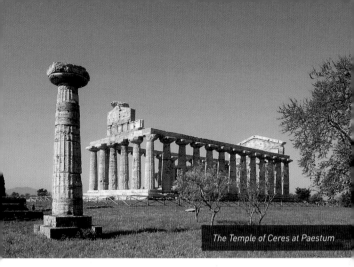

The Temple of Ceres at Paestum

BC **Temple of Neptune**. The roof has gone, but with its superb entablature and 14 fluted columns still standing, it is, together with Athens' Theseion, the best preserved of all the Greek temples. To the south, the **Temple of Hera** (also known, mistakenly, as the Basilica) is 100 years older and is Paestum's oldest, also predating Athens' Parthenon by 100 years. The northernmost **Temple of Ceres** was built around 500 BC, and was used as a church in the early Middle Ages, as attested by three Christian tombs.

Opposite the temples is an excellent archaeological museum (daily 8.30am–7.30pm; closed 1st and 3rd Mon of the month), a treasure trove of Greek and Roman finds excavated from the site.

PUGLIA

Known to many under its Roman name of Apulia, this region stretches from the 'spur' of the Gargano peninsula to the heel of Italy's boot, with gently undulating stony plateaux grazed by sheep and goats, and endowed with a wild, unspoilt beauty. Massive fortresses and fortress-like churches testify to the passage of the

Normans, then the German emperors in the Middle Ages. Among the groves of olive, almond and fig trees, the stones have been gathered up from time immemorial to build the smaller, but equally sturdy, corbelled *trulli* (houses with cone-shaped roofs) that crop up like so many mushroom clusters dotting the countryside. It is an exotically distant holiday destination popular with Italians and, increasingly, more adventurous Italophiles, both incredulous that this end-of-the-world piece of Italy is still part of Europe.

Gargano Peninsula

The peninsula's seaside resorts have good beaches among the pine groves, first-class camping and water sports facilities, and are a base for excursions and walks in an attractive hinterland of rolling hills. The scenic coastal circuit begins in **Manfredonia**, with historical attractions such as the 12th-century church of **Santa Maria di Siponto** (southwest of town). **Pugnochiuso** is among the best of the beach resorts, along with **Vieste**, where Emperor Frederick II left a castle from which to view the Adriatic; the pretty fishing villages of Peschici and Vieste climb up the rocky promontory here. Don't miss a spectacular recreation of the original 12th century basilica from wire mesh by the young Italian artist Edoardo Tresoldi in Santa Maria di Siponto.

Head inland through Vico to see the wild deer in the **Umbra Forest**. Perched on the Gargano heights south of the forest, **Monte Sant' Angelo** was a major medieval pilgrimage town, celebrated for its 5th-century sanctuary of **St Michael** (www.santuariosanmichele. it; daily July–Sept 7.30am–7.30pm, Apr–June and Oct weekdays 7.30am–12.30pm and 2.30–7pm, Sun 7am–1pm and 2.30–8pm (until 7pm in winter), Nov–Mar 7.30am–12.30pm and 2.30–5pm) in a grotto where the archangel appeared to the Bishop of Siponto three times. The sanctuary inspired the building of the great French island-monastery of Mont-Saint-Michel after Bishop Aubert travelled to Gargano to collect a piece of St Michael's red cloak. From a Gothic portico in the middle of town, beside the massive

13th-century **Campanile**, a staircase of 90 steps takes you down to the sanctuary's 11th-century bronze doors. Notice to the left of the altar the beautifully carved stone episcopal throne.

From the north coast resort of Rodi Garganico, you can take a 90-minute boat trip during the summer months, out to the pine-forested **Tremiti Islands**.

Trulli house in Alberobello

Alberobello

Alberobello . This agricultural town is the centre of Puglia's famous *trulli*, the white-washed cone-shaped houses with russet or grey dry-stone roofs dotting the landscape like giant spinning tops turned upside down. The dazzlingly white cone is formed by small limestone slabs set in a spiral without mortar to bind them. Although the region's oldest surviving *trulli* date back only to the 16th century, the construction technique is believed by some to be prehistoric, brought here perhaps from Greece or the Middle East.

It is a joy to wander Alberobello's two neighbourhoods of *trulli*, whose houses, shops and even churches – **Rioni Monti** and **Aia Piccola** – are protected as a *Zona Monumentale* (World Heritage Site). Shopkeepers are usually happy to let you onto their roof terraces for a striking view across a whole fairy-tale forest of some 1,000 *trulli* domes. Out in the country in and around vineyard and lime-clad **Locorotondo** and **Selva di Fasano**, you will find *trulli* (and *trulli*-inspired) farms, barns, grain silos and even petrol stations.

Northwest of Alberobello, a *strada panoramica* along a ridge overlooking the Adriatic coast leads to **Castellana Grotte** (www.

grottedicastellana.it; opening times vary), a spectacular cave system 60m (190ft) underground. Take a guided tour of the stalactites reaching down to fuse with stalagmites in columns of red, green and pink.

Last but not least is Puglia's crowning glory, **Lecce** ㊽, dubbed the Florence of the South because of its plethora of 16th- to 18th-century *palazzi* of local malleable limestone. Foremost is the **Basilica of the Holy Cross** (Santa Croce; daily 9am–noon, 4–7.30pm), the best example of the city's Baroque heyday; and the **Piazza del Duomo**, ringed by the rebuilt cathedral and buildings of similar pedigree. The **Roman Amphitheatre** in the heart of Lecce dates from the 2nd century AD and serves as a concert venue.

SICILY AND SARDINIA

SICILY (SICILIA)

Sicily is in many ways a country to itself, seemingly not part of Italy or Europe at all, and deserves a separate holiday to do it justice. However, for anyone with a few days to spare for a first glimpse, we suggest some highlights: the capital Palermo, the ancient Greek settlements and the coastal resort of Taormina.

Palermo

The bustling capital, **Palermo** ㊾, deserves the necessary effort to get into its colourful past. Cleverly integrating designs of Arab and Byzantine predecessors, the Norman palaces and churches join the crumbling grandeur of Spanish Baroque facades in momentary triumph over the chaos of the modern port city. It is not always an easy city to love, but few leave unimpressed. The intersection of Via Vittorio Emanuele and Via Maqueda is the town's historic centre – **Quattro Canti** (Four Corners) – within a characteristic setting of two great Baroque churches (San Giuseppe dei Teatini and Santa Caterina), the monumental 16th-century **Pretoria Fountain** by a

Florentine sculptor, and the piazza of the same name. The delightful Piazza Bellini includes the 12th-century church of **San Cataldo** with its three little red domes and Arabic inscriptions. It was used briefly in the 18th century as a post office, and has been restored to its bare Moorish beauty. Beside it, the restored Norman Gothic **La Martorana** (9.45am–1pm and 3.30–5.30pm, Sun 9–10.30am and 11.45am–1pm), partly remodelled with a Baroque facade and porch, has a fine campanile with four storeys of slim mullioned windows. Inside the porch, mint 12th-century **mosaics** show, to the right, Jesus crowning Sicily's Norman king, Roger I, and to the left, his admiral, Georges of Antioch, at the feet of the Madonna. In the nave are glittering mosaics of Christ Pantocrator (Omnipotent Lord) with accompanying angels.

West along Via Vittorio Emanuele, the **Palace of the Normans** (Palazzo dei Normanni; also known as Palazzo Reale; www.federico secondo.org; Mon–Sat 8.15am–5.40pm, Sun 8.15am–1pm) was originally built by the Saracens as a 9th-century fortress. It was later turned into a royal residence and an appropriate setting for the later brilliance and luxury of Emperor Frederick II's Sicilian court. Although it houses Sicily's regional government, tour buses line up for the jewel of the palace (and Palermo), one of Norman architecture's greatest achievements in Italy, the 12th-century **Palatine Chapel** (Cappella Palatina; same hours as the palace). The interior has a magnificent painted wooden ceiling with Arabic honeycomb

Palermo's busy port

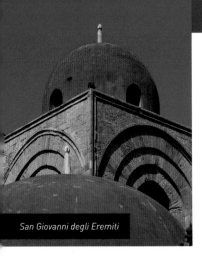

San Giovanni degli Eremiti

motifs and stalactite penden-tives. The **Byzantine mosaics** of the dome and apse depict Christ Pantocrator with the Evangelists, and Jesus bless-ing Peter and Paul; together with those of Ravenna, they are Italy's finest. The designs were a collaborative effort of Syrian Muslim craftsmen with Byzantine Christians.

The pink-domed church of **San Giovanni degli Eremiti** (Via dei Benedettini; Mon–Sat 9am–6.30pm, Sun 9am–1.30pm) is an intriguing example of 12th-century Arab-Norman design. Its exotic character is enhanced by the twin-columned 13th-century **cloister**, which is overgrown with tropical plants, orange, lemon and palm trees.

Housed in a 16th-century monastery, the wonderfully restored **Archaeological Museum** (Via Bara all'Olivella 24; www.regione. sicilia.it/bbccaa/salinas/index.html; Tue–Fri 9.30am–1.30pm and 2.30–5.30pm, Sat–Sun 9.30am–1.30pm) displays superb statues and sculpted friezes from Sicily's various archaeological sites, high-lighted by those from the Greek temples of Selinunte (600–500 BC), on Sicily's southern coast.

Offset the historical with the theatrical, and make a visit to Palermo's daily **Vucciria Market** (entrance near Via Roma and Corso Vittorio Emanuele), or better still the **Ballarò Market**, a raucous sprawling and exotic market with the spicy scents and sounds that transport you back to Moorish times. This is now the largest and liveliest market, overtaking the Vucciria, which has been reduced in size by Mafia-controlled modern development. Sicily's major port city offers fresh seafood in a remarkable variety of shapes and sizes, and no-frills trattorias within or near the market promise an excellent, inexpensive lunch.

Monreale

The hilltop suburb of **Monreale** 50 8km (5 miles) southwest of Palermo has Sicily's finest 12th-century **Cathedral** (www.cattedral emonreale.it; daily 8.30am–12.30pm and 2.30–5pm; chapel and terraces closed noon–3.30pm), as well as one of the best medieval mosaic cycles in Europe. Go to the back of the church to see its wonderful russet and brown stone chancel of interlacing arches, Gothic rose windows and Arab windows with pointed arches. The cathedral and the Arab-Norman Palermo were both declared Unesco World Heritage Sites in 2015.

In the grandiose interior, the luminous 12th- and 13th-century **mosaics** of the nave and apse depict the entire cycle of the Old Testament, complete with a 20m (66ft) Christ Pantocrator with saints, while aisle mosaics narrate miracles of the New Testament. The warm-hued human figures are thought to be the work of Venetian mosaicists.

The cathedral's lovely **cloisters** offer a moment of spiritual meditation along the arcades of delicate carved twin chevron-fluted columns and an almost sensual pleasure among the exotic flowers and trees and Arab fountain of its garden. It is understandably a favourite spot for wedding photos. It is also possible to climb the **tower** giving access to the roof.

Agrigento

Although **Agrigento** 51 is known as the birthplace of the Nobel Prize-winning dramatist Luigi Pirandello (1867–1936), it is the **Valley of the Temples** (Valle dei Templi; www.valleyofthetemples.com; daily 8.30am–7pm) that is its showpiece attraction. These magnificent temples date back to the 5th century BC. The **Temple of Juno**, with

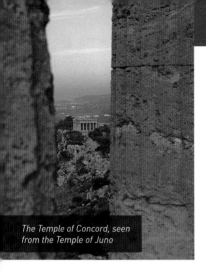

The Temple of Concord, seen from the Temple of Juno

a sacrificial altar, stands in majestic isolation high on a ledge at the eastern end of the Via Sacra. But it is the **Temple of Concord** that is the best-preserved Doric temple in Sicily (if not the world), thanks to its subsequent use as a church in the 6th century AD. The idyllic setting amid acacia and almond trees on a precipice overlooking the Mediterranean is enough to encourage you to worship a whole pantheon of Greek gods. Nearby is the oldest of the shrines, the **Temple of Hercules**, constructed in 500 BC, whose eight 10m (33ft) columns have been re-erected to give some idea of its original grandeur. In the western zone the Temple of Jove was considered the Eighth Wonder of the World, although it was never finished.

North of Temple Valley, next to the 13th-century Norman church of San Nicola, the small but important **Archaeological Museum** (Mon and Sun 9am–1.30pm, Tue–Sat 9am–7.30pm) has a fine marble statue of Ephebus (5th century BC); a reconstructed telamon, a 7.5m (25ft) sculpted male figure used to hold up a temple roof's entablature; and some fine Greek black and red Attic vases.

Taormina

Taormina ㊿. Sicily's most attractive resort town, already very popular in antiquity as a holiday spot for the Greek bourgeoisie from Syracuse, commands a splendid ridge-top view of the Mediterranean from its hillside villas and hotels. It is a port of call for countless cruise lines, but the international crowds can be avoided by those lucky enough to be spending the night – a *funivia* (cable car) connects the hilltop town with Mazzarò beach below.

No Sicilian *passeggiata* is more celebrated than a promenade on the elegant pedestrian shopping street of **Corso Umberto** and out along the **Via Roma**, or through the subtropical vegetation of the terraced **Public Gardens**. With picture-postcard panoramas south along the coast and to the volcano of Mount Etna to the west, the 3rd-century BC **Greek Theatre** (www.teatrogrecotaormina.com; daily 9am–7pm in summer, until 4pm in winter) is the only required site in town. It provides an evocative setting for summer festivals.

Excursions further up the mountain take you to two medieval fortresses, on foot to **Castello di Taormina** and, by bus, car (or foot) along a winding road, to **Castelmola** for grand views, although the summit of Etna is almost always swathed in clouds.

Syracuse (Siracusa)

Syracuse (Siracusa) ㉝. This east coast Corinthian settlement, founded in 734 BC, was the most powerful of Magna Graecia's overseas colonies and, under Dionysius (405–367 BC), a direct rival to Athens. In its heyday, its population was nearly treble the size of today's 118,000. It was here in the 3rd century BC that the famous mathematician Archimedes is said to have proven his water displacement theory in the bath, and then run naked into the street crying *'Eureka!'* (I've found it!). Today, the capital of Syracuse province is a cultured town of elegance and grace.

Syracuse's original settlement was the port island of Ortigia, joined by causeway to the mainland. Two pillars surviving from the Greek **Temple of Apollo** stand like a gateway, and the Spanish era has given it attractive 17th-century Baroque houses with iron balconies supported by floral carvings.

The graceful crescent-shaped **Piazza del Duomo**, surrounded by 17th- and 18th-century palazzi and the monumental facade of the cathedral (daily 8am–7pm), is the perfect place for breakfast. The church is an elaboration of the Greeks' Temple of Athena (5th century BC), its columns incorporated into the outside walls.

After many years of decay, the city – a Unesco World Heritage Site – has benefitted hugely from restoration work and Ortigia is looking lovelier than ever.

Famous Greek Links

Syracuse's principal excavated site, **Parco Archeologico della Neapolis** (daily 9am–2 hours before sunset, earlier during drama festival), is located on the northwest corner of the modern city. Rebuilt by the Romans to hold 15,000 spectators (one of the largest of the ancient world), the **Greek Theatre** (Teatro Greco) dates back to the 5th century BC when Aeschylus himself arrived to supervise productions of his tragedies. A classical drama festival is held here in May and June. The nearby **Paradise Quarry** (Latomia del Paradiso) provided the city's building materials and is now a pleasant garden of palm, oleander and orange trees. Its popular attraction is the cave that was dubbed **Orecchio di Dionisio** (Dionysius' Ear) by the painter Caravaggio in 1608 because of its acoustics.

Syracuse's history merits the world-class **Museo Archeologico Paolo Orsi** (www.regione.sicilia.it/beniculturali/museopaoloorsi; Tue–Sat 9am–6pm, Sun 9am–1pm), a crash course in understanding the Greek and other ancient cultures of the island.

Mount Etna

Mount Etna 🈴, Europe's tallest volcano is still very active as you will see from the tell-tale yellow sulphur stains of mini-eruptions as you approach the crater, where the lava beneath your feet is still warm. The summit currently stands at 3,350m (10,990ft) above sea level, but varies according to eruptions' destruction or lava deposits.

Etna continues to be highly volatile. The last decade or so has seen sporadic intense eruption and Etna started spewing ash columns and lava again in the summer of 2016. The craters are often

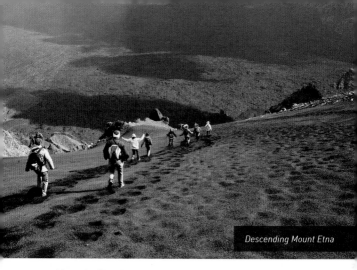

Descending Mount Etna

out of bounds. The simplest way of seeing the crater is the cable car from Rifugio Sapienza (www.funiviaetna.com), which includes an optional guided drive and walk to the summit. The energetic can go all the way up from the Rifugio Sapienza on foot. It takes around four hours – faster of course coming down. The summit can also be approached by the northern route via Linguaglossa. The climb on foot is a 6–7 hour round trip. From May to October, four-wheel-drive minibuses with guide will take you up to a height of 2800m (9186ft). For information and guides go to www.guidetnanord.com.

SARDINIA (SARDEGNA)

The Mediterranean's second-largest island (after Sicily) is well worth a holiday all to itself. Those curious to get a feel for its unique atmosphere should consider staying at small seaside resorts, combining meandering drives along Sardinia's coastline with excursions into the rugged hinterland. Prehistoric man dotted the island with mysterious cone-shaped *nuraghi* houses and watchtowers before it was colonised by Cretans, Phoenicians, Carthaginians and Romans.

Later, Sardinia became part of the commercial empires of Pisa, Genoa and Spain, and was annexed in 1718 by the dukes of Savoy. The Costa Smeralda is popular with the European yachting set and celebrities, and in August hotels are booked up months in advance.

Cagliari

The island's capital and main port is a largely modern city, but with a Spanish flavour to its older quarters up on the

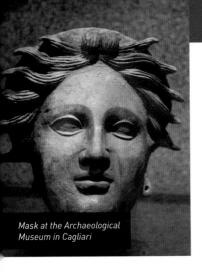

Mask at the Archaeological Museum in Cagliari

hill. The city's **Archaeological Museum** (Tue–Sun 9am–7.30pm) has some important bronze statues of warriors and priests found in prehistoric tombs and artefacts from the Nuraghic culture. The much-renovated cathedral has two superbly carved 12th-century pulpits, commissioned for the cathedral in Pisa. Before heading for the open road, try the excellent local cuisine, including Spanish-style fish stews and Genoese pasta dishes.

The **Cagliari to Muravera** road, which winds across the plunging ravines of the Sarrabus Mountains to the coast, is one of the island's most spectacular drives. Continue then up the coast to Lanusei and head inland across the rugged **Gennargentu Mountains**, covered with dense forests of cork oak and chestnut trees. Further to the north, just off the Nuoro–Dorgali road, is the secluded site of **Serra Orrios** ⑤, a well-preserved prehistoric village (signposted *Villaggio Nuragico*). A short walk along a marked path through the fields takes you to a group of dry-stone houses with two temples and circular ramparts in a lovely setting of eucalyptus and olive trees.

Archaeologists have located some 7,000 of these *nuraghi* structures around the island, believed to be parts of fortified citadels.

Costa Smeralda

The glittering **Costa Smeralda** on the northeast tip of the island is one of Italy's smartest resort areas, with beautiful beaches, five-star hotels, sports complexes and exclusive marinas for yachts and motor launches. It stretches around bays and rocky inlets from Olbia in the east to the promontory of La Maddalena. **Porto Cervo** is the coast's fashionable centre, but **Baia Sardinia** competes, with its craggy coastline. The little resort island and fishing village of **La Maddalena**, just a 15-minute ferry-ride from Palau, is the principal island of an archipelago of 14, most of them little more than piles of rocks.

Linked to La Maddalena by a causeway, the isle of **Caprera** was the last home of Giuseppe Garibaldi (see page 32), military leader of the Risorgimento movement for Italian unity. The house where he died in 1882 (his tomb is nearby) is now a museum.

The north coast road makes an enjoyable excursion along the dunes and pine groves lining the Gulf of Asinara. The fortress-town of **Castelsardo** stands high on a spectacular promontory overlooking the gulf. Inside its 16th-century cathedral, you can hear the sea crashing on the rocks directly below the foundations.

Alghero

Alghero 56, now a popular seaside resort on the northwest coast, has a pleasant Catalan flavour to its older quarters around the cathedral. Take a sunset stroll along the 16th-century Spanish ramparts.

There is good fishing to be had in the nearby bay of Porto Conte On the bay's southwestern promontory is the fascinating **Grotta di Nettuno** (Neptune's Grotto; daily May–Oct 9am–7pm, off-season until 4pm). Tours of these caverns, with their dramatic stalactites and stalagmites, are organised by boat from Alghero or on foot directly at the site, down a steep stairway in the cliffs.

Red Valentino store on Milan's Corso Venezia

WHAT TO DO

While you are wandering around the country's churches, *palazzi*, ruins and museums, you may wonder about the everyday life of the average Italian. The concept of *la dolce vita* easily outlived its introduction in the early 1960s and there is still a propensity for the sweet life. The Italian love of sport is contagious, the elegant shops are all too seductive, and the time-honoured theatricality extends from grand opera to colourful carnivals and religious processions.

SPORTS

Italian **football** attracts a huge following and in the major cities, the teams are studded with top stars: in Turin (Juventus and Torino), Milan (AC and Inter), Rome (AS Roma and Lazio), and Naples (Napoli). For millions, Sundays are less sacred for morning Mass than afternoon football matches. On a day when Italy is involved in a major international football match, streets all over the country are deserted.

Cycling races are hugely popular, especially the *Giro d'Italia* in May. Street and mountain bikes can be hired in most towns and resorts, and an increasing number of hotels have bikes for guests' use. Tuscany and Umbria are ideal for mountain biking and many tour operators offer guided or independent tours. **Motor racing** fans can see the Italian Grand Prix at Monza, near Milan, or at Imola (the San Marino Grand Prix), near Bologna.

On the beaches of the Adriatic coast, Italian Riviera, Sardinia and Sicily, **swimming** is a pleasure that requires a few words of warning. Conditions of water pollution vary from year to year, but avoid a dip in the immediate vicinity of major industrialised port cities: Genoa, Naples and Palermo. Look out for red flags warning about dangerous undercurrents, and check to see that beaches are patrolled by lifeguards. At most seaside resorts expect to pay for umbrellas, deck chairs and the use of changing cabins.

For water sports at the resorts, you can often rent equipment on the spot for **snorkelling** and **windsurfing** (particularly good on the lakes). **Scuba diving** is also popular, particularly off the islands and coasts of southern Italy. Some lake resorts also offer **water-skiing**.

Sailing is a popular sport around Sardinia and Sicily, and also on Tuscany's Argentario peninsula. **Canoeing**, **canyoning** and **rafting** are popular in the mountain areas of the north. Offshore **fishing** is popular all along the coasts; or freshwater fishing in the inland lakes and rivers, you will need a permit from the local municipality.

Hiking is the simplest, most exhilarating way of seeing the countryside, whether in the Dolomites or the Alps, around the lakes or trekking through the rolling hills of Tuscany or Umbria. Italy now has 25 national parks and more in the pipeline. The Gran Paradiso in Valle d'Aosta and Gran Sasso in Abruzzo offer some of the most spectacular mountain trekking. You can hire horses for **riding** throughout Italy – Tuscany and Umbria provide especially scenic terrain.

Golf enthusiasts can often play on local private courses, usually by producing proof of their home club membership. Venice has an 18-hole course at the Lido's Alberoni. On the Riviera, try Rapallo, San Remo or Garlenda (near Alassio). **Tennis** is less widespread than in other major

Windsurfing near Cagliari in Sardinia

European countries, but it is growing in popularity. Your hotel can help you find a hard or a clay court.

Skiing and snowboarding facilities are first-class in numerous resorts in the Alps and Dolomites, and world championships take place at Cortina d'Ampezzo and Val Gardena. The Via Lattea, the 'Milky Way' west of Turin, offers 400km (250 miles) of skiable pistes.

Keen road cyclists

ENTERTAINMENT

When Italians moved the melodrama of their lives indoors, they called it **opera**. Most famous of the high temples of this art is Milan's La Scala (www.teatroallascala.org), showcasing the works of Verdi, Bellini, Rossini, Puccini, and other Italian composers. The great stars and divas need a triumph here for true consecration. Its season is from December to mid-May. For good tickets you should plan well in advance (see page 149), but your hotel may be able to help with seats made available by last-minute cancellations.

The other great opera houses are La Fenice (www.teatrolafenice. it) in Venice, Florence's Teatro Comunale (www.operadifirenze.it), and the great Teatro di San Carlo (www.teatrosancarlo.it) of Naples. But Bologna, Parma, Perugia, Rome, and Palermo also have fine regional houses, which host performances from December or January until late spring or early summer.

In the summer, the unparalleled venue for **open-air opera** is Verona's ancient Roman Arena, a unique location for performances of *Aida* and other large-scale productions. In July and August, Rome's Baths of Caracalla provide a majestic setting for open-air performances. August's Puccini Festival is held at Torre del Lago in Tuscany, close to the villa where the composer lived. On the Adriatic, Pesaro honours its native son, Rossini, from mid-August to late September.

Orchestral **concerts** of symphonic and chamber music are also held in the opera houses, sometimes concurrently with the opera season. It is often easier to get tickets for these. Performances are also held in Milan's Conservatorio (www.consmilano.it) and Rome's Accademia Filarmonica Romana (www.filarmonicaromana.org), or the Accademia Nazionale di Santa Cecilia (www.santacecilia.it). Florence, Spoleto, Perugia, Ravenna, Rimini, Ravello and Stresa all hold important music festivals. Tuscany, San Gimignano and Lucca stage open-air concerts, while Amalfi's are given in the cathedral cloisters. Lovers of Neapolitan **folk music** can enjoy a whole

Inside Milan's La Scala opera house

week of it in September at the Piedigrotta festival.

A great open-air festival of **jazz**, **pop** and **rock music**, the Estate Romana (Roman Summer), is held in the parks and gardens of Rome. In the north of the city, near the sleek MAXXI Museum of Contemporary Art, is the Auditorium Parco della Musica

Films

One of the most enjoyable ways to polish your Italian is at the cinema, where most foreign films are dubbed. International film festivals are held in several cities, the most important in Venice and Taormina.

(www.auditorium.com), a vast, spectacular complex of three concert halls and outdoor auditorium. Italy's most important jazz festival is held in Perugia in July, and there is another in Alassio in September. For information about all Italy's music festivals (as well as theatre and film), see www.italiafestival.it.

For those seeking discos and **nightclubs**, Milan is the Italian hotspot, followed by Rome. Other large cities, especially university ones, have plenty of nightlife too. Outside towns, most of the action takes place in mid-summer in the open-air clubs of the coastal resorts. Cities offer scores of stylish **bars** where the pre-prandial aperitivo, from around 6–9pm has become a way of life. Cocktails come with a whole range or snacks and canapés, or often a whole buffet is included in the price of the drink.

Naturally enough, a visit to the **theatre** requires a good knowledge of Italian. You will find the best productions in Rome and Milan, the latter famous for Giorgio Strehler's Piccolo Teatro, followed by those in Florence and Venice.

SHOPPING

The Italian design sense has turned Italy into an emporium of style and elegance. The luxury goods of Milan, Venice, Rome and

Florence are among the finest in the world – jewellery, clothes, accessories, especially shoes, but also luggage and household goods and items of interior design. But don't expect to come away with many bargains.

There is an abundance of **gourmet delicacies**, which make the perfect gift. Consider the cheeses, salamis, Parma ham, Milanese sweet *panettone* brioche, Ligurian olive oil, Siena's cakes and famous *panforte*, a spicy fruit-and-nut concoction, local wines and liqueurs.

Many cities continue to be renowned for their **traditional crafts**: Naples' costumed hand-crafted figures for its nativity sets, Sorrento's *intarsia* (inlaid wood), Volterra's alabaster, Gubbio's ceramics, Florence's leather goods, Venice's glassware. For the rest, the widest range of Made-in-Italy products will be found in the large cities.

For quality goods, Italians prefer shopping in small boutiques. Family businesses often guarantee generations of craftsmanship and personalised service. If you want friendly treatment in the more expensive stores, you are ahead of the game when dressed appropriately. Even the most helpful sales assistant in a top-end boutique may be a little aloof towards customers whose image doesn't match what they are buying. Haggling, apart from in the markets, is a thing of the past. You can get an occasional small *sconto* (discount) when buying in volume or paying in cash; except among antiques, art and second-hand dealers, where negotiation is part of the business, you may get a cool response if you question the marked price.

Weekly **markets** are colourful open-air affairs with stalls selling flowers, food, fashions, household goods, crafts and much more besides. Antique markets, held in the larger cities, are a source of local handicrafts, although genuine bargains are rare.

Residents outside the EU are entitled to a VAT (IVA) rebate on goods over €155.

SHOPPING IN ROME

The capital's smartest and most expensive boutiques are conveniently concentrated in a compact pedestrian area around Via Condotti at the foot of the Spanish Steps. Here you will find the finest leather goods and of-the-moment fashions from all the predictable high-priests of style (Valentino, Armani, Prada, Gucci, Missoni).

For sheer exclusivity in **jewellery**, there is nothing like the imposing marble facade of Bulgari (Via Condotti), the ultimate monument to Roman luxury.

Two streets in Rome dominate the market in **art** and **antiques**. They are Via Margutta and Via del Babuino and other off-shoots of the Piazza di Spagna (as well as Via Giulia and Via Coronari).

On the outskirts of the chic shopping district around Piazza di Spagna, you will find mass-produced sweaters, jeans, and other casual wear. Moderately priced leather goods can be found on the Via Tritone, Via Nazionale and Via del Corso. For second-hand **bric-a-brac**,

An atmospheric shopping arcade in Bellagio on Lake Como

try the shops around the Campo de'Fiori and Piazza Navona. The Sunday morning flea market at Porta Portese in Trastevere is as much fun for the people-watching as for the occasional bargains.

SHOPPING IN FLORENCE

If it has ceded to Milan its place as Italy's fashion capital, Florence is still a centre of exquisite, if classic, elegance. Some of the best Italian designers started out in the city, and their flagship stores still line the main shopping streets. The thoroughfares for the smarter **fashion boutiques**, for men and women, are Via de' Tornabuoni, Via della Vigna Nuova, and Piazza della Repubblica and Via de' Calzaiuoli.

Florence is renowned for high-quality **leather goods.** The country's, indeed Europe's, finest craftsmen once clustered in small leather workshops around San Lorenzo and Santa Croce, but goods now come mostly from factories in the periphery. The leather school tucked away behind the church of Santa Croce's sacristy is still going strong, allowing you a glimpse at the traditional way of making leather goods such as handbags, wallets, gloves, belts and desk accessories. For cheaper leather goods try the stalls of San Lorenzo market.

The Ponte Vecchio is a picturesque place to shop for pricey but gorgeous gold and silver **jewellery**, designed with centuries of expertise. Less exclusive jewellery stores abound around town.

Intarsia – **inlaid wood** or **semi-precious stones** – is a venerated craft here, perfected in the 16th century. Furniture made in this way is likely to be expensive, but framed pictures of Tuscan landscapes or views of Florence are more moderately priced and, as souvenirs go, tastefully done. The town also specialises in bookbinding and beautiful stationery and paper products.

Antiques shops are centred mainly around Borgo Ognissanti, Via della Vigna Nuova, Via delle Fosse, Borgo San Jacopo and Via Maggio. Even if you cannot afford the often-prohibitive prices, they are worth visiting as veritable little museums of Renaissance and Baroque sculpture and furniture. If the creative geniuses are

long dead, master crafts-
men continue the tradition
of superb reproductions at
negotiable prices.

Just 27 km (17 miles)
from Florence, **The Mall** (Via
Europa, 8, Leccio Reggello;
tel: 055-865 7775; www.the
mall.it) is one of Europe's
most exclusive designer
shopping outlets. Labels such
as Gucci, Valentino, Alexander
McQueen and Bottega Veneta
can be had at up to 50 percent reduction on the recommended retail price.

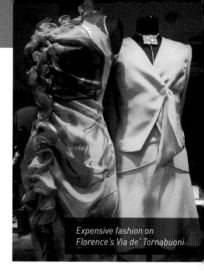

*Expensive fashion on
Florence's Via de' Tornabuoni*

SHOPPING IN VENICE

One of the great adventures of shopping in Venice is separating the
treasure-house from the tourist trap, distinguishing priceless gems
from pricey junk. By and large, the better, more expensive shops
are around Piazza San Marco. The shopping street of Mercerie has
quality boutiques growing progressively more moderate in price
as they approach the Rialto from Piazza San Marco; as does the
area west of Piazza San Marco. For cheaper purchases, head for
the Strada Nuova leading behind the Ca' d'Oro towards the station.

Bargains, or at least more authentic and tasteful products, are to
be found far from the main tourist centres, in artisans' workshops
on the Giudecca, in the Dorsoduro behind the Zattere – to be hunted
down or stumbled upon by chance.

Historical institutions that stand out among the **jewellery** and
glass shops can be found in Piazza San Marco. The famous Venetian
glassware poses a problem of quality and price. Some of it is

Venetian Carnival masks

depressingly ugly, but there is also an admirable renewal in both classic and modern design. Just hunt carefully. Necklaces of crystal or coloured beads are popular for children, the antique glass beads collectables for adults. Prices in the Murano island factories are rarely better than 'downtown', but you do get a free demonstration and transport thrown in. When choosing gifts, beware of non-authentic 'Murano-style' glass and counterfeit imports from Asia. If you want the goods to be shipped, always ask for handling and insurance rates before you buy, as they can frequently double the price.

Visit Burano to see intricate **laceware** being made in the time-honoured manner in the island's small museum. The real thing is exquisite but exorbitantly priced, with many lesser-quality, machine-made pieces from the Far East being passed off as locally handmade. Modern reproductions and interpretations of traditional patterns can be bought around Piazza San Marco.

The venerable craft of handmade **paper goods**, **stationery** and **bookbinding** is easy to find. You can give your fancy-dress outfits a touch of Venetian class with the finely crafted papier-mâché **masks** made by workshops for Venice's Carnival, but avoid the cheap imported counterfeits.

The range of **fashion boutiques** around San Marco is small but select, with an emphasis on top-class shoes and other leather goods made in the Brenta area outside Venice.

SHOPPING IN MILAN

Since the 1980s Milan has been a world centre for fashion design, drawing huge numbers of visitors – many celebrities among them – to the fashion fairs and flagship stores of top designers. Names such as Armani, Prada, Versace, Dolce e Gabbana, Gianfranco Ferre and Moschino all began their careers in Milan. The designer names are conveniently concentrated in a small, attractive area known as the Quadrilatero d'Oro (Golden Quadrangle), defined by Via Monte Napoleone, Via Manzoni, Via della Spiga and Via Sant'Andrea. The area around Corso Vercelli and Corso Magenta has excellent shopping at more reasonable prices, as does the area around the Piazza Duomo and Corso Vittorio Emanuele II. Bargain-hunters looking for jeans, shoes and cheaper fashions should head for the popular stores along Via Torino and Via Manzoni, or head for the factory outlets around town. You will find **art galleries** and **antiques shops** in the Brera neighbourhood and the side streets of Via Montenapolone.

Keeping up appearances in Milan's Quadrilatero d'Oro

FESTIVALS

The Italians' attachment to regional customs and religious festivals has dwindled in the 20th century, but many continue for the tourist trade. Here is a far from exhaustive list of some of the main processions and festivities around the country.

January Piana degli Albanesi (near Palermo): a colourful Byzantine ritual for Epiphany.

February or **early March** Venice: historical Carnival, masked balls and processions in magnificent costumes. Viareggio: more contemporary Carnival with parade of floats. Agrigento: Almond Blossom Festival in Sicily.

April Rome: Pope's Easter Sunday blessing.

May Assisi: Calendimaggio Christian and pagan festival. Naples: Miracle of San Gennaro (liquefaction of the saint's blood, also on first Sunday in May, 19 September and 16 December). Camogli (Riviera): Fish Festival, communal fish-fry in giant pan. Gubbio: wooden candle race, crossbow competition. Orvieto: Pentecost feast of the Palombella (Holy Ghost). Florence: Maggio Musicale (May–June), musical performances in various venues throughout the city.

June Pisa: San Ranieri, jousting and torchlit regatta on Arno river. Florence: medieval football game in costume. Spoleto: Festival dei Due Mondi (June–July), international theatre, prose, music and dance performances by leading artists from Europe and the Americas.

July Siena: first Palio (2 July, see page 102). Sardinia: S'Ardia – more dangerous than Il Palio (6–7 July). Palermo: festival of patron Santa Rosalia. Venice: Redentore regatta. Rimini: Festival of the Sea. Rome: Noantri street festival in Trastevere. Perugia and other Umbrian cities: Umbria Jazz, one of the most important jazz festivals in Europe.

August Siena: Second Palio (16 August). Venice: Venice International Film Festival held at the Lido.

September Naples: Piedigrotta, Neapolitan music and cuisine and the 19 September feast day of San Gennaro. Venice: historical Regatta.

October Assisi: Feast of St Francis. Perugia: Franciscan Mysteries.

December Rome: Christmas food and toy market on Piazza Navona. Assisi and Naples: nativity scenes in streets.

EATING OUT

The 'eating well' approach to life so treasured by the Italians is found in abundance at every meal. From an early morning coffee to an after-dinner *grappa*, eating and drinking here is always a memorable experience, perhaps even an art form.

WHERE TO EAT

For **breakfast** *(prima colazione)*, head for a *caffè* on the piazza, for an *espresso* or *cappuccino* with foaming hot milk (occasionally sprinkled with powdered chocolate), and a *cornetto* (jam- or custard-filled croissant). Breakfast is often included in your hotel rate, but the more expensive the hotel, the less likely this is.

Ideal for those adopting a healthy 'sightseer's diet' of one main meal a day, preferably in the evening, with just a snack for **lunch**, informal bars known as *tavola calda* serve sandwiches and hot or cold dishes at the counter, with limited table space. More and more bars are offering simple, one-course, inexpensive lunches of salads or pastas. If you want to picnic in the park or out in the country, get your sandwiches made up for you at the *pizzicheria* delicatessen. Ask for a *panino ripieno* (a 'stuffed roll'), choosing from the sliced meats and cheeses on display.

For **dinner**, it is useful to know that the more pricey

Venetian alfresco dining

restaurants *(ristoranti)*, are often the worst value. In the more informal family-run *osteria*, trattoria (and pizzeria, which serves much more than just pizza), the relaxed and delightful ambience is very enjoyable, and the food often has more character. A *rosticceria*, originally a shop specialising in grilled dishes, provides tables where guests can eat on the premises.

No matter where you are in Italy, restaurants must display the menu with prices in the window or just inside the door. By law all restaurants must also issue a receipt *(ricevuta)* indicating the name, address and IVA (VAT/sales tax) number of the premises. It is the custom to round up the bill with an additional 5–10 percent tip in addition to the service charge *(servizio incluso)*, which the waiter often does not receive.

If you want a quick sandwich, pastry, or just an espresso, soft drink, beer or *aperitivo*, head for a *caffè* or bar. In these it will cost more to sit at a table than to stand at the counter. A *gelateria* specialises in rich, creamy Italian ice cream.

Ristorante Ditirambo in Rome

WHAT TO EAT

The classic cuisine of Tuscany and Bologna and the pizza and pasta dishes of the south are available everywhere, but try regional specialities as you travel around the country. The very essence of Italian cooking is its simplicity: fresh fish sim-

> **By any other name**
>
> Cooking is essentially regional, and terminology for food and dishes may vary. There are, for example, at least half a dozen names for octopus or squid.

ply grilled; seafood served at room temperature as an hors d'œuvre (*antipasto*); thick, charcoal-grilled Florentine steak; seasonal vegetables without elaborate disguise, at most dressed with lemon, olive oil and pepper. Times are changing, but the following rule of thumb still applies: if it's not in season, it's not on the menu.

Many a trattoria sets out a table with an artistic display of platters of *antipasti*, where you are free to make up your own assortment (*antipasto misto*). Both attractive and tasty are the *peperoni* – red, yellow and green peppers grilled, skinned and drizzled with olive oil, garlic and a little lemon juice. Mushrooms (*funghi*), baby squash (*zucchini*), aubergine (*melanzane*), artichokes (*carciofi*) and sliced fennel (*finocchio*) are also served at room temperature. One of the most refreshing hors d'œuvres is the *insalata alla caprese*, slices of fresh mozzarella and tomato with fresh basil, drizzled with olive oil.

Try tuna fish (*tonno*) with white beans and onions (*fagioli e cipolle*) and olive oil. Mixed seafood hors d'œuvres (*antipasto di mare*) may include scampi, prawns (*gamberi*), mussels (*cozze*) sardines (*sarde*), squid (*calamari*) and octopus (*polpo* or *polpetti*).

Ham from Parma or San Daniele is served paper thin with melon (*prosciutto con melone*) or, even better, fresh figs (*con fichi*). Most salami is tasty, though commercially produced, but look in particular for the local products of Florence, Genoa, Naples and Bologna.

Soups are the thick mixed vegetable (*minestrone*) or a simple clear soup (*brodo*). *Brodo* may have an egg beaten into it (*stracciatella*).

Pasta

Italian restaurants traditionally serve **pasta** as an introductory course, *il primo*, not as the main dish. It is said that there are almost as many different shapes of Italian pasta as there are days of the year – well over 300. Each sauce – whether it be tomato, cheese, cream, meat or fish – calls for its own kind of pasta. Many restaurants offer one or two home-made pastas daily; the commercially processed pasta can be no less delicious.

Spaghetti with pesto

Besides the classic spaghetti, the worldwide popularity of pasta has familiarised us with *tagliatelle* ribbon noodles (known in Rome as *fettucine*), baked lasagne with layers of pasta, meat sauce and béchamel, and stuffed *ravioli*. From there, you launch into *tortellini* (reputed to be modelled on Venus's navel), *linguine*, flat *pappardelle*, short *penne* and ribbed *rigatoni*.

The **sauces** are no less abundant or savoury. The most famous is *bolognese*, known as *ragù*, made of minced beef, tomato purée and onions and never served with spaghetti but with *tagliatelle*. Other popular sauces range from the simple *aglio e olio* (garlic, olive oil and chilli peppers), *marinara* (tomato, onions, garlic and herbs), *funghi* (mushrooms), *matriciana* (bacon and tomato), Genoese *pesto* (fresh basil and garlic with olive oil, pine nuts and parmesan) and *vongole* (clams), to the succulent *lepre* (hare in red wine) and more unusual *al nero*, pasta blackened by squid ink.

For prince and peasant alike, Lombardy's Po Valley **rice** fields have made risotto a worthy rival to pasta, particularly in the north.

The original version is cooked slowly in white wine, beef marrow, butter and saffron, and served with Parmesan cheese. Variations are endless: try those with mushrooms, chicken or seafood and seasonal vegetables.

Main Courses

For the main **meat** dish beef (*manzo*), pork (*maiale*), lamb (*agnello*) and chicken (*pollo*) are most often served simply charcoal-grilled or roasted (*al forno*). Try *cotoletta alla Milanese*, egg and breadcrumbed veal cutlet from Milan, *scaloppine al limone* (veal fillets with lemon) or *vitello tonnato* (veal in tuna sauce). The popular *saltimbocca* (literally 'jump in the mouth') is a Roman veal-roll with ham, sage and Marsala wine, while *osso bucco* is stewed veal shin. Calf's liver (*fegato*) is served in a Marsala wine sauce, *alla milanese* in breadcrumbs, or *alla veneziana*, thinly sliced and fried with onions. In the south, meat is often cooked in a tomato and garlic sauce (*alla pizzaiola*).

The **fish** you see displayed on ice is prepared very simply: grilled, steamed or fried. For a main course, look for *spigola* (sea bass), *triglia* (red mullet), *pesce spada* (swordfish) and *coda di rospo* (monk or angler fish). Be careful when ordering the *fritto misto*. Although this 'mixed fry' usually means from the sea, it can also contain breaded chicken, calf's liver, veal and vegetables.

Aristocrats among the **vegetables** are truffles (*tartufi*) and big boletus mushrooms (*funghi porcini*), simply grilled. Try red peppers stewed with tomatoes (*peperonata*) or aubergine (*melanzane*) – sometimes stuffed with anchovies, olives and capers.

Fading traditions

A traditional Italian lunch (*pranzo*) is a true gastronomic event, to be shared and savoured with friends and family at leisure. This is still the case on Sunday but on weekdays an increasing number of Italians, especially in the cities, now grab lunch on the go and have dinner as their main meal.

Cheese

Of the cheeses, the famous parmesan (*parmigiano*) is sometimes eaten separately at the meal's end, not just grated over soup or pasta. Try the blue gorgonzola, *provolone*, creamy Piedmontese *fontina*, the pungent cow's milk *taleggio*, or ewe's milk pecorino. Ricotta can be sweetened with sugar and cinnamon as a dessert.

Desserts

First and foremost, **dessert** means *gelato*, the best ice cream in the world. Ice-cream parlours (*gelateria*) often serve better ice cream and more varieties than the average trattoria. Look for *gelateria* that make their own ice cream, piling their unusual creations high, like multi-coloured mountains of temptation. The coffee or fruit-flavoured shaved ice, *granita*, is always refreshing.

When well prepared, *Zuppa inglese* (English soup) should be a thick 'soup' of fruit, cream, cake and Marsala wine. You may prefer the creamy *tiramisù* (pick me up). *Zabaglione* is made of egg yolks, sugar and Marsala wine, and served warm.

Italy's **fruit** is always surprisingly sweet: grapes (*uva*), peaches (*pesche*), apricots (*albicocche*) and wonderful fresh figs (*fichi*), both black and green. On Italian menus at least, *Macedonia* is a fresh fruit salad. When berries are in season, don't miss them.

REGIONAL SPECIALITIES

Rome goes in for hearty meat dishes. Its *saltimbocca* veal rolls have gone around the world, but you mustn't wander too far from the Eternal City to get a real *stufatino* (beef stew) or *coda alla vaccinara* (braised oxtail with vegetables). Romans also claim the best roast kid (*capretto*) and spring lamb (*abbacchio*). In the Jewish Ghetto try the *carciofi* prepared *alla giudea* or *alla romana* – whole baby artichokes, crisply deep-fried.

Tuscany produces excellent roast meats; *cacciagione* (game) is popular in season. *Pollo alla cacciatore*, 'hunter's style' chicken, has a tomato sauce embellished with mushrooms, shallots, herbs and ham. The charcoal-grilled T-bone *bistecca alla fiorentina* is often big enough to cover a plate and usually serves two people well. Adventurous palates enjoy the *trippa alla fiorentina*, tripe with tomato, marjoram and parmesan cheese. On the coast, look out for the *cacciucco*, a spicy fish stew of the sea's bounty in a slightly spicy tomato broth. *Baccalà* is dried salted cod. Tuscans are known as 'bean eaters': try any variation of *fagioli*, white beans; they are a principal ingredient of *ribollita, a thick and* wintery soup.

Umbrian cuisine has great finesse. The roast suckling pig *(porchetta)* is especially fragrant with fennel and other herbs, and look for a succulent spit-roasted wild pigeon *(palombacce allo spiedo)*. Umbrians are proud of their *cacciotto* and *raviggiolo* ewe's cheese. In season, the truffle rules. The supreme pasta dish is served *ai tartufi neri* (with black truffles).

Milan has contributed its risotto, *cotoletta alla milanese* (breaded veal scallop), *osso buco* and sweet *panettone* brioche to the nation. But it's kept for itself the *casoeula* – pork and sausages stewed in cabbage and other vegetables. Milan is also famous for its *bollito*, a boiled beef dish with sausage, chicken, white beans, cabbage, potatoes and a tomato sauce. To fend off the autumn rains, the cornflour *polenta* served with so many savoury Lombard dishes becomes *polenta pasticciata*, a stout pie of mushrooms and white truffles in a béchamel sauce.

Fresh pizza

Spaghetti frutti di mare (seafood pasta)

The choicest herb in superb **Ligurian** pasta sauces is the basil of Genoa's pesto, best with the local *trenette* (large-size spaghetti). Rosemary is sprinkled on flat rounds of bread –*focaccia* – with olive oil. Wild aromatic greens are mixed with ricotta cheese in the ravioli-like *pansoti*, always served with a creamy walnut sauce. Liguria's fine olive oils rival those of Tuscany and Puglia. On trattoria menus, *misto di mare* is determined by the morning's catch from the fish-rich coastal waters.

Cooking in **Alto Adige** or South Tyrol is mainly Austrian-style. Home-cured ham, *Speck*, is generally cut in paper-thin slices. In the mountains, try *Knödelsuppe*, a chicken or beef broth with simple dumplings. Austria meets Italy with *Spinatspätzle*, gnocchi-like spinach noodles with bacon and cream. *Friuli-Venezia Giulia* also continues the cuisine of the Austro-Hungarian empire – goulash and barley soup. Here, the great ham is *San Daniele*.

In **Venice**, the Adriatic specialities include cod, 'tenderised' for the great *baccalà mantecato* (cream of dried cod), and *grancevole* – red Adriatic spider crab. The combination of liver and onions, *fegato alla veneziana*, knows few rivals. Pasta appears less frequently than risotto, as popular here as in Lombardy, particularly with scampi or mussels, as well as *risi e bisi*, rice and green peas. Beef carpaccio is sliced raw and as thin as Parma ham and served with an olive oil and mustard sauce. Delicious *cicchetti* are fresh, bite-size bar food (similar to Spanish tapas).

Bologna has an uncontested position of leadership in Italian gastronomy. Its specialities are the mainstays of the national cuisine: *tortellini* pasta stuffed with different meats or cheeses; *costolette alla bolognese* (breaded veal cutlets with ham and cheese); and *lasagne verde*, baked green pasta with beef *ragù* and béchamel sauce. The classic Bologna *mortadella* has little to do with the imitations found elsewhere. The star of neighbouring Parma is its *prosciutto* (air-cured ham) and parmesan cheese (labelled *parmigiano-reggiano*).

A classic dish of **Turin** is *vitello tonnato* – a delicious blend of cold roast veal and tuna fish served with a mayonnaise sauce, gherkins and capers. Not to be confused with the fondue from across the Swiss border, the *fonduta* of Piedmont is a hot dip of buttery *fontina* cheese, cream, pepper and white truffles that put this region on the culinary map. Its coffee houses, filled with confections and locally made chocolate products, are some of the nation's best. Most famous are the sublime *gianduiotti*, studded with hazelnuts.

In the South

In **Naples**, the tomato is king. It is used in the simplest pasta, for which *alla napoletana* just means 'with a tomato sauce'. The classic pizza *(margherita)* uses local mozzarella cheese made of buffalo milk, with tomato sauce and basil or oregano. A handy version is the *calzone*, pocket-size pizzas filled with ham and mozzarella and folded in a half-moon. The seafood is excellent. Have morning coffee with a crisp Neapolitan *sfogliatella* croissant filled with sweet ricotta cheese. The *cannoli*, the south's great dessert, is stuffed with ricotta.

In **Puglia** try the *agnello allo squero*, spit-roasted on a fire of twigs perfumed with thyme and fine herbs; or *cutturidde*, baked with onion, parsley, tomatoes and sprinkled with *pecorino* cheese. *Gnemeridde* are chitterlings of baby lamb roasted or stewed with ham, cheese and herbs. Also try any of the great fish stews. The region's unique *pasta orecchiette* (little ears), is usually served with a sauce based on *cima di rape* – slightly bitter turnip greens.

The coastal resorts of **Sardinia** cook up a pungent fish soup *(cassola e pisci)* and roast eel *(anguidda arrustia)*.

Inland, kid *(capretto)* and suckling pig *(porceddù)* are roasted on the spit, as is the island's greatest delicacy, wild boar *(cinghiale)*. There's a great variety of bread, the best being charcoal-baked *civriaxiu* and wafer-thin unleavened bread *casta da musica* (music papers). Try them with the local *pecorino*, ewe's cheese.

Sicily has a rich culinary heritage. The *melanzana* (aubergine) is prepared in myriad ways, best perhaps simply grilled or in the *alla norma* sauce, with fresh tomatoes and mozzarella cheese. The Arab legacy lives on in the abundance of citrus fruit and almonds that appear in the island's desserts. Sheep's milk ricotta cheese is a favourite ingredient in many delicious puddings, such as *cassata*.

WINES

Italian wines are undergoing a resurgence and there are ample opportunities for tastings, with wine routes and a rapidly growing number of enotecas (wine bars). Although the Italian wine spectrum includes far more than just **Chianti**, these are the most recognisable and are exported worldwide. The best Chianti Classico are produced in an historically designated area between Florence and Siena (see page 97) and distinguished by the *gallo nero* (black cockerel) label.

Slow food

The Slow Food Movement (www.slowfood.com), founded in Piedmont in 2006, tries to counter the spread of modern fast-food culture. The movement has been so popular that it now has over 100,000 members in five continents.

Of the other Tuscan wines, the most appreciated reds have traditionally been the refined Vino Nobile di Montepulciano and the powerful Brunello di Montalcino. But Super-Tuscans, a loose-knit family of brilliant but quirkily named *vini da tavola* that burgeoned in the 1980s, are now some of Tuscany's great stars. The most notable Tuscan white is the smooth dry Vernaccia di San Gimignano.

Umbria produces notable white wines, predominantly Orvieto, but also Grechetto and some outstanding reds such as Torgiano Rosso Riserva and Sagrantino of Montefalco.

North of Tuscany's Chianti region, popular wine producers are centred around Verona and Lake Garda in the **Veneto** region, notably the well-known Valpolicella, Bar-

Sample the local wine

dolino and Soave. The areas near Conegliano and Valdobbiadene produce the popular sparkling white Prosecco that makes a wonderful *aperitivo and is served in every bar*. Neighbouring **Friuli-Venezia Giulia** is best known for the dry and aromatic Tocai, now renamed Friulano, and the highly-prized and expensive dessert wine, Picolit.

Puglia has made huge improvements in its wines. Look out for Primitivo di Manduria, a heady red, the Locorotondo and Martina Franca whites and the dessert wine Aleatico. **Sicily**'s wines are also looking up. Good quality reds are produced from the local Nero d'Avola grape variety; also worth trying are the dry red Carasuolo di Vittoria province and the up-and-coming wines from the lava-enriched foothills of Etna.

Among aperitifs commonly drunk, bitters such as *Campari* and *Punt e Mes* are refreshing with soda and lemon or orange. For after-dinner drinks, try the aniseed-flavoured *sambucca* with a *mosca* (literally a fly) coffee-bean in it, or try Veneto's fiery *grappa*, distilled from grapes. An *amaro* (bitter) can be enjoyed pre- or post-meal.

TO HELP YOU ORDER

A table for one/two/three. **Un tavolo per una persona/ per due/per tre.**

I would like... **Vorrei...**

The bill please. **Il conto per favore.**

MENU READER

aglio garlic
agnello lamb
aragosta lobster
basilica basil
birra beer
bistecca beefsteak
burro butter
calamari squid
carciofi artichokes
cavallo horse
cinghiale wild boar
cipolle onions
coniglio rabbit
cozze mussels
fagioli beans
fagiolini green beans
finocchio fennel
formaggio cheese
frittata omelette
frutti di mare seafood
funghi mushrooms
gamberetti shrimps
gamberi prawns
gelato ice cream
insalata salad
lumache snails

maiale pork
manzo beef
melanzane aubergine
olio oil
olive olives
pane bread
panna cream
patate potatoes
peperoni peppers
pesce fish
piselli peas
pollo chicken
polpo/pólipo octopus
pomodori tomatoes
prosciutto ham
riso rice
salsiccie sausages
spinaci spinach
tonno tuna
uova eggs
verdure vegetables
vino wine
vitello veal
vongole clams
zucchini courgettes
zuppa soup

A–Z TRAVEL TIPS

A SUMMARY OF PRACTICAL INFORMATION

A

ACCOMMODATION (See also Camping, Youth Hostels)

Italy has a great variety of accommodation in all categories, from luxury villa hotels and palatial apartments to small family-run hotels, rustic retreats and B&Bs. You are unlikely to find many real bargains but standards are reasonably good and accommodation is strictly regulated.

Hotels Every hotel, called *hotel* or *albergo*, is classified in categories by stars from one (basic) to five (luxury). Hotels can be grand guesthouses, chic chalets, hip boutique hotels converted fortresses, Zen-like spa-hotels or ecohotels. Breakfast is usually included in the price. During high season, some resort hotels require guests to stay a minimum of three nights on half-board *(mezza pensione)*.

B&Bs Italy has seen a boom in B&Bs, both in cities and regions. The quality of accommodation is variable but places are generally clean, simple and welcoming. In the main cities, chic guesthouses have replaced the outdated *pensione*, a category that no longer officially exists. For full up-to-date listings visit www.bbitalia.it or www.caffelletto.it.

Do you have any vacancies? **Avete camere libere?**
I'd like a single/double room **Vorrei una camera singola/matromoniale**
...with bath/shower/private toilet **...con bagno/doccia/gabinetto privato**

Spiritual Retreats Italy abounds in religious retreats that have been transformed into leading luxury hotels, but you can also find monasteries run by religious organisations that provide rooms and meals for guests at reasonable rates. Visit www.monasterystays.com for convents and monasteries throughout the country.

Self-catering Apartments, villas, houses and other self-catering accommodation provide a cost-effective alternative to hotels, and can sometimes be rented for as little as a couple of nights. Villas are quite pricey but standards are high and many enjoy superb locations. For a variety of options see www.rentvillas.com, or www.luxuryretreats.com.

Agriturismo If you have a car, consider staying on a **farm**, in a cottage, a modernised farmhouse, or a 17th-century castle, and enjoy such activities as grape-harvesting, mushroom-gathering, fishing, horse riding or golf. For details contact Agriturist, the National Association for Rural Tourism at www.agriturist.it or www.agriturismoinitalia.com.

Mountain Huts The Italian Alpine Club (CAI) owns around 500 hundred *rifugi* or **mountain refuges** and detailed information can be found on their website (www.cai.it).

Tourist Tax The Tassa di Soggiorno, the tourist tax, may come as a nasty surprise at the end of your stay. The cost varies from region to region and depends on the star rating of the hotel. In Como for example you will be charged from 70c (1 star hotel) to €2.50 (4 star hotel) per person per night, so a couple staying in a four-star hotel for four nights would have to pay an extra €20. The tax is levied on a maximum number of nights, which can be anything from 4–10. Young children are usually excluded. If you have prepaid your hotel bill, the tax will not have been included (or mentioned) – it is always charged when you check out at the hotel. B&Bs and residences are also included, usually at a slightly lower rate.

AIRPORTS

Rome and Milan are Italy's principal gateway cities, but scheduled international flights also operate to Genoa, Naples, Turin, Venice, Florence, Pisa, Palermo and other major centres. The following website lists links for all of the Italian airports: www.aeroporti.com.

Rome is served by two international airports. Fiumicino (or Leonardo da Vinci; www.adr.it/fiumicino) lies about 30km (18 miles) southwest of the city centre. It is mainly used for scheduled flights. Fiumicino has a domestic and an international terminal, and the Leonardo Express direct train every 15–30 minutes brings you to Stazione Termini, Rome's main rail station. The journey takes half an hour.

Ciampino (www.adr.it/ciampino) is 16km (10 miles) southeast of the city centre and mostly serves charter flights.

Terravision coaches run between Termini station and Fiumicino and Ciampino. Buy tickets online, www.terravision.eu, at the airports' Terravision kiosk or Termini's Via Marsala entrance.

Milan has two airports, Malpensa (www.milanomalpensa-airport.com), 45km (28 miles) northwest of the city centre, for international traffic, and Linate (www.milanolinate-airport.com), about 7km (4 miles) to the east, mainly for domestic and European flights.

The Malpensa Express train links Malpensa Airport with Milan's Cadorna station in the centre every 30 minutes from 4.30am–11.30pm, taking 40 minutes (www.malpensaexpress.it). There is also the Malpensa shuttle bus every 20 minutes (6am–12.30am) from Terminals 1 and 2 to Milano Stazione Centrale, taking about one hour. From Linate the Starfly bus service (www.starfly.net) to Milan's Central Station operates every 30 minutes from 7.45am–10.45pm, and takes about 30 minutes. The cheaper No. 73 bus operates every 10 minutes (5.35am–0.35am) from the airport exit to central Milan. Taxi fares from airports to the respective city centres are at least 10 times higher than the bus fares.

What time does the train/bus leave for the city centre?
A che ora parte il treno/pullman per il centro?

B

BICYCLE HIRE

Cycling is a convenient way to get around the narrow streets of Italian cities, particularly those where the centres are now barred to traffic.

Bike hire is widely available in cities and resorts. An increasing number of hotels are now set up for cyclists. For details of accommodation and biking itineraries visit www.italybikehotels.it.

BUDGETING FOR YOUR TRIP

Italy is one of the most expensive holiday destinations in Western Europe. Prices of accommodation vary widely but in high season in cities and tourist resorts you can expect to pay €150–250 for a comfortable double room with bath, €90–130 in a simple hotel or B&B. Count on €35–60 upwards for a three-course evening meal with half a bottle of wine in a restaurant, and €16 or so for a pizza and beer. Drinks and coffee taken at the bar are a good deal cheaper than those at a table with waiter service. Entrance fees to state museums, galleries and gardens range from €5–16; entrance is free for EU citizens under 18 and over 65 and those aged 18–25 normally get a 50 percent discount. Private museums have their own rates and discount policies.

C

CAMPING

There are more than 2,000 official campsites in Italy, most of them well equipped. For details of sites visit www.camping.it. Most of the sites are along the coast and in the mountains. Sites are normally open from April to September.

Is there a campsite near here? **C'è un campeggio qui vicino?**
Have you room for a tent/caravan? **C'è posto per una tenda/roulotte?**
May we camp here? **Possiamo campeggiare qui?**

The *Camping Card International* (http://campingcardinternational.com), a pass that entitles holders to modest discounts and insurance coverage, is required at many campsites. It can be obtained through your country's camping or automobile association. It is inadvisable to camp outside official sites. If you do so, ask for advice from the local tourist office, choose sites where there are other campers, and always ensure that you have the permission of the property owner.

CAR HIRE (See also Driving)

The major international car hire companies have desks in the arrival area of Italy's airports. The best rates are usually found by booking directly with an international company and paying before you leave home. Check that the quoted rate is all-inclusive and beware of costly insurance excess in the small print. You must be over 21 to rent a car, and you will need a full, valid driver's licence, held for at least a year, which must be shown at the time of pick-up. You must also produce your credit card; cash deposits are prohibitively large. There is nearly always a charge for a second driver.

I'd like to hire a car. **Vorrei noleggiare una macchina.**
...for one day/a week **...per un giorno/una settimana**
I want full insurance. **Voglio l'assicurazione completa.**

CLIMATE

In the Alpine region, winters are long and cold, but often sunny, while summers are short and pleasantly cool. The northern lakes and Po Valley see cold and foggy winters and warm, sunny summers. The rest of the country, even the northern Ligurian coast, has mild winters. Summers are dry and hot to scorching, depending on how far south you go, but sea breezes often compensate for the heat.

The best time to visit the Ligurian and Adriatic coasts is from May/

June to September. Before or after this it can be rather chilly and wet with most hotels closed and beaches practically deserted. The best time to visit the cities is spring or autumn – between April and June or in September and October – when the weather is most pleasant. However, the streets can be just as crowded. The average maximum daily temperature in Rome in July and August is 30°C (86°F) and can drop to 11°C (5°F) in January. In Milan in July and August it is 28°C (82°F), and 5°C (0°F) in January.

CLOTHING

In northern Italy in winter, you will need boots and an overcoat, but in the south a lightweight coat will be adequate. During early spring and late autumn, bring light to medium-weight clothing and rainwear for brief but regular showers. Summer evenings can be cool, so pack a jacket or wrap. Comfortable walking shoes are indispensable. Remember that Italy's churches are places of worship as well as works of art and architecture, and you should dress respectably – shorts, miniskirts, bare shoulders and midriffs are frowned upon and may even mean that you are not allowed entry.

CRIME AND SAFETY

Cases of violence against tourists are rare, but petty theft is an endless annoyance, and tourists are easy targets. Check whether your home insurance policy covers theft or loss of personal effects while abroad; if not, it is wise to take out separate insurance.

Take usual precautions against theft; don't carry large amounts of cash; leave your valuables in the hotel safe; and never leave your bags or valuables in a parked car, whether in view or in the boot. The main danger is from pickpockets, especially around tourist attractions, busy markets and buses. Beware of gypsy girls with babies – while they distract your attention begging for coins, an accomplice may be behind you dipping into pockets and bags. If you have a shoulder bag, wear it across your body – it's harder to snatch.

Make photocopies of your tickets, driver's licence, passport and other vital documents to facilitate reporting a theft and obtaining replacements.

Any theft or loss must be reported immediately to the police. Obtain a copy of the report in order to comply with your travel insurance. If you lose your passport, you must also inform your consulate or embassy (see page 235).

> I want to report a theft. **Voglio denunciare un furto.**
> My wallet/passport/ticket has been stolen. **Mi hanno rubato il portafoglio/il passaporto/il biglietto.**

D

DRIVING

Motorists bringing a vehicle into Italy need a full driver's licence, Vehicle Registration and insurance documents. The use of seat belts in front and back seats is obligatory; fines for non-compliance are stiff. It is also mandatory to switch on dipped headlights outside built-up areas during the day. A red warning triangle and reflective jackets must be carried in case of breakdown. Motorcycle riders must wear helmets. The use of handheld mobiles while driving is prohibited. The ACI (Automobile Club d'Italia; www.aci.it) or the AA (www.theaa.com) give on-line information worth consulting before your departure.

Driving conditions. Drive on the right, overtake on the left. Give way to traffic from the right. Speed limits: 50kmh (30mph) in town, 90kmh (55mph) on main roads, 130kmh (80mph) on motorways.

Dual carriageways *(superstrade)* and most motorways *(autostrade)* are skilfully designed for fast driving. Italian *autostrade* are toll roads – take an entry ticket from an automatic machine when you enter the motorway, and pay at the other end for the distance travelled. Don't enter exclusive 'TelePass' (automatic toll meter) lanes, unless your vehicle is equipped with a receiver and you are setup with the system, or you will be forced to reverse.

Rules and regulations. Italian traffic police *(polizia stradale)* are authorised to impose on-the-spot fines for speeding and other traffic offences, such as driving while under the influence of alcohol or stopping in a no-stopping zone. All cities and many towns and villages have signs posted at the outskirts indicating the telephone number of the local traffic police headquarters or *Carabinieri* (see Police). Police have become stricter about speeding, a national pastime, and there are now hidden speed cameras.

Fuel. Petrol stations on motorways are generally open 24 hours; others often close for lunch, opening from 7am–12.30pm and 3pm–7.30pm, and may close on Sundays and holidays. Many offer self-service by an automatic machine that accepts notes and sometimes credit cards. In the south, cash is still preferred.

Parking. A blue-and-white sign with a 'P' indicates legal parking places. Many towns and cities have Blue Zone parking, usually limited to one or two hours. Payment is by meters or scratch cards, available from tobacconists. For longer stays, try to find a supervised car park *(parcheggio custodito)* near your hotel and leave your car there. Be sure to check opening hours, as few are accessible 24 hours a day. Many larger towns have multi-storey car parks *(autorimessa* or *garage)*, as well as car parks outside the centre with bus connections into town. Many historic centres are restricted traffic zones *(Zone a Traffico Limitato* or ZTLS). If you ignore warning signs you will almost certainly incur a fine by post (hired cars are no exception). If your hotel is within the restriction zone, call in advance so the hotel can inform the police of your licence number and obtain a temporary transit permit.

Don't park in places marked by yellow and black stripes, or where it says 'Zona Rimozione' (removal zone), 'Zona Verde' (green zone), 'Zona Pedonale' (pedestrian zone), or in a 'Sosta Vietata' (no parking) or 'Divieto di Sosta' (no stopping) zone; if you park there, your car will likely be towed away.

If you need help. Should you be involved in a road accident, dial the all-purpose emergency number 113, or 112 for the *Carabinieri*. Every 2km (1.5 miles) on the motorway there's an emergency call box marked 'sos'. If you require breakdown or road assistance call 803 116, but you will be charged; be sure that you have breakdown insurance coverage before you leave home. If your car is stolen or broken into, contact the Urban Police Head-quarters *(Questura)* and get a copy of their report for your insurance claim.

Road signs. Most road signs in Italy are international. Some written signs you might also come across are included below.

Curva pericolosa Dangerous bend/curve
Deviazione Detour
Divieto di sorpasso No overtaking
Divieto di sosta No stopping
Lavori in corso Road works/Men working
Pericolo Danger
Rallentare Slow down
Senso vietato/unico No entry/One-way street
Vietato l'ingresso No entry
Zona pedonale Pedestrian zone
ZTL Limited traffic zone

DISABLED TRAVELLERS

Hotels and restaurants are legally required to provide access for the disabled. Specialised tour operators can offer customised tours and itineraries, eg Flying Wheels Travel (www.flyingwheelstravel.com) and Accessible Journeys (www.disabilitytravel.com). Village for All (www.villageforall.net) is a database of accessible hotels, farmhouses, museums, beaches and other venues.

E

ELECTRICITY

220V/50Hz AC is standard. An adaptor for continental-style sockets is needed; American 110V appliances require a transformer.

EMBASSIES AND CONSULATES

Contact your embassy or consulate if in trouble (loss of passport, problems with the police, serious accidents). All embassies are in Rome, but many countries maintain consulates in other cities.

Australia: Via Antonio Bosio 5, tel: 06-852 721, www.italy.embassy.gov.au.

Canada: Via Zara 30, tel: 06-854 442 911, www.canadainternational.gc.ca/italy-italie/.

New Zealand: Via Clitunno 44, tel: 06-853 7501, www.mfat.govt.nz.

Republic of Ireland: Via Giacomo Medici 1, tel: 06-585 2381, www.dfa.ie/irish-embassy/italy/.

South Africa: Via Tanaro 14, tel: 06-852 541, http://lnx.sudafrica.it/.

UK: Via XX Settembre 80/a, tel: 06-4220 0001, www.gov.uk/government/world/italy.

US: Via Vittorio Veneto 119/A–121, tel: 06-46741, www.usembasssy.it.

EMERGENCIES

In an emergency, if you don't speak Italian, find a local person to help you, or talk to the English-speaking operator on the assisted service, tel: 170.

Please can you place an emergency call to the ...?
Per favore, può fare una telefonata d'emergenza ...?
police **alla polizia**
fire brigade **ai vigili del fuoco**
hospital **all'ospedale**

General emergency assistance, carabinieri 112
State Police 113
Fire 115
Ambulance 118
Coast Guard 1530

G

GAY AND LESBIAN TRAVELLERS

Gay life in Italy is becoming more mainstream, especially in the north. Bologna, Milan, Turin and Rome all have lively gay scenes and Taormina in Sicily and Rimini on the Adriatic coast are two of the main gay resorts. arci-gay (www.arcigay.it), the national gay rights organisation, has its headquarters in Bologna (Via Don Minzoni 18, tel: 051-095 7241), but has branches in many other cities.

GETTING TO ITALY

By Air. Rome's Leonardo da Vinci (Fiumicino) and Milan's Malpensa airports (see page 227) are the main intercontinental gateways, and there are direct flights from European cities to many other destinations. From Milan and Rome there are regular scheduled flights to some 30 destinations within Italy. From the UK, British Airways (www.ba.com) and Alitalia (www.alitalia.com) operate services to major Italian cities; the main low-cost carriers are easyJet, (www.easyjet.com), Ryanair (www.ryanair.com), Jet2 (www.jet2.com) and Thomson (www.thomson.co.uk). From the US there are daily flights to Rome and Milan from New York, Atlanta, Chicago, Miami and Los Angeles. The main carriers are Delta (www.delta.com), Alitalia (www.alitalia.com) and American Airlines (www.aa.com).

Package tours are offered by a wide range of tour operators and travel agents. The Italian National Tourist Office (www.enit.it) has details of tour operators offering tours and special-interest holidays, including language, art and architecture courses.

By road (see also Driving). The road system in Italy is very manageable from north to south including ferry connections to Sicily and Sardinia. It is accessible through France, Switzerland and Austria. For route planning and details on the cost of petrol, road tolls levied on French and Italian motorways, and the Swiss motorway road tax, visit www.viamichelin.com.

By rail. For information on rail travel and rail passes, contact Voyages-SNCF (http://uk.voyages-sncf.com/en/), or visit www.seat61.com. Italian State Railways (Ferrovie dello Stato Italiane) or will help plan an itinerary: www.fsitaliane.it. Within Italy, tel: 8488-88088. The journey from the UK to Milan, via Paris on Eurostar (www.eurostar.com) and the overnight Thello sleeper car to Milan or Verona takes just over 14 hours (16 hours to Verona).

InterRail and Eurail passes are valid in Italy but a rail pass for Italy only is unlikely to be an economical way of travelling in Italy, since supplements, not covered by passes, are levied on the faster trains which normally require seat reservations. Although less frequent these days, be aware of the Italian *sciopero* (train strike) that can last from a few hours to a few days.

When's the next bus/train to ...? **Quando parte il prossimo autobus/treno per ...?**
single (one-way) **andata**
return (round-trip) **andata e ritorno**
first/second class **prima/seconda classe**
What's the fare to ...? **Qual è la tariffa per ...?**

GUIDES AND TOURS

Local tourist offices and major hotels can help you find qualified guides and give you a list of tours. Private tour guides give you access to lesser-known sights and shopping and it is best to book in advance from home during high season. In the main centres tourist office websites (available through www.enit.it) give details of local guides and tours.

> Can you recommend a sightseeing tour/an excursion? **Può consigliare un giro turistico/una gita?**
> We'd like an English-speaking guide. **Desideriamo una guida che parla inglese.**

H

HEALTH AND MEDICAL CARE

It is highly advisable to have health insurance, which usually comes as part of a general travel insurance policy. EU citizens are entitled to free emergency hospital treatment if they have a European Health Insurance Card (ehic) available from post offices or online at www.ehic.org.uk. You may have to pay part of the price, so keep the receipts so that you can claim a refund.

If you need medical care, ask your hotel concierge or contact your embassy to find a doctor (or dentist) who speaks English. In an emergency you can call 118 for an ambulance.

Tap water is safe to drink unless there is a sign reading 'Acqua Non Potabile'.

HOLIDAYS

Banks, offices, most shops, and some museums close on the following days (shops and offices may also close on local feast days):

1 January *Capodanno/Primo dell' Anno* New Year's Day
6 January *Epifania (La Befana)* Epiphany
25 April *Festa della Liberazione* Liberation Day
1 May *Festa del Lavoro* Labour Day
2 June *Fiesta de la República* Republic Day
15 August *Ferragosto* Assumption
1 November *Ognissanti* All Saints' Day
8 December *L'Immacolata Concezione (Forte dell 'Immacolata)* Immacu-

late Conception
25 December *Natale* Christmas Day
26 December *Santo Stefano* St Stephen's Day
Moveable date: *Lunedì di Pasqua* Easter Monday

L

LANGUAGE

Despite the many different dialects around the country, standard Italian is understood by everyone. Staff at the major hotels and shops in the cities and resort areas will usually speak some English, so you can easily get by without a word of Italian. However, it is polite to learn at least a few basic phrases. Local people will welcome any attempt you make except in major tourist cities like Venice, where locals may insist on showing off their English.

The Berlitz Italian Phrase Book and Dictionary covers most of the situations you are likely to encounter during your travels in Italy. Also useful is the Berlitz Italian-English/English-Italian Pocket Dictionary, which contains the basic vocabulary you will need, plus a menu-reader supplement.

M

MAPS

Tourist offices give away basic street plans and regional maps featuring a selection of local information. More detailed maps are on sale at newsstands.

I'd like a street plan of... **Vorrei una pianta della città...**
I'd like a road map of this region **Vorrei una carta stradale di questa regione**

MEDIA

Newspapers and magazines. You can find newspapers in English at airports and most city-centre newsstands *(edicola)*. The *Wall Street Journal Europe* and *International Herald Tribune* are available on the day of publication, as well as UK broadsheets, including *The Times, Guardian, Telegraph,* and some tabloids.

Radio and TV. The Italian state TV network, the RAI *(Radio Televisione Italiana)*, broadcasts three TV channels, which compete with many other independent channels. All programmes are in Italian, including British and American feature films and imports, which are dubbed. Most hotels and rental properties have cable connections, which show cnn, BBC World, and Sky, all offering world news in English.

The airwaves are crammed with radio stations, most of them broadcasting popular music.

MONEY

Currency. In common with most other European countries, the official currency used in Italy is the euro (€). Notes are denominated in 5, 10, 20, 50, 100, 200 and 500 euros; coins in 1 and 2 euros and 1, 2, 5, 10, 20 and 50 cents.

Banks and currency exchange. Most banks are open 8.30am–1.30pm and 2.30–4pm, Monday–Friday. In the south, opening hours tend to be later in the afternoon.

Money can be changed at currency-exchange offices *(ufficio di cambio)* in main stations and airports and privately owned offices, located around town. However, the exchange rate or the addition of a commission makes the latter's transactions less advantageous than those offered by banks. The same applies to foreign currency or traveller's cheques changed in hotels, shops or restaurants.

ATMs. Cashpoints *(Bancomats)* outside banks are widely available, and are the easiest way of obtaining cash in euros, drawn on either your bank, travel money card, or credit card. Check with your bank at home to make sure that your account and pin number are authorised for international withdrawals. Look for correlating symbols on the cash machine and the back of your card.

Credit cards, traveller's cheques. Most hotels, many shops, service stations and restaurants honour major credit cards. Traveller's cheques (eg Thomas Cook and American Express) can be changed in cities and tourist resorts, but are no longer widely accepted. In small towns, especially in the south, it is best to have some cash handy. Take your passport or national identity card along whenever you go to a bureau de change *(cambio)*.

> I want to change some pounds/dollars/traveller's cheques.
> **Voglio cambiare delle sterline/dei dollari/traveller cheque.**
> Can I pay with this credit card? **Posso pagare con la carta di credito?**
> Where is the bank? **Dov' è la banca?**
> Where is an atm? **Dov' è il bancomat?**

O

OPENING TIMES

Banks are generally open 8am–1.30pm and 2.30–4pm Monday–Friday. Currency exchange offices at airports and major railway stations are open until late in the evening and on Saturday and Sunday.

Churches generally close at lunchtime, approximately noon–3pm. They discourage tourist visits during Sunday services.

Museum and art gallery opening hours vary enormously and may change from one season to the next. They are usually Tuesday–Saturday 9 or 9.30am–4pm, and in some cases 5–7pm, and until 1pm on Sunday. Closing day is generally Monday. If Monday is a holiday, some museums and galleries close the following day. Check times with the local tourist office before you set out. Large city museums often have late-night summer openings, until 10pm or later.

Post offices normally open from 8.15 or 8.30am–1.30 or 2pm Monday–Friday, until noon on Saturday and on the last day of the month. Main post offices in larger cities keep longer hours.

Shops traditionally open Monday–Saturday 8am–12.30 or 1pm and from 3.30 or 4pm–7.30 or 8pm, but an increasing number, especially in northern Italy, are open all day Monday to Saturday, and some on Sunday, too. Many shops close on Monday morning and/or Saturday afternoon and on Sunday. Food stores generally open earlier, closing on Wednesday or Thursday afternoons. There is a limited number of stores open during August: a sign saying *chiuso per ferie* with dates, indicates they are closed for holidays. In coastal resorts shops will open all day, every day in high season.

P

POLICE

The municipal police *(vigili urbani)* wear navy blue or white uniforms and white helmets. They direct traffic and handle routine police tasks. Some municipal police act as interpreters. Look for the special badge on their uniforms. The *Carabinieri*, a paramilitary force, wear light brown or blue uniforms with peaked caps, and deal with violent or serious crimes and demonstrations. The Questura, their headquarters, also deals with visas and other complaints, and is a point of reference if you need help from the authorities. The *Polizia Stradale* patrol the highways, issue speeding tickets and assist with breakdowns (see also Driving).

Italy's borders, ports, airports and railway stations come under the jurisdiction of the national police *(Polizia di Stato)*. In an emergency, dial 112 or 113 for police assistance.

Where's the nearest police station? **Dov' è il commissariato di polizia più vicino?**

POST OFFICES

Post offices, identified by a 'PT' sign, handle mail and money transfers and generally open Mon–Fri 8am-1.30pm (main offices until around 7.30pm), Sat until noon. Hours may vary.

Stamps *(francobolli)* can also be bought at tobacco shops and at some gift shops and hotels. Mail is sluggish; ask for Posta Prioritaria, an express service that costs just a bit more but gets to its destination much faster.

Postboxes are painted red; the slot marked 'Per la Città' is for local mail, 'Altre Destinazioni' is for all other destinations. The blue box is for international post.

> Where's the nearest post office? **Dov' è l' ufficio postale più vicino?**
> A stamp for this letter/postcard, please. **Un francobollo per questa lettera/cartolina' per favore.**

PUBLIC TRANSPORT

Taxis *(tassì or taxi)* don't cruise, but can be picked up at taxi ranks in main squares of cities or ordered by phone. Extra charges for luggage and for trips at night and to airports are posted inside the cab. It is usual to round up the fare.

In addition to **bus** *(autobus)* services, some big cities operate trams/ streetcars *(tram* in Italian). Naples has four funicular *(funicolare)* routes. Rome, Milan and Naples have underground/subway *(metropolitana,* abbreviated *metrò)* systems. Where required, remember to punch tickets to validate them before boarding, or you will risk a stiff fine regardless of being a non-Italian speaker.

Buy **tickets** for buses and trams in advance at tobacco shops, news-stands or bars. There are Metrò ticket machines at metro stations.

Rome's buses can be crowded, but they are an inexpensive means of transport and a rambling introduction to the city. Tickets are valid for 100 minutes and can be purchased in books of five from tobacconists, newsstands, vending machines and the atac (Rome's transport authority, www.atac.roma.it) offices. One-day, three-day and weekly tickets are also available. The tickets are also valid on Rome's metrò, although the two lines (A and B) have a limited number of stops in the city centre. A third line (C) is under construction to link Grottarossa north of the Vatican to Pantano in the southeast (estimated date of completion 2020). Rome has a bike-sharing scheme whereby you purchase a pre-paid card at ATAC offices (at Termini, Spagna and Ottaviano stations on Metro A) and top it up at the dozen or so PIT tourist offices around the city. Visit www.roma-n-bike.com. For boat cruises along the River Tiber go to www.battellidiroma.it.

Florence now has a fully pedestrianised centre and is easily covered on foot. The bus network, run by ATAF (www.ataf.net), provides small electric buses skirting the centre and a good service out to the suburbs such as Fiesole.

Milan is served by atm buses and trains and the Metropolitana Milanese, made up of four lines. Information and tourist tickets are available at the atm office on the mezzanine floor of the Duomo metrò station or at Stazione Centrale. For details, see www.atm.it.

In **Naples**, buses are crowded and slow, but they are the only means of transport in some areas. The small-scale but convenient metrò connects the Stazione Centrale in the east with the Stazione Mergellina in the west.

Venice's water buses (vaporetti, and the smaller and faster moto-scafi) ply the Grand Canal and shuttle between islands. Tickets are available from most landing stages, tobacconists, shops displaying the ACTV sign and tourist offices. All tickets must be punched at the machines at the landing stages; failure to do so or travelling without a ticket will incur on-the-spot fines. Apart from single tickets (€1.50, valid for 75 minutes) there are passes valid for 12, 24, 36, 72 hours and a week. The system is quite complex; for details go to www.actv.

it. Venice has about six water-taxi *(motoscafi)* stations. Theoretically rates are fixed but they tend to vary according to distance; clarify the destination and price before boarding. This also applies to trips by gondola.

By coach. Italy has a vast network of coaches (long-distance buses) called *pullman*. Information on destinations and timetables are posted at coach terminals, usually situated near the town's railway station, and can be obtained from local or regional tourist offices (see page 248) or sometimes from your hotel.

By train. Italy has a comprehensive and efficient train network, with some of the lowest fares in Europe. The main operator is the state-owned Trenitalia (www.trenitalia.com) though private operator NTV (Nuovo Trasporto Viaggiatori, www.italotreno.it) is now competing with high-speed trains between main cities. Tickets can be bought and reservations made at travel agencies and railway stations or bought online (www.trenitalia.com or www.italiarail.com). For long-distance trains, tickets must be bought in advance. If you live in the UK, tickets can be bought through International Rail on 0871 231 0790. On most journeys children under the age of four travel free; aged 4–12 inclusive they pay 50 percent.

When's the next bus/train/boat/plane for...? **A che ore parte il prossimo autobus/treno/traghetto/aereo per...?**

What's the fare to...? **Quanto costa il biglietto per...?**

I want a ticket to... **Vorrei un biglietto per...**

single (one-way) **andata**

return (round-trip) **andata e ritorno**

first/second class **prima/seconda classe**

I'd like to make seat reservations. **Vorrei prenotare un posto.**

Italian trains are classified according to speed. Trenitalia's fastest train is the 300 kmh (186mph) Frecciarossa (Red Arrow), followed by the Frecciargento (White Arrow) and Frecciabianca (White Arrow), both up to 201kmh (125mph). Tickets that include a seat reservation must be booked in advance for all three. InterCity trains (IC) are less swish but still provide a fast service between main cities, and again require seat reservation. Espresso (E), Regionale (R) and other local trains are the cheapest and slowest, stopping at local stations. Validate your ticket in the platform machine before travelling or you face a stiff fine.

By boat. There are regular car-ferry or hydrofoil connections to the main islands; see www.enit.it for inter-island ferry operators. Ferries and hydrofoils also operate between towns and sites on the northern lakes of Como, Garda and Maggiore.

By plane. Alitalia, Meridiana (www.meridiana.it) and other domestic airlines have flights between Rome and/or Milan and some 30 Italian cities and less frequent service to a number of provincial airports. Detailed information is available at travel agencies.

R

RELIGION

Although Italy is predominantly Roman Catholic, all major religions have congregations in the large cities. Check local newspapers for details, or ask at your hotel or the local tourist office.

S

SPAS

Italy has some 340 spas and health resorts that use thermal waters for rest, recreation or treatment. Many are clinical, therapeutic spas but there is an increasing number of health and beauty centres, especially in Tuscany and Ischia, which are dedicated to pampering.

T

TELEPHONES

Public phones are increasingly hard to locate. Some take coins and credit cards but the majority accept only phone cards (schede telefoniche), sold in various different euro denominations from tobacconists, newsstands and post offices. Instructions are given in English.

To make an international call, dial 00, followed by the country code (Australia +61, Ireland +353, New Zealand +64, South Africa +27, UK +44, US and Canada +1), then the area code (often minus the initial zero) and finally the number. When dialling within Italy remember that codes are an integral part of the number and should always be included.

You must insert a coin or a card to access a dial tone even when making a toll-free call. Be aware of exorbitant hotel charges for direct calls and service charges for toll-free calls on their phone lines.

International calls: 170 (English-speaking operators)
International enquiries: 176 (English-speaking operators)

EU mobile phones can be used in Italy, but check their compatibility before you leave. Charges for using a UK-based mobile to make and receive calls and texts abroad are high. It may be worth purchasing an Italian 'pay as you go' SIM card to use during your stay. Currently, there are four mobile phone operators in Italy: TIM, Vodafone, 3 and Wind.

TIME ZONES

Italy follows Central European Time (gmt+1). From the last Sunday in March to the last Sunday in October, clocks are put ahead by one hour. When it is midday in Rome it is 3am in Vancouver, 6am in New York, 11am in London and 8pm in Sydney.

TIPPING

Tipping is not taken for granted in Italy although a bit extra will always be appreciated. A service charge of 10–15 percent is usually included on restaurant bills, if not add 10%. For quick service in bars leave a coin or two with your till receipt when ordering. Most hotel prices are quoted as all-inclusive *(tutto compreso)*, and the service charge is included, but at luxury hotels iva (vat/sales tax) is added to the bill; ask if you are unsure. Porters, doormen and service-station attendants all expect a tip of a euro or two, depending on the situation. Taxi drivers do not expect a tip but will appreciate it if you round up the fare to the next euro.

> Thank you, this is for you. **Grazie, questo è per Lei.**
> Keep the change. **Tenga il resto.**

TOILETS

Toilets may be labelled with a symbol of a man or a woman or the initials WC. Wording may be: **Uomini** for men, **Donne** for women; **Signori** (with a final i) for men; **Signore** (with an e) for women.

> Where are the toilets? **Dove sono i gabinetti?**

TOURIST INFORMATION OFFICES

As tourism is such a vital factor in Italy's economy, there is an elaborate network of information offices that provide useful maps and brochures. For general information, the state tourist office enit *(Ente Nazionale Italiano per il Turismo*, www.enit.it), has offices in major foreign cities as well as regional capitals. The organisation publishes detailed brochures with information on accommodation, means of transport, general tips and useful addresses for the whole country.

When in Italy, look instead for the apt *(Azienda di Promozione Turistica)* for more detailed regional sightseeing information; they occasionally help as well with hotel and camping accommodation. Worth considering are the tourist passes available in major cities that offer free public transport, free or discounted access to museums plus the advantage of being able to skip the queues.

Italy ENIT head office: Via Marghera 2/6, Rome, tel: 06-49711, www. enit.it. The call centre on freephone 060608 will answer all your practical queries. 'Enjoy Rome' (Via Marghera 8a, 00185 Rome, tel: 06-445 1843, www.enjoyrome.com) is a very informative private tourist office.

Australia and New Zealand Level 2, 140 William Street, East Sydney NSW 2011, Australia, tel: (61) 02 9357 2561, email: sydney@enit.it.

Canada 69 Yonge Street, Suite 1404, Toronto, Ontario, M5E 1K3; tel: 416-925 4882, email: toronto@enit.it.

UK 1 Princes Street, London W1B 2AY, tel: 020-7408 1254, email: info.london@enit.it.

US Chicago: 3800 Division Street, Stone Park, IL 60165, tel: (312) 644-0996, email: chicago@enit.it.

New York: 686 Park Avenue, New York, NY 10065, tel: 212 245 5618, email: newyork@enit.it.

V

VISAS AND ENTRY REQUIREMENTS

For citizens of EU countries, a valid passport or identity card is all that is needed to enter Italy for stays of up to 90 days. Citizens of Australia, New Zealand and the US and Canada also require only a valid passport.

Visas *(permesso di soggiorno)*. For stays of more than 90 days a visa or residence permit is required. Regulations change from time to time, so check with the Italian Embassy before travelling.

I've nothing to declare. **Non ho niente da dichiarare.**
It's for my personal use. **È per mio uso personale.**

Free exchange of non-duty-free goods for personal use is allowed between EU countries. Refer to your home country's regulating organisation for a current complete list of import restrictions.

WEBSITES AND INTERNET ACCESS

www.enit.it Official site of Italian state tourist board, UK and Ireland.

www.italiantourism.com Official site of Italian government tourist board, North America

www.italymagazine.com Online version of Italy Magazine with articles on all things Italian.

www.agriturismo.com Details of more than 1,200 farm holidays and B&Bs.

http://emea.venere.com Useful site for booking accommodation online. Wi-fi access is available in airports, train stations and other public places. Most hotels offer Wi-fi and internet facilities, often chargeable. Internet cafes can be hard to come by outside of the larger towns.

WEIGHTS AND MEASURES

Italy uses the metric system.

YOUTH AND STUDENT HOSTELS

Italy's youth hostels *(ostelli della gioventù)* are open to members of Hostelling International (HI, www.hihostels.com). Membership cards and information are available from national youth hostels associations (in the UK visit www.yha.org.uk). Alternatively, you can purchase temporary membership for a small fee on arrival at the hostel. You should reserve well ahead in summer. This can be done online through HI for a small fee.

INDEX

INSIGHT ⊙ GUIDES POCKET GUIDE

ITALY

First Edition 2017

Editor: Tom Fleming
Author: Jack Altman and Patricia Schultz
Head of Production: Rebeka Davies
Picture Editor: Tom Smyth
Cartography Update: Carte
Update Production: AM Services
Photography Credits: Alamy 67; Anna
Mockford and Nick Bonetti/Apa Publications
59, 94, 96, 105, 117, 123, 124, 128, 130, 157,
158, 207; Annabel Elston/Apa Publications
152/153; AWL Images 1; Bigstock 147, 197;
Bill Wassman/Apa Publications 40, 114, 184,
187; Britta Jaschinski/Apa Publications 74,
216; Chris Coe/Apa Publications 17, 18, 25,
27, 68, 76, 79, 80, 82, 84, 90, 101, 106, 113,
121, 126, 132, 135, 138, 142, 145, 151, 155,
162, 185, 189; Chris Godet/Apa Publications
202; Claude Huber/Apa Publications 173;
Dreamstime 23, 35; Frances Grandsden/
Apa Publications 87; Getty Images 4MC, 6L,
213; Glyn Genin/Apa Publications 21, 118,
137, 141, 148, 194, 204, 211; Greg Gladman/
Apa Publications 5T, 31, 168, 171, 174, 176,
178, 180; iStock 4ML, 4TL, 5TC, 5M, 5MC,
5M, 14, 111; Jerry Dennis/Apa Publications
71, 209; Jon Davidson/Apa Publications 73,
89, 109; Leonardo 7R; Ming Tang-Evans/Apa
Publications 5MC, 6R, 7, 11, 42, 45, 49, 51,
53, 54, 57, 61, 63, 65, 200, 214; Neil Buchan-
Grant/Apa Publications 12, 32, 165, 166, 191,
192, 203; Phil Wood/Apa Publications 182;
Photoshot 37; Ros Miller/Apa Publications 28,
210; Shutterstock 4TC, 220; Steve McDonald/
Apa Publications 99, 103, 223; Susan Smart/
Apa Publications 92; Sylvaine Poitau/APA
Publications 198, 219; Turismo Torino 161
Cover Picture: Shutterstock

Distribution
UK, Ireland and Europe: Apa Publications
(UK) Ltd; sales@insightguides.com
United States and Canada: Ingram Publisher
Services; ips@ingramcontent.com
Australia and New Zealand: Woodslane;
info@woodslane.com.au
Southeast Asia: Apa Publications (SN) Pte;
singaporeoffice@insightguides.com
Hong Kong, Taiwan and China:
Apa Publications (HK) Ltd;
hongkongoffice@insightguides.com
Worldwide: Apa Publications (UK) Ltd;
sales@insightguides.com

**Special Sales, Content Licensing
and CoPublishing**
Insight Guides can be purchased in bulk
quantities at discounted prices. We can
create special editions, personalised
jackets and corporate imprints tailored
to your needs. sales@insightguides.com;
www.insightguides.biz
All Rights Reserved
© 2017 Apa Digital (CH) AG and
Apa Publications (UK) Ltd

Printed in China by CTPS

Contact us
Every effort has been made to provide
accurate information in this publication,
but changes are inevitable. The publisher
cannot be responsible for any resulting loss,
inconvenience or injury. We would appreciate
it if readers would call our attention to any
errors or outdated information. We also
welcome your suggestions; please contact us
at: hello@insightguides.com
www.insightguides.com

31192021277569